B WADE, D.
Wade, Dwyane,
A father first :how my life became
bigger than basketball /

A FATHER FIRST

A FATHER FIRST

HOW MY LIFE BECAME BIGGER THAN BASKETBALL

DWYANE WADE

WITH MIM EICHLER RIVAS

WILLIAM MORROW

An Imprint of HarperCollins*Publishers*

Grateful acknowledgment is made to the following for the use of the photographs that appear in the insert: pages 1, 2, 3 top, courtesy of the Wade family; page 3 middle and bottom, courtesy of the Marquette University athletic department; page 4 top, by Victor Baldizon/NBAE/Getty Images; page 5, by John W. McDonough/*Sports Illustrated*/Getty Images; page 6, by Jesse D. Garrabrant/NBAE/Getty Images; all other photographs by Bob Metulus Images.

HarperCollins books may be purchased for educational, business, or sales promotional use. For information please write: Special Markets Department, HarperCollins Publishers, 10 East 53rd Street, New York, NY 10022.

FIRST EDITION

Designed by Jamie Kerner

Library of Congress Cataloging-in-Publication Data

Wade, Dwyane, 1982–
   A father first : how my life became bigger than basketball / by Dwyane Wade. — 1st ed.
      p. cm.
   ISBN 978-0-06-213615-2 (hardback) 1. Wade, Dwyane, 1982–
2. Basketball players—United States—Biography. 3. Fatherhood—United States. 4. Fathers and sons—United States. I. Title.
   GV884.W23W34   2012
   796.323092—dc23
   [B]   2012020583

12 13 14 15 16   DIX/RRD   10 9 8 7 6 5 4 3 2 1

To my grandmother, Willie Mae Morris,
my first teacher in life

And to Zaire, Zion, and Dahveon,
for teaching me what it truly means to be a father first

I'm stronger because I had to be. I'm smarter because of my mistakes. I'm happier because of sadness I've known and now wiser because I learned the lesson.

—Author unknown, often cited by Pastor Jolinda Wade

CONTENTS

A FATHER FIRST

PROLOGUE

HOMECOMING

Friday afternoon
March 11, 2011
At home in Miami

"What?!"

I'm alone in my bedroom just before dozing off to sleep when I sit bolt upright to stare at the BlackBerry in my hand. It looks like some alien object, blinking like crazy. I can't stop staring back at it and the shocking e-mail that just came in.

My heart is pounding as I inhale and exhale and try to catch my breath. I'm usually good at keeping my emotions in check—but not right now.

I reread the eight words of Jim's e-mail. Jim Pritikin is the attorney representing me in the very painful, very public, drawn-out custody battle for my sons, nine-year-old Zaire and almost four-year-old Zion. With no warning, no explanation, Jim's message tells me the judge has made a final decision.

It's over.

"What?!" I repeat, still talking to myself, now even louder than before.

Still trying to grasp this moment, I take another deep breath and mentally rewind the tape, replaying recent events that might offer some clue as to what this really means.

No more than ten minutes earlier, after a grueling practice, I'd headed upstairs to lie down for a quick rest. The previous night on the Heat's home court, at the buzzer, we'd won a hard-earned victory against the Los Angeles Lakers, not only landing a playoff spot—and breaking out of our five-game losing slump—but also putting a stop to the Lakers' eight-game winning streak. But there was no time to celebrate. By Friday morning at practice, my teammates and I were back on the grind. We had work to do. With LeBron James and Chris Bosh in their first season with the team, there was enormous pressure on us to prove the Heat's naysayers wrong, on the one hand; and, on the other, live up to supersized expectations to win a championship.

Of course, for me that pressure was nuthin' compared to what had been going on with the ordeal of the custody case. Most of the time I'm a pro at blocking out all kinds of drama. Sometimes to a fault. But that just was not possible when the safety and well-being of my sons was at stake. Not when my ability to be there for them as their father was being threatened.

You know, none of this ever made sense. When Siohvaughn and I first separated—a short time after baby Zion arrived, when Zaire was five years old—I just assumed we'd figure out a fair way for each of us to spend time with our sons. Was I naïve? Apparently. But I was following the example set by my mother and father, Jolinda and Dwyane Wade Sr., who divorced, coincidentally, after the same number of years being married. My sister, Tragil, and I—five years and a few months old, respectively—were the same ages as my sons at the time of the break-up with their mom and me. As tough as our circumstances were in those years, our parents sent a clear message that even when moms and dads aren't married anymore, they can overcome their differences and make decisions together for whatever's in the best interests of the children.

If you love your kids, seems to me, you do everything in your power to make sure they aren't robbed of their relationships with their father or their mother.

Sitting there in my bedroom, it hits me that after everything my boys have lived through over the last three and a half years—not only the divorce proceedings but this past year's custody dispute—everything in their lives is about to change dramatically. A mix of extreme emotions and questions bombard my thoughts. How do I explain to Zaire and Zion what these changes mean for them? How do I reassure them while they are dealing with all of these new uncertainties?

Before I even begin to answer those questions, I'm taken back to the memory of something that happened to another boy, age eight and a half, who—twenty-one years earlier—felt he had also been left on the doorstep of uncertainty.

The year was 1990, late in the summer before his third-grade year at school. Not too hot anymore but not cold yet, either. The place was the Southside of Chicago, on the corner of Fifty-Ninth and Prairie, not the projects but a place hard-hit by poverty and drugs, where the sound of gunfire was more or less constant and knowing someone who died young was a reality.

The boy I'm remembering is me.

"DWYANE!" TRAGIL CALLED FROM THE SIDEWALK, UP TO THE stoop of our three-story apartment house where I was sitting with our grandma—the two of us watching the street, as usual. My sister gestured for me like it was no big deal, getting me to come on down, as if she wanted to ask me something.

Whatever it was she wanted, I didn't need any encouragement to hustle down the steps, taking them in twos and threes, so fast I almost lost my footing on the sidewalk and came close to falling down splat on my hands and knees. At the last minute, though, I regained my balance, and sprinted over to my sister, eager to hear what was up.

If you had asked Tragil in those days what she thought about my future in the NBA, she would have laughed and said, "That boy?" She remembers me as being pretty uncoordinated, and even accident-prone. She and my two older sisters, born to our mother before she and our dad married, used to tease me and say, "How you fall when nothing there?"

Tragil, thirteen years old, going into the eighth grade, just shook her head and laughed. "C'mon." She nodded toward the direction of the bus stop. "You wanna go to the movies with me?"

Not even bothering to ask what movie or how this turned out to be my lucky day, I immediately answered, "Yeah!" and took off down the sidewalk, not wanting to give her the chance to change her mind. There was no point trying to hide how happy I was about going somewhere, anywhere, with Tragil—who most of the time was running off someplace to hang out with her friends and didn't want her kid brother tagging along.

Tragil knew me well, maybe better than anyone. She knew that what most people saw in me as a shy person was actually someone with a lot of inner confidence and a strong sense of wanting to be different; but she also knew that at times I was unsure of myself in front of others. She later taught me the word *introvert* and explained that's why I was quiet and seemed shy. But I grew up watching everything and paying serious attention, with an active mind full of thoughts and dreams—even though I might not have said a lot. Tragil knew all that. She also knew that the other reason I tried to tag along with her and her friends was because our mother always used to tell me, "You go on now, you go follow your sister."

Mom wanted me to make sure Tragil wasn't getting into any trouble, that she was safe, so that became my job, just as my sister was raised to protect and look out for me—Jolinda Wade's only son, the youngest child and only boy in the household. Even when our mother's own troubles took hold, getting her deeper into drugs and a relationship with an abusive boyfriend, she still did whatever she could do to keep us safe. There is no question I worried about my mother when she was out at night, and loved her so much I couldn't sleep because I wanted her to come home and let me know she was okay. But there is also no question that Jolinda Morris Wade's love for her children—and her desire to see us achieve our dreams—was the most important truth of my early years.

Looking back, I can't remember when various worries started to wear on me. I do know that by eight years old, the things that would shock most adults who weren't exposed to what we were had started to become normal. Drugs were a major part of the culture, a way of life, and so were the gangs who controlled the corners—the Gangster Disciples and the Black Disciples, or GDs and BDs, as they were often called. In the Englewood area of Chicago's Southside where we lived, you could get anything. Weed, crack, heroin, and any substances in between. Everything was in plain sight: people snorting, smoking, shooting, getting busted, being handcuffed by the police and carted off right out in the open for using and/or selling, many going to jail or winding up dead.

Our dad—who lived in a somewhat better neighborhood, also on the Southside, but much farther south and west from where we were—visited us fairly often. He might just come by and check in or take us out to do something fun, or, on occasion, have us stay with him overnight. Whenever Dad was staying at his girlfriend's house, her two sons who were around my age included us in whatever games they were playing or planning. And, yeah, basketball was at the top of that list!

Dad was by no stretch of the imagination what you'd call well-off, as he now and then reminded us that he did pay child support. But compared to how we were living—no phone, sometimes no electricity, often hungry, yet too proud to tell anyone—Dwyane Wade Sr. had stability. Dad was employed for most of his working years by Anderson

Printing Company, in their delivery business, getting up at five o'clock every morning, day in and day out. That meant he usually came to see us on weekends—or every other weekend, and sometimes it was a month or two months between visits. On the Saturdays when he was supposed to be coming, Tragil and I would wake up early and go wait by the door for hours to watch for the first sight of his old sky-blue Chevy chugging down the block. The minute we saw it, we raced each other to greet him.

On some of those Saturdays, something would apparently come up, and Tragil and I would wait all day, with every sighting of a car down the street getting our hopes up until it finally drove up close enough for us to see that no, it wasn't him. On those occasions when we'd wait at the door all day long for Dad to arrive and he never showed, there wasn't much we could do to hide our hurt.

Later, when I became a father, these experiences would stay with me as reminders to be careful about making promises to my children. This was something that was especially true during the prolonged divorce proceedings—when the boys and I couldn't see each other for long periods. Whenever we did see each other, we'd part not knowing when we'd see each other again.

Those days when Dad didn't show up were among the few instances when I can remember Mom really getting mad at him. Otherwise, my parents were almost never critical of each other in front of us.

All of that was less in my thoughts than it was in Tragil's on that day when she and I hopped on the bus to go to the movies. My sister might have realized that I was about to reach a dangerous time in my life. With Mom not around as much and Dad coming by less—as he got involved in doing more to take care of his girlfriend's boys—Tragil had been making a lot of offhand comments lately. She'd say, "Sons need fathers!" and "Dads can teach things mommas can't." Maybe she knew I was getting closer to the age when hanging out on the corners would be an obvious next step, and had decided she'd better do something before it was too late.

Many members of our extended family had gone in that direction, some gaining clout in the GDs, others in the BDs. For a while, that meant nobody messed with me, by virtue of who those relatives were. But that was about to end now that my turn was coming. Clearly.

That's what you did when you got to be ten, eleven, even eight or nine: you fell in line. If you had the maturity, you fell in line. You might come in as a watch-out kid, your job being to watch out for everyone in case there was any sign of the police. Then you'd graduate to holding the drugs and, from there, go on to selling them. And so on. I'd never actually said to my sister, "I know there is gonna come a time soon when I'm gonna be put in that position," because that would be as unnecessary as saying the day after Sunday is Monday.

Those were just the facts of our lives that I chose to ignore that day, especially once Tragil and I got to our seats on the bus on the way to the movies. Off on our end-of-summer adventure together, I wanted to enjoy the ride and block out the somber feeling that something else was coming to an end: childhood. So I did what was in my nature—to appreciate the present moment—and just paid attention to sights outside the bus window.

The bus ride did seem to go on a lot longer than I'd expected. I knew that the movie multiplex my sister's friend had told her about was not so far away. But I didn't care how long it was taking. Tragil, usually much more talkative than me, didn't say anything and seemed content to see me so happy. How far we had gone, I couldn't tell, except we were still on the Southside. The neighborhoods seemed to be improving block by block. The farther from our house we rode, the safer and more family-friendly the streets began to look.

At West Seventy-Ninth and Marshfield, I got my bearings and realized this was where my father's girlfriend, Bessie, lived. At the bus stop, I looked over into the back lot of one of the three-story apartment houses and recognized it from Dad having brought me to play there. That was when, to my surprise, I spotted Donny, one of Bessie's sons.

Seven years old, Donny was in the back lot by himself, wielding this big toy sword like he was doing battle with a tree and then mixing in karate moves to defend against imaginary opponents. Looked fun to me. Real fun.

Tragil didn't waste any time before asking, "You wanna stop and go play with Donny?"

"Yeah . . . ," I began, hoping not to sound too excited since we were having our brother-sister day together. Probably, I thought, we were just stopping by for a short while and then going on to the movies later.

"Let's go, then." Tragil jumped up and led the way so we could get off the bus before the doors closed.

While my sister went up to Bessie's apartment—where there were usually different people stopping by—I joined Donny in the back lot to get in on the sword battle. Before long, Donny's older brother, Demetrius, showed up with a basketball, plus a couple of other kids he knew. Now the games could begin! The alley alongside the building became our makeshift court while we rigged up a crate that had no top or bottom to serve as the hoop. Demetrius was head and shoulders above all of us—in height and skills. But given the unstoppable competitive streak in my DNA, I was determined I'd catch up one day.

The hours flew by. When Tragil finally came out to the alley to get me, we were still in the thick of the game, having so much fun I'd completely forgotten about our earlier plans.

"You ready to go?" she asked with a little smile, like she knew the answer.

"No." Had to be honest.

"Well, you could stay, if you want. You could stay the night."

"Cool." I started over to Demetrius, who had the ball. Then I turned around to Tragil again to ask when she was coming back to get me.

"I'll come back, Dwyane. I'll come back tomorrow." She may have hesitated before leaving after that, maybe to stay and watch us play, maybe not wanting to go back home to her own uncertainties. She might have even known, before I'd figured it out, that she probably wasn't returning there anytime soon.

A day went by without Tragil returning to get me. The fun of hanging out, plus knowing I was going to be around my dad more often, must have distracted me from worrying. It took me about a week before I realized Tragil wasn't coming for me at all. At first, I didn't want to believe that. But then I counted the days in my head, one by one, how she hadn't been back that following day, or the day after, and so on, and finally there was only one conclusion: she wasn't coming back. Then it dawned on me that the plan was never to go the movies, that for some reason, she had decided to trick me.

It took some time before I could grasp what my sister was doing. She was getting to be that age herself, close to high school, when she would have to figure out a plan for her security, how to make her way in the world. She had been taking care of me all these years and now she had to take care of herself.

Years later, Tragil told me how hard it had been to walk away that day in the alley. She was proud that beforehand she had spoken her mind to Dad, telling him he needed to step up and take a more active role in looking after his son, and she was even prouder that he agreed. Her plan had worked, she said, mainly because one of the most important lessons Mom had taught Tragil was to be strong and to say how she felt but also to remember that there is a time, a place, and a way to do so. That's how she had been successful in speaking to Dad. But Tragil couldn't explain anything to me back then.

My sister recalled, "I got to see you playing, enjoying yourself, and I was about to cry my eyes out, so I had to walk away fast. I didn't want you to see me crying."

Our mom had placed her faith and trust in Tragil and expected her to make that most unselfish of decisions, to get me into a situation where there would be more opportunity to have a better life, to go after dreams that might not have been possible if I had stayed where I was. Tragil did it for Dad, too, who stepped up in many ways, working on our father-son relationship, which wasn't always easy but laid the groundwork for what I have with my own sons. Tragil did it for our mother, above all, so Mom could find the strength to overcome all that stood in her path—and become the living miracle she is today.

Looking back, I give my sister so much credit for what she did for me and for all of us. But in those first days and weeks away from the only home I knew, the truth is that I felt lost, alone, and overwhelmed by everything that had changed instantly the moment she hurried away.

Still, deep down, I understood that Tragil had saved my life.

THE POWER OF THAT MEMORY HELPS ME PUT JIM'S NEWS about custody into perspective this Friday afternoon. I force myself to exhale and release some of the pressure that's been building all this time.

Very few people other than those most close to me know how hard this has been on me. My ex had fed the press so many untruths that to this day, some of the public, including loyal basketball fans, aren't aware they've been proven false and retracted. The damage these accusations caused led me to file a defamation suit against her immediately. One of the most damaging of these claims was that I had given her an STD. This was disproven almost immediately and the lawsuit she had used to put that lie out there was withdrawn. But it's impossible to undo this kind of damage. For the record, the accusation wasn't true, is baseless, and was eventually seen by the custody judge as part of the all-out effort to alienate the boys from me. Then there were her accusations that I had been physically abusive. Again for the record, these were also false. I've learned over my years in the NBA that there are some knocks that come with the territory—and I've gained a thick skin. But where I drew the line was when absurd charges were also filed against my sister Tragil and my girlfriend, Gabrielle Union, and allegations were made against members of my family, as well as friends, whose only guilt was loving me and wanting to see me have time with my sons.

Gossip did just as much damage. In the press, I was painted as a poor lost kid who was taken in by my ex and her mom in high school and never would have ever made it without their efforts. Then, it was said, I left once the going got good. We've all heard stories like that before so they sound true—even though the facts don't back them up. On top of that, when my ex filed a suit for damages on behalf of the boys against Gabrielle, the press went to town to portray Gabrielle as a home wrecker. The court threw out that suit, of course, and Gab and I rose above the noise, becoming closer in the process.

All of this was shocking and regrettable. But the issue of alienation—what the court sees as one parent's repeated attempts to prevent a child from having a healthy relationship with the other—was the most disturbing. When I filed for divorce in May 2008, I asked for joint custody. Siohvaughn then sued for sole custody. That was the beginning of the longest custody trial in Cook County family court history.

I believed—and still do—that children need their dads and their moms in their lives, and I never set out to fight for full custody. Siohvaughn is a most loving, caring mother and the boys love and adore her just as they do me. But it had become clear to me, even with court orders that she comply with a visitation schedule allowing my sons to travel twice a month from Chicago to Miami—usually in the care of Tragil—that she was going to disregard orders and throw up every and any excuse to keep me from seeing them. Something had to give. I kept hoping for a reasonable resolution, but that seemed less and less likely as the changing teams of lawyers on the other side threw up hurdles.

It got so bad that I had to start going to court and filing multiple motions just to talk on the phone to the boys. More worrisome was finally hearing their voices but knowing the words they were saying weren't their own. And then, more and more frequently, were last-minute claims that Zaire and Zion were sick and couldn't travel for their visitation with me. Or there were other excuses. Or no excuses at all. The breaking point came in early 2010 when we couldn't even locate my sons and their mother, the most frightening moment of my life.

That was the turning point for me—when I decided that I had to seek full custody. If this had to be a fight, then by God, I had to fight for my sons.

Here I am now, a roller coaster of a year later on this Friday afternoon following a tough practice, not long after trudging up the stairs to close my eyes for an hour or so. I had begun to brace myself for a decision that wouldn't be in my favor. The judge, a woman, had indicated that her verdict was most likely coming within six weeks or so. By now I knew that custody cases often tend to be weighted toward keeping kids with their moms. Siohvaughn's lawyers had argued forcefully that between extensive travel and the demands of my NBA and business schedules I wouldn't have time to meet my responsibilities as a full-time single dad. The truth was that I had created a schedule that would let me spend more time with them than many nine-to-five fathers. Still, there weren't many well-known stories of full-time single dads in the National Basketball Association.

Then there was the blow of the court-appointed outside expert who had expressed real concern during the trial about how much the boys had suffered emotionally from being alienated from me by their mother; we had expected her to recommend I be awarded full custody—but, in the end, she advised against it.

All of that had been weighing on me. Plus, this was one of the Fridays when Tragil was supposed to pick up the boys in Chicago and fly with them to Miami for our regularly scheduled weekend. Until they were safe on the flight, I wasn't going to relax. But even so, I was able to smile, imagining the two of them bounding in the front door—Zaire with his big personality and infectious laughter, Zion with his great powers of observation and his one-of-a-kind sense of humor—and of course the hugs and joy that would follow.

Just before sinking into sleep, I reached for the BlackBerry to have it closer for checking messages in case anything was happening with the boys or if my sister had any updates. And that's when, seconds later, the sound of Jim's e-mail caught my attention, causing me to click on it, sit up in the bed, and react with a couple of incredulous "What?'s" before leaping to my feet, again reading those eight words:

DWYANE HAS BEEN AWARDED CUSTODY OF THE CHILDREN

"What . . . ?" I say out loud once more in a high pitch. "You gotta give me more than this, Jim!"

I'm out of my mind, talking to the BlackBerry and to myself.

I call Lisa Joseph, my business manager and point person on just about everything, who works under the umbrella of Henry Thomas (a.k.a. Hank), my sports agents at Creative Artists Agency (CAA). Hank at that moment is trying to get Jim on a conference call. Jim, unbeknownst to any of us, is in the middle of another court case and unable to answer the phone. Apparently Jim had gotten the news on his way into court and only had enough time to send that message.

"Lisa, did you see this e-mail?"

"Yes, but I don't know what it means!" she says.

My heart starts beating even faster, as she clicks off to call Hank, while I see Jim's phone number come up on my screen.

Grabbing that call, and then hearing Lisa and Hank conferenced into the line, too, I listen to Jim say in a voice that's all out of breath, "Oh my God, you just got full custody of the boys!"

In my wildest dreams, I could never have believed what Jim has just confirmed. I want to cry, jump, scream, and shout, and, above all, praise God. But Jim brings us back to the ground and asks, "Have you talked to your sister?"

"No, not yet . . ." My heart almost stops. Suddenly, boom, I panic that something could have happened to stop Tragil from picking up the boys.

"Call her now," Jim says, calmly but urgently, not wanting to worry me. The documents had been released to my ex's attorneys at the same time that my sister was supposed to have picked up the boys and were already in the Town Car with a driver and well on their way to the Chicago airport. But anything could have thrown off the timing. There was a stop she was going to make to pick up our sister Deanna's nine-year-old son, Dahveon, who was going to be visiting me in Miami for the weekend with his cousins. What if they were running behind?

In a full sweat, now out of breath, I call Tragil, asking in almost stutters, in a low voice, "Is . . . is everything . . . are . . . my sons safe?"

The minute she tells me they are in the car, sitting in the backseat on the way to the airport, the weight of the world lifts off my chest and now my tears start to fall. I explain Jim's e-mail, which Tragil also got.

We just keep saying, "Oh my God," so grateful that the struggle is over. I'm crying like a baby for joy and Tragil starts crying like a baby, too.

I can hear Zaire's voice from the backseat, asking, "T.T.?"—as he calls his aunt Tragil—"What's wrong? Don't cry!"

She says, "Oh, honey, nothing's wrong, everything's fine." The boys clearly have no idea what's happening.

I ask Tragil not to say anything to the boys and tell her I want to explain everything to them in the right way at the right time, so they understand that having their main home base with me won't change anything about how much their mother loves them and will continue to be in their lives. Even if it's going to take time, I have to explain why we'll keep the faith that she and I will find that open line of communication so that both of us are their parents no matter what.

Meanwhile, I'm leaving nothing to chance and add security at both the Chicago and Miami airports. Once that's in place, I race downstairs to share the news with Gabrielle—who is there for the weekend—Rich Ingraham, my chef, and a group of friends who've stopped by. More tears follow, along with hugs and prayers of thanks.

Then, in the middle of the excitement and celebration, it hits me—they're not just coming for the weekend this time. They're here for good, not returning to Chicago at the end of the weekend as they normally would.

That's when I immediately switch—like BOOM—into full-time single-daddy mode, calling Lisa Joseph back and asking her to call Brand Jordan to get clothes and shoes sent over ASAP and to check right away with the school and preschool so we can have the boys enrolled by Monday. I also want to set up appointments with their Miami doctors. In our appeal to the court for custody a lot of legwork had already been done. We had already put up security gates and kid-proofed the house for their visits but having extra safety supplies would be good. What we needed was a desk where they could be all set up to do homework. Then there's Shellye Martin, my longtime interior designer, who has been working on designs to make the guest bedroom where they sleep more kid-friendly. "Oh, and I want to talk to Shellye about how fast we can get the bunk beds. And bedding, don't forget the bedding!"

Suddenly, I'm like Dwyane Wade, the director, on the phone marshaling the troops, talking about how I need this done, that done, and how fast. Wow! This is not usually my MO but when the responsibility I asked to have is given to me, what else am I going to do but rise to the challenge?

AND THAT WAS WHEN I REALIZED SOMETHING ELSE THAT paved the way for this book. First, it occurred to me that there was no guidebook out there that defined and detailed what being a great full-time single dad really was. Where was the game plan for getting this right? Well, if there wasn't one, then I would need to draw from the past and do the legwork to create one of my own.

Fatherhood, to me, isn't something you do for awards or acclaim. It's a privilege and a huge responsibility. Of course, the recognition I've been given has been flattering—except I don't think it makes sense to honor me for what I should be doing in the first place. That said, I do hope that by opening up in ways I haven't in the past, I can encourage other fathers or father figures to get more involved with their kids' lives.

Another reason I'm writing this book is for Zaire and Zion. My hope is that in retracing some of my steps in life, both successful and not, I can pass on important lessons taught to me by others and that I had to pick up on my own. But I also want them to know there are no shortcuts or easy answers to being a father first, my life's mission. I want them to know I'm learning still, sometimes on the fly.

Who really tells you how to be a dad? No one. Which is why I want to share my discoveries about how every child is different and you therefore have to parent each differently. I want to address the priorities I'm a stickler for—my beliefs about respect, responsibility, hard work, having dreams, and always being open to learning. Just as important, I want my boys, including my nephew Dahveon, to know they are my best teachers when it comes to being a good father.

For those men who are dads but not fully engaged as fathers, I want to urge you not to miss out on the greatest rewards and blessings that your children represent in your life. A lot of guys have approached me and asked how to become more involved when circumstances have kept you out of your kids' lives. Hopefully you'll find useful suggestions in my story. Aside from an abundance of reading materials, many communities provide all kinds of classes that promote the values of coparenting, which I can't stress enough.

My sincere hope is to inspire both fathers and mothers who may feel challenged by single parenthood or by your current situation. I'm really writing for all parents, including those foster parents or relatives who raise kids that may not be biologically their own, as well as coaches, teachers, advocates, and mentors. By investing our love and energy and time in young people and in their development, we change and heal our world.

And, finally, I wanted to write this book for the kid in every single person out there so you can know the power of love and your own possibilities. If my story and the stories of my loved ones have taught me anything, it's the simple truth that you have to play your heart out until the buzzer sounds no matter how disastrous the score may seem at times, because giving up is not an option.

I can't promise that will always win you an NBA championship. But as my mother used to say when encouraging me to strive to do great things, to lift others as well as myself, "Your life is bigger than basketball."

And that saying brings me back to Friday night, waiting for my boys to arrive. I had to gather my thoughts and feelings so I could give my sons the news that inspired this book in the first place. After all the uncertainty, I could assure them that after everything, they were now home.

And, finally, so was I.

PART ONE

The way to redeem your past is not to run from it, but to try to understand it, and use it as a foundation to grow.

—Jay-Z, *Decoded*

CHAPTER ONE

GO GET YOU A GAME

FRIDAY EVENING
MARCH 11, 2011
AT HOME IN MIAMI

YES, IT'S TRUE—I LOVE THE ROAR OF THE CROWD.

When the fans are with you, their voices come together in a big booming rush of sound that you can actually feel in your body—almost like a wave that lifts you and carries you past your own limits.

I love the chants, the stomping of feet, the eruptions of cheers, hoots, and hollers. Besides the fact that I'm lucky to do what I love for my living, I'm blessed every day on the job with the joy of hearing fans and announcers call my name. Not to mention various nicknames—from "D-Wade" to "Flash" to just "#3."

But as much as I love the music of the crowd when they're with me, none of that comes close to the thrill of hearing my sons call out my most favorite name of all: "Daddy!" Any time, anywhere, any day.

So, needless to say, on the evening of Friday, March 11, when I open the door to greet Tragil and the boys, hearing their chorus of "Daddy! Daddy!" it's enough to bring on another batch of tears.

Zaire bounds in first. No surprise there. But Zion somehow edges his brother out and takes a running leap up into my arms for the first hug. Swinging him up on one side of me, I lift up Zaire in my other arm. (Yeah, I'm strong.) Then, spotting Dahveon—nicknamed Dada—shyly standing off to the side, I gesture for him to come on over to get in on the action.

Group hug!

This is crazy. This is pure happiness.

Tragil, fighting her tears, joins in, along with Gabrielle and some of our friends who have been helping out for most of the afternoon, arranging appointments at schools, shopping for extra clothes and school supplies, measuring for the bunk beds, and making sure the kitchen's stocked with more than a weekend's worth of kid-friendly food. My mantra all day to everyone has been that we need to establish a set routine that gives them a sense of normalcy and security. Routine, I've learned, is key.

Meanwhile, we're all also trying to be restrained, not wanting the boys to suspect something dramatic is up. That conversation needs to happen. But not yet.

"Let me look at you three. C'mon now."

We break out of our hug so I can admire each one of the boys, rubbing on their heads, giving each a compliment, and then more hugs. Can't help myself. In the parenting school I come from, love and praise are fundamentals. As basic as the air we breathe. Love comes first, second, and last. Always.

I start with my nephew Dahveon—whose father hasn't been on the scene regularly in his life. Same age as Zaire, Dada's an old soul, sensitive but also fun-loving. After his mom, my sister Deanna, gave her okay for him to start traveling with his cousins to visit me, Dada quickly became a steadying force for them. And for me. During the worst challenges of the custody battle, when my visitations with the boys were so infrequent and my relationship with Zaire was strained as a result, I'd invite Dada to come for a visit, too, and he always made Zaire feel more comfortable and able to enjoy the fun.

Dada and I high-five and low-five as I tell him how much I appreciate his help. So proud of himself, he struts off, then stops to show me one of the latest dance moves from Chicago.

Zaire, never one to stand still, waits excitedly to confirm that everybody's going to the Heat game the next day. When I assure him that the game is early enough for the three boys to attend, he does a couple of dance moves he's learned from Dada to show his pride. Everyone cracks up. Not a shy kid whatsoever, Zaire has that ability to let his spirit lift the spirit of others. In fact, before I can say much more, he starts making small talk with the other adults in the room—like a seasoned conversationalist. He throws in comments on everything from the latest YouTube music video he's seen to traffic on Biscayne Boulevard. And he's hip, too, coming up with his cool little catchphrases to respond to the adults, saying, "Yeah, yeah, that's what I'm talkin' 'bout."

"Zaire," I start to laugh, "you don't know nuthin' 'bout that. You just makin' comments like you know." I hug him again, amused. He shrugs, enjoying my admiration, full of his nine-year-old swagger.

I swear, if I could live my childhood over, I wouldn't mind being Zaire Wade at his age. He's an all-around cool kid, with a lot of personality, excellent athletic skills, and a real gift of gab, all on top of being very handsome. Not that I take the credit. Yeah, I see some Wade in his expressions and features but he has his mom's eyes and lips. And that outgoing, talkative side of him is much more like her than me.

Zion got his mom's smarts big-time. But as far as looks go, he's a mini-me. Pictures of me at his age look so much like him we have to check closely to tell who is who. He scans the room, making sure nobody is standing close by, and motions me closer to say something. When I lean down to hear, he jumps up again, hugging on my neck, laughing.

"Zion, you are awesome, ya know that?" I say and watch his face light up.

"I know," he nods.

Like his brother, Zion has major confidence. For someone not even four years old, he is smart beyond his years. Sometimes too smart. It's crazy how well he can converse with adults. Being a Gemini, though, he can be as standoffish as he can be friendly.

Unlike Zaire, who is Mr. Mayor, holding court wherever he goes, Zion looks at everyone with a crooked eye. Takes him a while to warm up. When he does, though, he loves you unconditionally. But he's very careful in general, which to me, someone who now most likely has some trust issues of my own, might be a good thing. In some ways, because the boys were prevented from seeing me for long periods, Zion and I are just getting to know each other. We're definitely going to be making up for lost time.

One of the many special traits that I admire about Zion is how he is just his own little person. He doesn't feel the need to be as passionate about basketball—say, like Zaire and Dada, who are both getting into it as players. Especially Zaire. Zion likes getting into the mix but apparently he has his own dreams. I'm not sure what they are yet, but whatever he throws himself into in the coming years, I mean—watch out world!

When our arriving travelers hear snacks being offered, the three boys dash off together to the kitchen to see what Rich has cooking.

This is when Tragil and I have a chance to talk and hug again in relief and joy. A few people close to us understand the hell of these last several years but she is perhaps the only person who has been there at almost every step of my journey. Right now, Tragil knows that I have my own process for making decisions and that I'm intensely thinking through how to talk to the boys about the custody news. She also knows that part of that process, painful as it is, involves reflecting on the past and our own childhood.

My sister has always said that one of her jobs in the family has been to remember everything that's happened along the way. "So I can remind you in case you forget" is what she says.

Not that I've forgotten anything. It's just that up until now, I've had to block a lot of it out.

But no more. If I want to be the Daddy I promised myself as a child that I was going to be, it's time to go back there and do the remembering myself.

Whenever I go hunt for memories from childhood, the most vivid recollections that come to mind are of my grandma and me sitting out on the stoop of our apartment building on the corner of Fifty-Ninth and Prairie. Probably the earliest memory I have of the two of us out there together took place on a night in early spring 1987, a few months after my fifth birthday.

There's a sound track that accompanies this memory: a radio blasting R&B from someone's apartment, a boom box across the street with the bass turned all the way up and somebody rapping to the beat, police sirens and gunfire at enough of a distance not to run and hide, and car tires screeching as they speed along the wet pavement of Prairie Avenue.

And then, in the middle of that hum of the nighttime sound track could be heard the sad vocal of my grandmother crying and praying out loud: "Oh Lawd, Lawd, please help me get outa this mess. Lawd, please help me with these children caught up in they trouble, Lawd."

There were many nights when I heard her cry and pray like that. Why this night stands out, I don't know, except that this could have been the first time that I made a promise to myself never to do the things, whatever they were, that made my grandma sad and worried like she was. Not because of how bad those things were (even though I had some general ideas already) but because of how much I loved my grandmother and wanted her to be happy.

Grandma had lived in the apartment on the top floor of the three-story building since the early 1970s, along with her son Roger, our uncle, who worked as a security guard in those days. We had only moved into the apartment on the first floor the year before. As Tragil could better recall about the previous four and a half years since my birth, they had been turbulent for us and for our mom, especially after she called it quits with Dad. With our mother's initial descent into the clutches of drugs, Tragil and I were separated from her at different times when we stayed with friends and relatives, while our two older sisters, Deanna and Keisha, in their teens, stayed with other family members. Dad remained in the picture but probably didn't know the extent of our situation. The thing was that even when she was "in her madness"—as we would say to refer to Mom's battles—a lot of people loved and believed in her, and went the extra mile to help out with her kids until she was able to get on her feet and have us all under one roof again.

At last, that day had come when Mom got off drugs and found a steady part-time job. Grandma was then able to talk the landlord into letting us move into the same building as her. When we arrived, the landlord and his family lived on the second floor but pretty soon he moved out and my aunt Barbara started renting that apartment. Because of his close relationship with Grandma, the landlord was lenient with Mom on those occasions when the rent was late. When the electric bill was late, that was another story. We had a hot plate and lights that we'd hook up to an outlet in the hallway and we had to run to unplug the cords whenever the landlord was coming.

None of those worries bothered me and Tragil much. At first. We were struggling, yeah. But we had our momma back and we were a family again. We had our own bedroom, Tragil and I, that we shared. We'd go shopping as a family once a month, with help from welfare, and we had a regular schedule. Some of my happiest really early memories of my mother come from this period. Nothing specific, just plain and simple mother love, like glimmers of light you spot at a distance on the surface of the water, the further you get from the memories.

Because, unfortunately, all of this was short-lived.

A new man came into my mother's life. Young as I was, I understood that he brought the drugs into our place, once it became apparent that the first-level apartment was a prime location for dealers to do their drops, and soon enough as just a place to sell from. What I didn't understand was how it was he got to come into our house and control our mother, beating her, like she would say, breakfast, lunch, and dinner, and then attempt to control us. My mom was on dope again before long, all for reasons I couldn't fathom until much later. She didn't think that I knew or that I'd ever seen her shoot up. It would have been too shameful for her to accept that I was ever in the room when she was tapping for a vein to hit and putting the needle in.

Right before I turned five was the first time the police raided the apartment.

Whenever my mother's boyfriend or anyone shady was around, Tragil would get us into our bedroom at the back of the apartment and lock the door. No one who ever came around laid a hand on us. But she had always prepared me for the pounding on the front door by the police. Our escape route was to run out the back door and up the outside staircase, two flights to Grandma's back porch. Tragil would push me out first and then follow. Once again she was willing to sacrifice getting caught as long as she got me out of there first.

This time, thankfully, we both hit the stairs running at full speed. The police had been staking out the place but hadn't come around to the back. At the top of the steps, we desperately knocked on our grandma's back door, calling out for her in loud whispers, "Grandma, it's me Dwyane!" "Grandma, it's Tragil, can we come in?"

No answer.

Scared to death that she wasn't there, we were so relieved and lucky to find Uncle Roger at home. We flew inside and then raced to the front window on the other side of the apartment and looked down to see our nightmare: Mom in handcuffs being dragged to the patrol car. They'd found nothing in terms of drugs but they took her anyway only to hold her overnight and release her in the morning.

And now, a few months later, our grandma was out on the front porch on a rainy spring night, praying and crying because of what drugs had done to her daughters and sons and nephews and nieces and grandchildren. So that's what caused a switch to flip in my mind— seeing how much pain and stress the madness had brought to her—and I knew for certain right then that this woman, this rock of the family, my grandmother, would not have one more child to cry about when it came to me. And my decision to be different was not one of judgment of right and wrong on anyone else, only that I didn't want to be the cause of Grandma's worries and hurt. The thought was unbearable that she could one day be hurting at night for something I'd done or something I was doing.

And that was that.

Of course, I had other memories of this period in time out there on the porch where Grandma usually kept her chair just under the over- hang. In warmer weather, we'd stay outside farther down on the stoop, sitting there for hours, late into the night. And Grandma would watch the goings-on in the neighborhood, keeping an eye out not just for her own kids and grandkids but for everyone. Nowhere in the world was safer to me than my spot sitting behind my grandma. No matter how many times she'd say, "Go on in, chile, time you go to sleep," I'd say, "I don't wanna go to bed, I'm not tired!" and then proceed to curl up right behind her and fall asleep there.

At sixty-five years old, Willie Mae Morris, born and raised in Jack- son, Mississippi, mother of nine, including my mom, was more to me than a mothering/grandmother figure. She was probably closer to a mentor, teaching me fundamental lessons for life—that later would carry over to basketball. Grandma taught me the importance of family, of loyalty, of looking out for loved ones. She tried to teach me patience and forgiveness, too.

"When somebody do you wrong or do somebody wrong that you love," Grandma would say, "gettin' back at them ain't the way."

At five years old, I'd heard all that "two wrongs don't make a right" stuff. But, frankly, I already knew that if you didn't stand up and answer someone who disrespected you or somebody in your family— that would be seen as weak. You had to fight back.

You can ask Tragil about that. Not long after I started kindergarten, she began telling me about a bully from her school who'd been teasing her, taking her book bag, messing up the stuff inside, and throwing everything on the ground, and scaring her. Finally, when he did it in front of me after she stopped by to walk me home from school one day, I went ballistic and let him have it. Me, a skinny little five-year-old boy, hauls off and punches this sixth-grade badass in the nose?! Naturally, he turned around and punched me twice as hard in my nose, at which point Tragil stopped being afraid of the bully and chased him down the street to get vengeance, but he outran her. The fight would have been broken up by older kids. They may have whispered something later about who some of our family members were. Whatever was said, after that the bully backed down completely.

Grandma's point was to let it go. "Can't fight water under the bridge." She emphasized that forgiveness wasn't about weakness. "You gotta move on, learn to forgive," she explained. "But you never forget." That was my grandmother's belief and she repeated it: "Forgive but don't forget." Then, looking at me straight in my eyes, she asked, "Understand?"

I nodded but it took me years to really understand. Still, in the meantime, she had started to teach me what it meant to be tough in a different way.

Willie Mae Morris was so tough. She could walk down the streets, through the most dangerous parts of the neighborhood, and nobody would mess with her no matter what was going on. There was this aura of pride and dignity that everyone admired, which came along with the fact that she was obviously a godly woman. Grandma commanded a presence and a toughness.

Nothing intimidated Grandma, not even the police. And nothing scared me more than the police. So whenever they came around, I hid right there on the porch behind Grandma and no harm would ever come to me—because I think the police had a respect for Willie Mae Morris, too. She was like the patron saint of the neighborhood and as long as she was sitting there on the stoop or down in the grass in front of the building, they almost never tried to come in on a bust.

Of course, almost is not never. After that first raid, there would be others. I was terrified that the next time they would take Mom away and not let her come home.

The cure for the fear, as far as I could tell from Grandma, was to be on my toes, to use my senses, paying attention to sights, sounds, and smells, learning to read people—anticipating their next moves by little clues. By being watchful, my fear wouldn't overpower me so much and I could enjoy the entertainment value of all these interesting characters who all passed by 5901 Prairie Avenue.

Grandma loved to have me watch with her, too. And her laugh was contagious and unforgettable. Her laugh would ring in my head forever—the music of someone holding on to joy as hard as she held on to faith.

Whenever something positive happened, Grandma would remind me of it often, teaching me to value happier memories. We talked so much about the day I graduated from kindergarten at the Cockrell Child Parent Center that it stands out as a highlight of childhood. The school was for pre-K and kindergarten, before I'd continue on at Betsy Ross Elementary, which Tragil attended. For the graduation ceremony, I came dressed in my best clothes—a little suit I'd been given by a member of the family—and I wasn't sure if Mom was going to make it. But lo and behold, when I stood onstage I looked out and spotted her there in the crowd, waving and smiling proudly, pointing me out to the people around her.

Grandma loved any occasion that brought others together. That stoop was like her office—with everybody stopping by for a visit. My sisters and their friends would come by, as would neighbors and aunts and uncles and cousins, sometimes even sitting down on the steps with her before heading off to wherever they had to go. Except for me. I'd hang with Grandma, in the best seat in the house, right behind her, to watch and listen, enjoying the show. As scared as I was of the police, I eventually started to have a running inner monologue—me pretending I was a stand-up comedian or something—about the different officers. Like there was one of them who moved in a robotic motion, his head rotating from side to side, and his eyes always hidden behind his shades. He was the one I nicknamed "Robocop."

Whenever he headed our way, I'd just think to myself, *Okay now, here comes Robocop*, and chuckle under my breath. Somehow that made him not as mean. I'd share my inside jokes with Tragil and with my only friend of these years, a kid who started as a bag boy carrying drugs when he was all of five.

That was a damn shame. And most people at the time would have agreed. But, again, that was the culture, the way of the world that we lived in: that eventually everyone was going to be connected or related to the gangs in some capacity, part of the industry that was all there was.

No one spoke too much to me of the history of the Chicago gangs. The older folk, however, could remember that they originally formed to be of service to the needs of the community, like a social fraternity for belonging, when your own family couldn't be there for you or when other institutions let you down. When politicians and even church leaders had no answers for the problems in the community, the gangs stepped in and actually fulfilled important functions. That changed over time. Still, for a struggling, mostly poor, all African American community like ours, where pretty much the only white people we encountered were the police (and they were all white then), gangs like the GDs and the BDs offered protection and options. The drug trade wasn't just one option; it more or less became the only option, what ruled every aspect of life—*the* answer.

All this reality played itself out over the years as I watched the main players and the supporting cast of characters go about their daily business in plain sight. This wasn't out of the norm for kids my age, either. But maybe, as a serious spectator, I paid extra attention. I knew who sold what and where. By the time I left, I'd seen over the course of my time every corner, every signal, every handshake for the exchange of money and drugs. Since the police watched, too, the dealers had to keep changing it up, trying different stuff for the handoffs so as not to look shady. There was an art and a science to these moves. The buyer would have the money in a hand and the seller had the drugs in a hand. The two would approach, act cool like they knew each other, do a kind of "what's up" hesitation, and then in a blink—*slap!*—the handshake exchange was done and did. So smooth. Into the pocket.

Now the twist in this story is that whatever any of them might be doing on the corners or down the street, whenever they passed by my grandma's porch a noticeable change occurred. All of a sudden, they'd stand up straighter than before and greet my grandma with the most polite, courteous attitude. They always began with "How you doin' Momma Morris, you need anything?"

No doubt they'd go right back to their ways as soon as they were out of her sight. But when they walked past this sixty-five-year-old woman sitting out on our porch, it was straight-up respect. Total. The unwritten law seemed to be that you couldn't just walk by and not say "How you doin' Momma Morris?"

The respect was something that I picked up on very young, something that as her grandson gave me pride, that I vowed to carry with me from that time forward, and that I have in me still.

MY PARENTS, IN DIFFERENT WAYS, WERE BOTH DREAMERS. And each is responsible for planting the seeds of dreams in me—in soil that was already enriched by the general landscape.

Let me add that my serious interest in basketball didn't happen until I was about nine years old. Even then, the odds were very much against me having any real success as a baller. But growing up how and where

I did before that age gave me some unusual skills that would serve me down the line in overcoming those odds.

For starters, I was Chi-town born and bred, Southside, too, and if you didn't love basketball a little, I'm sorry, but that meant there was something wrong with you! Besides that, Chicago weather, no matter what the season, was like growing up in a climate of extremes that amounted to built-in endurance training.

Fall was my least favorite season. Not because of school. Through-out childhood, school was a positive outlet for me. In spite of being a quiet kid, I was one of the better students and liked the fun activities, including games and classroom projects. There was safety and struc-ture. There was a space to forget worry. But outside and back at home, with the days getting shorter and nights longer, when Mom wasn't home I couldn't stay out on the porch behind Grandma as late. The chill in the air was also a reminder that winter was coming.

I could appreciate the sight of the leaves turning the colors of red and gold. Yet the mood of the world around me seemed less festive than in other seasons. The emotion wasn't something I wanted to name, but in hindsight, I'd call it sad. What I did like about the season as I turned six and then seven was getting to move off the porch and go follow Tragil on the weekends and evenings when she was going out with her friends.

If Mom saw that my sister was leaving to go somewhere and said, "Wait five minutes and then you go follow her," that was my cue to be on a mission. Out of there like lightning, I kept myself at a distance while following the trail, careful to avoid tripping or making any extra noisy moves that would tip off Tragil or her friends. The trick was never to take my eyes off them but to stay hidden by ducking behind cars. It never occurred to me that I was developing skills for the basketball court. However, I couldn't have asked for a better early obstacle course with all the weaving and darting between parked cars and trash cans, plus the ducking down and then jumping up and running some more after that. Half the time Tragil would spot me ducking behind a car or almost tripping over my growing feet. But she wouldn't say anything. I think she wanted me to honor Mom's request to look after her.

Winters in Chicago were brutal, the worst, but somehow they didn't bother me as much as fall. After the first heavy snowfall of the season, I'd go out that next morning all layered up to walk to school, not able to feel anything because of the numbing cold, and imagine I'd landed on another planet and this was how we had to walk in our space suits. I maximized opportunities for fun, making snow angels and snowmen and the best snowballs in the neighborhood. Along with having a good arm for throwing, I had my own strategies for being sneaky at throwing snowballs at people—like Tragil and her friends—and then ducking and hiding so they never knew who was responsible.

Most winter nights were too cold for sitting outside late to watch for Mom when she wasn't home. Instead, I'd wait up indoors by the window, often falling asleep there on the window ledge inside. In the morning, I'd find that someone had picked me up and carried me back to bed. In those instances, I'd run to check in on my mother, and most of the time, to my relief, she would be there in her bed, asleep.

Then came the rainy season, otherwise known in Chicago as spring.

Since everything appeared to be gearing up for summer, spring brought me excitement for what was to come. The first weeks of spring were my idea of breaking out of jail, coming out of the Chicago winter, and getting to go outside to play again. Or, as in the case of the rainy days, play outside on the porch for hours while Grandma sat in her chair under the overhang watching the street.

In just sneakers, jeans, and a sweater, no more winter coat or snow boots, I was out again, breathing the smells of the springtime in the city, waiting for sunnier days, singing, "Rain, rain, go away, come again some other day," which always got a chuckle out of Grandma.

With a hard little rubber ball someone had given me, I made up rules and regulations for the Rain Game, as I called it. The object of the game was to hit the ball on the wall and elsewhere and get it to come back to me. Out on the window was a metal ring that I would attempt to hit, like scoring a basket, and then ricochet at the right angle to land back into my hands. If the ball hit the ring and then rolled downstairs, the points didn't count. That also meant I'd have to run after it in the rain and get all wet. At six and seven years old, my ball-handling skills weren't half bad. Even if they were based on that little hard rubber ball.

The Rain Game helped me pass the time until my favorite season arrived. With the first sign of summer, Grandma would move her chair closer to the edge of the porch and let me sit on the stoop, even run around the front yard and play on the grass. As hotter days wore on, she'd let me go follow Tragil and go places with my cousins, all of us coming up with different games and adventures.

My happiest summer days, as I remember them, had to do with getting to watch or play basketball. Many of these memories are connected to my real introduction to the sport through my father. Dad—or Daddy, as I still called him in those days—was the person who first put a basketball in my hands. He was the first person to embody the deep passion for playing that I'd later discover in myself.

Sundays in summer meant that if Tragil and I were lucky, Daddy would swing by and pick us up after church and take us to watch him play. Tragil used to brag to her friends that our daddy was taking us over to the park in his neighborhood for his regular game in a summer men's league. When he'd show up as promised and load the two of us in the back of his old sky blue Chevy, I can recall the faces of the other kids watching us go off with this good-looking young workingman— like a celebrity, in a way.

That feeling of being special, of wanting others to see that our daddy loved us and was taking us to his game, stayed with me for days. Sometimes weeks. And so did every detail of the game and the festivities afterward. Most of the men on my father's team were working guys like him, so this Sunday basketball game was the highlight of their week. A lot of the guys brought their families—wives and grandparents and kids all on blankets with coolers and picnic baskets packed to the brim or fixings for barbecuing right there at the park.

Nobody ever had to ask me, "Are you hungry, son?" I was always hungry.

These Sunday games were no mere hobby or pastime to Daddy. The court was his stage, his place for taking all those dreams he used to harbor for doing something important with his life, for becoming a star. At various points, Big Dwyane, as Mom used to call him to differentiate from me, wanted to be a recording artist, a professional baseball player, and, yeah, get into the NBA. In time to come, I'd understand that he wanted out of the hard life and he wanted that for us, too. But he didn't necessarily know how to express the fact that those desires to give us something better came from love. Daddy was definitely rough around the edges.

Nowhere was that more evident than on the court. I mean, he was so tough. Of all the guys, Dad was always the one fixing to get into a fight. Anytime you heard arguing in a game, that was Dwyane Wade Sr. chewing out somebody for something. He was also intimidating as hell and as athletic as athletic gets. Not the best shooter, Dad, about six foot three, was a high flyer. Very muscular. He could outrun, steal, rebound, and do it all—except he couldn't shoot threes worth a damn. He could go to the basket, slashing like crazy, and dunk so hard the ground shook. That was his game. And he was good at his game.

In what turned out to be my first school of basketball, Dad played with a lot of guys who were also good. Once a lot of the local league players got older, they developed specialties. There might be that one guy who was a shooter. All he had to do was shoot. Then you had the point guard, who specialized in ball handling and control. Then you had the slasher like our dad. Over the years, I had a chance to study him and all the specialists and learn a lot from watching. For example, on Dad's regular team there were two guys named Michael—who went by Big Mike and Little Mike. And, not surprisingly, Little Mike was really little and Big Mike was really tall and athletic. The two had all these moves they'd worked out together, with Little Mike throwing lobs to Big Mike, who would then make child's play out of easy baskets. Those two looked masterful to me.

The moment Daddy dropped us off back home, I'd start working on Uncle Roger to let me borrow his basketball. On the days when he went to work as a security guard, I'd have to ask Grandma for permission to take it for a few hours. Roger was a cool uncle, not a super-talkative guy, but then neither was I, and occasionally he would come outside and give me pointers on dribbling or bring a baseball to play catch with me.

And then something happened that today is still not clear in my mind. No one explained what it was but one day I came up to return the basketball that Grandma had let me borrow and found Uncle Roger at home—staring blankly out the window. He barely registered my presence, like he didn't know me. The most I could get out of anyone was from one of my aunts, who told me, "Roger got real sick and he was in the hospital."

When I asked if he was going to get better soon and be himself again, my aunt didn't say another word.

Uncle Roger was never the same again, never able to go back to work, never interested in coming outside on hot summer days to play with me. The fact that nobody had a better explanation for what happened was troubling. On some deep level, I was even angry about the terrible communication and had this thought—*you know what, when I get to be in charge of a household, we're gonna talk about important things that are happening and not sweep them under the rug.* And in that thought, I came across the awful truth: that I was in charge of nothing. The fear that a similar or worse fate as Uncle Roger's would come to my mother only intensified.

Somehow, without me having to say anything, at my lowest moments, the part of Jolinda Wade that was her true self—her God self, as she would say—would let her out of her inner prison and be Mom. High or not, she'd take my hand and look right at me and ask, "Who your favorite girl?"

"You, Momma" was the only answer and the only truth.

Then, especially on those long summer days when she wanted to get out of the house and do something to make me happy, we'd borrow Uncle Roger's basketball and walk over to the park.

As it so happened, Washington Park, one of the most famous, popular parks in Chicago, ran adjacent to our neighborhood. In my seven-year-old mind, the park was as big as a city, complete with a huge swimming pool area and different playgrounds, and a series of basketball courts lined up as far as the eye could see. Like how I imagined heaven to be!

To get to the courts, Mom and I only had to walk six blocks or so. A part of me couldn't wait to get to the park and another part of me wanted these hours to last as long as possible. So while Mom carried her box of vino—like Wild Irish Rose, nothing fancy—and a blanket or chair she'd set up in the grass to sit, I'd dribble on up ahead and then dribble back, warming up for the competition.

Probably the most vivid of our summer outings to the park happened one July afternoon in 1989, when I was about seven and a half. Tragil, who had just turned twelve, had gone swimming with her friends and my mother had said, "You and I, let's go have us a date."

When we got to the basketball courts at Fifty-Third Street, before Mom could set up her chair and find a good spot where she could watch me play, the first order of business was to find a game where they'd let me in.

As she always did, Mom pushed me ahead of her and said, "Go get you a game, baby, go on."

If it was anyone but my mother, I would have just stood around, hoping for an opening. But this was what she told me to do and I had to find a way onto one of the courts. That day, as usual, most of the pickup games with younger players already had their teams set. The older guys, a lot of them in their forties, were in the middle of games that appeared to be even more closed. As I knew from Daddy's games, the men in their thirties and forties were hard-core about their minutes on the court and only had so much time to be at the park. But having had better luck in the past getting in on games with older players, I tried with them first.

"Cool if I come in?" I asked one of the men who looked like he was an organizer.

"Not today" was the answer.

At the next court, I couldn't even get anyone's attention.

At the third court, the older guy in charge started to say, "Not today," too. But he was interrupted by one of the guys on the opposing team, who argued with him. "C'mon, let the little man play." Fine, the main dude said, "You take him."

With that, I signaled to Mom, who nodded proudly and made herself comfortable on the grass nearby. As she would later say, she was not only my favorite girl but my first true cheerleader.

Now that the hard part of getting myself a game had been accomplished, the real fun began. And I have to admit, nobody saw me coming. The team that took me must have thought they were giving some kind of charity to a little kid. The other team must have been ready to take a breather and run right past me. Well, guess what? I surprised everyone, mostly by being one of those testy players—by using everything I had to my advantage and by exploiting the opponent's disadvantages. When the guy who didn't want me to play started to dribble the ball—watch out!—I was low to the ground and had no trouble grabbing it and tearing off with it, then posting up and putting it in!

By the end of the day, I was something of a hero.

The joy of this particular summer afternoon that I had shared with my mom, like others, couldn't last forever. I knew that. And I accepted that, just because of my hours of watching the reality show that was life from our porch. Mom said as much that evening after she called to me and said, slurring her words slightly, "Baby, time to go home."

I said all the things that a seven-year-old would say, that I was having so much fun, that I didn't want to stop playing basketball, and so on. But I helped her up anyway so we could leave.

To cheer me up, Mom then told me something I wouldn't hear again until many years passed. "Remember, baby," she said, with a dreamy expression on her face, "your life is bigger than basketball. Remember that."

Not sure what she was trying to tell me, I remembered and believed that had to be the case—because she said so. Also, because she had been the one to say, "Go get you a game."

I got that lesson. I figured out, at that age, that the world wasn't going to bring me my dreams. That job was going to be up to me.

Twenty-two years later, I could look back and recognize that's exactly what I did. And hopefully, as I announced to the three boys on Friday, March 11, 2011, that it was their bedtime, I could find an opportunity to pass on one of the most motivating lessons of my childhood.

But in the meantime, I was going to read them my favorite book, a story about change. Maybe you've read it. The title is *Green Eggs and Ham*.

CHAPTER TWO

PRAYERS, PROMISES, AND DREAMS

SATURDAY AFTERNOON AND EVENING
MARCH 12, 2011
AMERICAN AIRLINES ARENA, DOWNTOWN MIAMI

WHEN THE TIME COMES TO SHARE THE NEWS ABOUT THE
custody judgment with my teammates and the Heat staff, I make the decision not to say anything before our game against the Grizzlies. As usual,
everybody's doing whatever it is they usually do to get into that place of
mental focus that we need to have before a game. This day, some of the guys
listen to music, others are reading. Scratch that. Chris Bosh is reading.

The only person that I choose to pull aside before the game and tell
about my getting full custody of the boys is LeBron James.

He reacts with the same surprise, joy, praise, and relief as everyone in my inner circle has expressed so far. But since he knows we have a game to play, he does a good job of not letting on to the other guys.

That being said, it's hard to hold back all that pent-up emotion that comes pouring out of me during the game that follows, so much so that I'm thinking that some of the guys have to suspect some kind of added level of intensity and freedom from me on the floor.

But in spite of that hunch, as soon as we return to the locker room when the game is over and Coach Erik Spoelstra asks for everyone's attention so I can say a few words, I'm surprised to look around and see everyone staring back at me with big smiles.

Well, yeah, we had a great game. But this emotion I'm feeling from everyone is more than about how we played. Not that I expect the guys to come to tears over my news. Too much manly pride. Too much testosterone.

Still, it means the world to me to hear the cheers and feel the support when I announce that my custody ordeal has come to an end and that finally I get to be Daddy, who I've fought so hard to be. Everyone in the Heat organization has been like family all along, being there for me during the hardest days.

Of course, other than the insanity of what was reported in the media during the divorce and custody battles, the guys still know few of the details from behind the scenes. That was my choice, both to protect my family's privacy and to prevent all of that internal emotional pressure from hurting my game and, by extension, the team.

And, as I think about it in these moments, keeping my emotions boxed in like that has always been for better and for worse. On the plus side, I can see that part of what drives me—my will—comes from the fact that I've always had to fly under the radar to prove myself; so not letting anyone know what's going on has given me a needed edge. Part of it may be a mental glitch, just the way I'm wired, but blocking out the turmoil allows me to play harder and better under pressure. That goes for injury, illness, and whatever is happening off the court. Some people call it being in the zone—a kind of hyperfocus that requires you to set all the noise of the day aside, to become a warrior the minute you change out of your street clothes and into your uniform. To do that, I've had to learn not to allow hurt, anger, fear, or negativity mess with my head, but instead to transform the internal pressure cooker into the competitive engine that drives me.

On the minus side, I've also built up a high tolerance for the causes of distress and, unfortunately, learned to tolerate toxic situations much longer than I ever should have.

But standing in the locker room after announcing "The court has awarded me full custody of Zaire Blessing Dwyane Wade and Zion Malachi Aramis Wade," I'm starting to think that can change. At twenty-nine years old, I get to unlearn some of those old coping mechanisms and write a new chapter.

Even if most of the guys didn't know the details, as I listen to the cheers coming from an entire locker room of NBA players and coaching staff, I know they share the sense that justice has prevailed. After all, as a team we share the value that family comes first, something that our team president, the legendary Pat Riley, often reminds us right before he emphasizes what comes next: the will to win.

If the game today was any indication, no one will have to worry that the weight now lifted from me means that I'll play with any less intensity.

For one thing, having my boys there with us courtside to watch the game had given me added fuel—and that's an understatement. For another, that intensity is a fact of who I am—bred into me not just from the childhood I lived but from the history of what came before me.

MY MOTHER NEVER USED TO TALK MUCH ABOUT WHAT HER younger life had been like, growing up as one of nine children, raised by a single mother. From time to time, she'd answer questions. But not at length. Mostly, I felt robbed of getting to experience her true personality or how smart she really was, or even how beautiful she was before being in her madness.

Jolinda Morris had been a natural beauty. Tragil and I would study pictures of Mom in her teens—and compliment her soft, pretty features, with her big, soulful eyes, mysterious smile, and a fine complexion someone once compared to milk chocolate.

"Well," she'd laugh and admit in her smoky voice, "you know the thing I always wanted to be first was a model."

A great dream! Was it a stretch? Not to me. Yeah, I was biased because I was a boy and she was my mother and we were so closely connected. And still are. But in those old pictures you could see the sparkle in her eyes of someone who was going places, someone who believed she was marked by destiny. Then, after she traveled the world as a fashion model and achieved independence, her plan was to find a good man and they'd have twelve children together. Mom had it all mapped out—complete with a storybook house and a white picket fence.

What happened?

Only later, after we became adults, did Tragil and I start to ask that question of Mom and began to piece together the puzzle. Without blame or self-pity, my mother went back to where the dreams originated, growing up with eight siblings, the daughter of two country kids from Mississippi who'd come up to Chicago without the skills needed to thrive in the labor force or for raising children.

"All they knew," Mom would say, "was how to make babies."

"Did you know your father?"

"We knew Dad but he wasn't around."

That left her mother—our grandma—not much time except for work. Willie Mae kept three jobs at a time. "Your grandma was a workaholic who made sure that we had the necessities we needed to survive. I always appreciated that. And her independence."

Grandma also liked to have something to drink at the end of the day. Mom explained: "That was her way of releasing her cares and enjoying herself, being able to party a little bit and have a good time." As a little girl, my mom looked up to her mother very much. "More than once, I made the statement that when I grew up I wanted to be just like my mom. Your grandma was the prettiest woman in the world back then. She had this long beautiful hair that was a showstopper, and when she dressed to go out with her face made up, I'd look at her and think life would be magic if I could grow up to be like her."

Mom later wondered if, by trying to follow her mom's ways, she'd brought a curse upon herself without knowing it—that one day she'd turn too much to drinking and partying to escape the hardships of her life. But there was another more important puzzle piece, I guess you could say, and that came from her feeling different from everyone else.

This was how she put it, looking back: "I was that kid who was used to going off to be by myself. The 'special' one with a vivid imagination full of stories I could make up. I would talk to shoes, bunny rabbits, kind of like a schoolteacher." Not happy in the circumstances she was living, Jolinda used to do a lot of writing "to get out of the real world." Even though people told her how cute she was, she recalled, "I didn't think that I was cute at all." Then, fighting low self-esteem, she began to write stories of her Cinderella dreams and share them with her siblings on special occasions like Christmas and Easter.

Everyone encouraged her writing. Her being special and being different soon became a powerful thing. That is, until one day when her dad stopped by and he heard her reading one of her stories. He said she was crazy and in fact told Willie Mae that she needed to put that child away. "I was so angry with him," my mother remembered. "He didn't know me. And what did he mean, 'put me away'?"

On the one hand, that left a young Jolinda Morris to feel like she needed to find herself a man who would value all she had to offer. On the other, her mother was raising her to be strong and independent, with the familiar refrain: "You don't need a man, you can take care of yourself."

The social scene at school added another layer. At first, as one of the smartest kids in the classroom, Mom found a positive outlet in the world outside the house. But that started to change toward the end of elementary school. "I didn't think of myself as one of the pretty girls so to me I became a nerd," she said. "I wanted to hang with the popular people. So I got out of my lane and went into the lane with them. And they drank." Those fifth- and sixth-grade kids would go to a place called the Chicken Shack and someone would pass around some sweet peppermint schnapps. "Yeah, that was my first little drink I drank, and after a few sips I could approach people and feel confident, like I was somebody else, and before long learned to be anyone I wanted to be."

Teachers talked to Mom all along about her academic potential. But no one reinforced that message at home. At sixteen she gave birth to my oldest sister, Deanna. She told me, "I was a baby myself, having a baby. For a minute, though, I was happy. She was so very precious to me. My best little friend in the world." About my sister's daddy, Mom said, "First one to catch my eye and then break my heart. When I got pregnant by him, at least four or five other girls were pregnant by him, too."

The next year, a friendship that turned into a relationship, but no real love, led to her getting pregnant with my sister Keisha. At seventeen, about to be the mother of two little girls, Mom dropped out of high school. "My life was going down at that point. But I was trying hard. I started working at a plant called Wilson and Jones. I was still home with mother, but I was taking care of my girls, being independent and responsible and thought that would take away how disappointed I was in myself. Except it didn't. The shame set in because instead of making it out, I'd come to a place called failure. The big *F*. And I was the smart kid who had the promise."

For the next year, she tumbled into the first downward spiral. No drugs but hard drinking. "Just drinking to drink" is how she described it. "I was embarrassed. I was miserable. I was really lonely."

The dreams didn't go away but they seemed to get shelved, from how I interpreted her past. Being an introvert—something I could understand—she had trouble starting up conversations. As a result, she just continued doing what she was doing, working, taking care of her babies, drinking, and feeling out of place.

But then, one day, she saw this interesting, cool cat go gliding down her sidewalk on a skateboard and everything changed. This was a story I heard many times whenever Tragil and I would ask, "How did you and Dad ever get together?"

"Big Dwyane went by on that skateboard and I thought he had the prettiest smile I'd ever seen in my life. I remember saying, mmm, he and I would make some pretty babies."

As a seven-year-old I was shocked at that comment. But Tragil, twelve at the time, only laughed and said, "Well, you did!"

Mom later admitted the only reason she even approached Mr. Dwyane Tyrone Wade to introduce herself: "I was young and alcohol let me be outspoken, whereas if I was sober, I wouldn't have said anything to him."

Anyway, she was the one that started flirting. Dad never knew that part of the story about Mom spotting him. His version was that he saw her first. He was about fifteen years old then, a little younger than her, and to him Jolinda Morris was the prettiest, most witty, most intelligent girl on the block. "She had two kids already," he said about the day she approached him, "and meeting the prettiest girl on the block made me the man." At the time he and his friends worked part-time at McDonald's and Burger King. So, Dad decided, "My dream was to feed her and her babies and then I would marry her." He wanted to be the knight in shining armor for Jolinda.

Pretty soon they were boyfriend and girlfriend, and that was the ballad of how our parents met. Details of their married life together are hazy from this point on. But I know from the way they spoke of each other, even as the years passed, that there was always a lot of love in the bond they had.

Serving in the U.S. Army in the early years of their relationship,

Dad was stationed in Panama when Mom was getting ready to give birth to their first baby together. He was upset not to be in Chicago for the birth, but he managed to call Mom in the hospital and was able to give my sister her name.

"Tragil," Dad supposedly told her on the overseas phone call, and spelled it, explaining that each letter stood for something important that he cared about. As the story goes. He didn't remember it that way. Dad said, "Well, I was looking to give her a beautiful name and I was in an airplane flying over the desert so I looked in the dictionary I had with me for a word related to the desert. *Tra* came up about desert and I flipped to another page and something about *gil* so I combined them to make Tragil" (pronounced "Trah-gill").

That military side of Daddy wasn't easy for my mom. As she also said, "Big Dwyane was not an angel." At the same time, Mom was quick to mention that Dad was a very hard worker and was responsible for his family, not just supporting her and Tragil but also being a dad to my older sisters, as close to a father as they ever had.

Before I arrived on January 17, 1982, Mom and Dad had gone back and forth for months about what to name me. Mom was so excited after three girls to be having a boy that she wanted to name me Blessing.

Dad said simply, "Blessing? No way." He wanted to name me Aramis.

"Aramis?" Mom asked. "No. If not Blessing, let's call him Joe."

"Joe? No." Dad probably said, "Hell, no." He wanted Aramis or nothing.

Where he came up with his names, we never knew. But in the end my parents couldn't compromise on Blessing or Aramis or Joe. So they named me Dwyane Tyrone Wade Jr. Not the coolest, most distinctive name, I know. Even so, it's been sturdy over the years and has served me well. Besides, I could tell in hearing the story many times that I was named with love from both parents—something every child should be blessed to hear. And meanwhile, when I became a father, my sons' mother and I joyfully gave Zaire the middle names Blessing

Dwyane and gave Zion the middle names Malachi Aramis. They love their names!

From what I gather, Mom and Dad had issues before they broke up for good. When they were together, both were focused on the children. They were struggling, for sure, but there was stability. We had a roof over our heads and nobody had to go hungry. Life was not perfect, though. Both of them probably saw the fading of their dreams to make something important of themselves and to get out of the grind. Still in their twenties, they had four kids to support with no time to pursue fantasies of fame and fortune. And so reality boxed them in—reinforcing the likelihood that Jolinda wasn't going to be a model or a writer and Big Dwyane wasn't going to be the next Marvin Gaye or Reggie Jackson or the most interesting cool cat gliding through the neighborhood and turning the heads of all the beautiful women.

Partying might have become the needed escape from disappointment, a way to feel good and have that taste of glamour and excitement that the dreams used to provide. Like Mom, Dad had grown up without a father in the household and had been raised by a single mom as one of eight children. His mother drank, and as he would say, "The apple doesn't fall far from the tree." So he followed suit, picking alcohol as his drug of choice. And he was a hard-drinking man. He would dabble in drugs, though not like Mom, who besides drinking was regularly getting into other substances—weed, acid (occasionally), or "tac" (PCP), which was snorted. But nothing harder. Not yet.

When Mom and Dad divorced, they may have consciously made a pact not to tell us kids why. Or it might have just seemed like the right thing to do. Whatever the reason, by not getting into a blaming contest over the breakup, they spared us the additional hurt that often comes to children of divorce.

Reflecting on the truth of the matter years later, Mom explained that she controlled the relationship at the start, but when Big Dwyane began to grow up and have more control, even distancing himself, she was lost. "Without control in the marriage, well, I didn't know what to do anymore," she recalled. "My ground fell out. So now here's this guy who I don't know anymore and I thought if I had another baby it'd bring us together." That baby turned out to be me. They did come together to celebrate my arrival. But by then they had grown too far apart, according to my mother. She felt that she was the one to blame, that she didn't do enough to keep him from pulling away. She didn't see any option but divorce.

Daddy disagreed and even fought the breakup. Mom didn't want to be the needy one, she would say. She wanted to be the independent woman her mother raised her to be, one who didn't need a man. So she left with all four of us. Daddy tried to get her to come back and almost succeeded. But something stopped her, possibly pride, or just not wanting to have to put up with the challenges of his ways.

Whatever it was, Mom remembered that "when I stepped back in the house again I said, 'I can't do this.' There was a chance my marriage could have got back, but, no, I was selfish. I wasn't thinking about y'all. That was your only father. I wasn't thinking about my babies. I was thinking about me. And when I left, my life went to hell."

THE WORST OF THE NEXT FOUR YEARS OF OUR MOTHER'S DE-scent into addiction didn't register as deeply with me as it did with Tragil. For one thing, I was a toddler and preschooler, protected from the specifics. For another, unlike my sister, who went from five years old to nine in this phase, I had no earlier memories of having that stable household, with enough to eat and two parents together at home at night.

But Tragil had something that kept her going: the same intensity of purpose that our mother managed to reinforce in both of us. Just as I was later told to follow my sister and report back on her, Mom laid down the law as soon as I was born that all my sisters were to watch and care for me. Tragil wouldn't let the other two come near. She would insist, "He's my baby," holding me, cradling me in her arms, spoiling me as much as our mother did. In hindsight, Tragil admitted, "I went into nurturing way before my time."

In the past, Mom had partied mostly to escape loneliness and disappointment, to forget her shame and numb the pain of loss. But now drugs were like self-punishment—and never strong enough to wipe out the part of Jolinda that was in that place called failure, wearing the big *F*. That was when she graduated to snorting and smoking crack, eventually moving toward heroin. Part of it may have been the attempt to make some money to support us and then dipping into the stash. There was an unwritten law against sampling your own wares that even little kids knew you had to obey. The slippery slope.

This was that time period when we lived with friends of our mom's and other relatives who took us in. Tragil had a third-grade teacher who helped. And then there was Grandma. She would tell my sister, "Now, you take care of Little Dwyane. Momma's gonna get on her feet. Don't you worry. But I don't want you to be no kinda trouble to other people."

Tragil listened and taught me, young as I was, not to be no kinda trouble.

Being the proud woman Willie Mae Morris was, she also insisted that we learn to hold our heads high, not to be ashamed of our situation, and especially not to tell on Mom. On her own, Grandma probably fussed at our mother to no end. But with Tragil and me the message was that the instability was temporary. Even if it was difficult or uncomfortable, the rule was "Don't embarrass your mother."

Tragil once asked if I remembered us living with our uncle Eddie, not far from Fifty-Ninth and Prairie. I didn't. Apparently he had nothing, just a lower bunk bed where we could sleep. She said that he didn't even have a toilet, only a hole in the floor and a hose. But he knew we needed shelter and was able to provide it.

Grandma would coach my sister on how to keep herself and me bathed, how to use an old-fashioned scrub board, and how to patch my jeans, which I kept ripping because of my numerous falls. Meanwhile, we had enough clothing to wear. Grandma had a close friend who happened to work at the local Laundromat and would call Grandma to come pick out the nicer children's clothes whenever people left laundry unclaimed. By example, Willie Mae was teaching Tragil how to be resourceful, how to keep the two of us from looking raggedy and untended, how to carry ourselves with self-respect.

No matter where we stayed, my sister could remember Grandma showing up at some point with a bag of food, just checking in. That was true even when we moved into her building with Mom. Grandma would always check on us. Her first question would be "You children hungry?"

Seemed to me like our grandmother was so much better off than us. But Willie Mae just had the knack for stretching the little that she did have into just enough. When she wasn't doing a paid job, she'd volunteer at various church food drives, and come away with groceries for us.

At those moments when she became desperate over the fact that no one could locate our mother, Grandma would tell Tragil to put out the word that I was sick. However the grapevine worked, very quickly the news would reach Mom and she would rush to find us to make sure nothing was seriously wrong. Those occasions were often followed by stretches when we'd be back with Mom—staying with other people— and she'd be fighting to get herself back on track, to be able to support her children under one roof. Dad wanted that, obviously, and would have been willing to help. But Mom had her own issues with pride that kept her from admitting how badly she needed help.

And that was a problem that would haunt me, too. Not only was I overly proud but, being born a Capricorn, I was also extra stubborn. Even when better days were upon us, with all four kids back with Mom and living in the apartment at 5901 Prairie, that didn't change. By the time the hardest period really kicked in, a couple of years later, I was already set in my prideful ways.

• • •

"BOY, GET BACK IN THE HOUSE!" TRAGIL YELLED AT ME ON A gloomy Saturday morning in the fall, a few months after the start of second grade at Betsy Ross Elementary.

Moments earlier I had been inside our apartment and realized she had managed to slip out the front door—she had cleverly left it open so as not to alert me to the fact that she was going somewhere. That's when I took off after her. With no jacket, I galloped through the hall, out of the building, and down the steps, scanning to the right and left for any sign of her or her friends.

Right then she called to me from across the street. Thirteen-year-old Tragil was waiting there alone, arms folded across her chest, ready to put up a fight if I refused to go back inside.

Hanging my head, I trudged back up the steps. For a minute, I paused before going back inside to decide whether I should go see Grandma or not. In those days, my older sisters, already about seventeen and sixteen years old, were rarely around. Mom was at home. But so too were her boyfriend and a couple of other men.

That was par for the course when a drop was going to happen soon. If there were drugs for sale in the apartment or the vicinity, any extra people hanging around would be an indication of business transactions—an excuse for a police raid. No matter what was happening, Tragil and I had been taught that when we heard that knock at the door and the bellowing voice of "Police! Open up!" we should always answer, "My mother's not home!"

Somehow, whenever that happened, the time it took to answer was enough stalling for the boyfriend and his guys to be out the back door and gone, taking all the drugs and paraphernalia with them.

Feeling sad because I wanted to be with my sister and not stuck in the house on a Saturday, I comforted myself with the thought that Mom was at least safe in the house. Just knowing where she was helped ease my mind a lot—although, to be honest, I was less concerned about my mind at the moment than I was about the empty pit in my stomach.

Hunger was starting to get old.

Obviously, by this time I couldn't avoid making the comparison between how we were living and how most normal kids were. Not having the new clothes or new shoes was tough. But not getting to eat when I was hungry: that was almost as terrible as the times when I didn't know where Mom was. What was really messed up was the fact that sometimes I didn't eat when food was available—all because of pride and stubbornness.

Case in point: There I stood downstairs on the front stoop, famished, and Grandma was up on the third floor with a stocked kitchen so she could start to cook for Sunday's meal. All I had to do was to go knock at her door and say, "Grandma, I'm starving," and she would have put down a huge spread just for me. But I couldn't bring myself to do that. Afterward, if my grandmother found out that I was hungry and hadn't told her, she'd get mad and say, "I'm gonna call you every day to come up here and eat, you hear me?"

Seriously, she would scream my name out her window until I came upstairs, but I was tormented inside: relieved that I'd get to eat but feeling guilty for doing so. The real issue was that I didn't want Grandma to even think that Mom wasn't feeding us. That was my mother and I didn't want her to look bad in my grandmother's eyes.

The dilemma had me starting to think about asking for a job as a watch-out boy. I'd seen how kids younger than me in the neighborhood would get tipped now and then with a few dollars just for watching— something I did anyway. The thought of the candy that a couple of bucks could buy made my mouth water so much I could taste the sweetness. But here too, sugar fiend though I was, the fear of Grandma finding out how I came by that money had always kept me from going outside the law. A healthy fear.

Besides, if I could hold out, Tragil might come home later with something for me to eat. Maybe even a glazed doughnut or two that she knew I craved. If not that, tomorrow was Sunday, and after church, there would be open house at Grandma's—with her country cooking and as many helpings as I wanted of Willie Mae's soul food.

With the comfort of those thoughts, I ran back into our apartment, leaving the door open for Mom's boyfriend and his guys, who seemed like they were getting ready to leave in a hurry. Not sure where my mother was just then, I checked first in her bedroom.

Not there. Thinking maybe I heard the water running in the bathroom—sometimes a clue that Mom was in there, possibly getting high—I decided not to think about it but just to sit down on the floor next to her bed, turn on the TV, and watch some Saturday-morning cartoons.

No more than three or four minutes later, I recognized police radio sounds that didn't seem to be coming from the TV show. Before I had a second to stand and run to the back of the apartment and get up to Grandma's, the police raid was under way—with as many as three officers coming in my direction.

In my nightmares, I had witnessed this moment in a kind of slow motion. But now it was happening in real time: my heart pounding in my throat, heavy footfalls approaching, and the shiny metallic glint of a gun coming through the bedroom doorway.

At that same split second of seeing the silver gun and two policemen stepping into the room with it, I try to slide underneath the bed. Not fast enough! They spot me and in SWAT team speed the two rush to drag me from under the bed, grabbing my shaking body and putting the gun to my head. One of them says in a heavy whisper, "Don't say anything. You walk and take me to where your mom is." The other one pushes me, the one with the gun at my head, whispering next to my ear, "Now."

Aware for sure that Mom's in the bathroom doing drugs, I'm not thinking about the gun to my head. I'm thinking about how I can possibly warn her that the police are here, so she can flush the drugs down the toilet. So I'm walking slow, real slow, hoping she heard the radios and the police and the footsteps into the apartment. There's three policemen behind me, one holding the gun at the back of my head, and I stop at the bathroom. I knock on the door.

No answer.

"Mom?" I try to make my voice express alarm that something isn't right.

"Yeah, what you need?"

"Mom, open the door."

"No, boy, leave me alone."

I can tell by her answer that she's picked up on my warning.

One of the police, not Robocop, but another officer who used to wear shades a lot, too, is about to push in the door but just then my mother opens it. No drugs or signs of drug use. Even if the toilet has apparently just been flushed, nobody can prove that there has been drugs.

The police abruptly move me out of the way and then grab Mom, putting the gun on her, demanding that she tell them where the drugs and the guns are hidden.

They tell my mother that someone called the station and complained that a person was in our building with a gun and was waving it out the window, threatening people who were walking by. Mom assures them there has been a mistake. When they search the apartment, unfortunately, they find measuring scales that supposedly have drug residue on them.

For a second time, I had to watch my mother be put in handcuffs, jammed into the back of a police car, and taken down to the station. Out on the porch, fighting back the tears, too proud for anyone to see me cry, feeling anger starting to fill up that hole in my stomach, I picked up the little rubber ball and started to hit it as hard as I could against the building.

Just then, Tragil came running, out of breath. She knew what had happened. After she told me to go back inside, she'd seen the police creeping up to the house from their stakeout. But it was too late for her to come and get me.

"I'm sorry," my sister said, breaking down. "I'm so sorry."

Of course, there was nothing for Tragil to be sorry about. And I told her so.

In hindsight, I was probably still in shock, not to mention frantic about when Mom would come home. Fortunately, she was not forced to stay overnight, returning to the house even before the sun went down, to my great relief.

Out on the stoop with Grandma, I saw Mom walking up to the house, looking like she'd just been on an errand or something. Before she could get halfway up the walk, I was at her side, bouncing up and down, so happy to have her home.

That night I slept soundly. I woke up early the next day, excited that we were all going to church. Halfway down the block, at 5921½ Prairie, the Revelation Missionary Baptist Church, presided over by Pastor Mary L. Box, occupied half a storefront and may have sat thirty-five people at the most. Mom didn't go regularly but had said she was thinking about it. That was her—not one to build up anyone's hopes in case she didn't show. We knew she was going to try. There had been times when Tragil and I would be up front, singing with the choir, getting ready to do our solos, and we'd see Mom come in quietly in the back just to hear us. Other times, she'd bring some friends with her that we didn't know, some of the group kind of smelling like stale wine and cigarette smoke.

If anyone had the nerve to stare or, worse, make a comment, Tragil and I would glare right at that person. That was our mom and she was there, same as the rest of them, to find a space of peace, of love, and of forgiveness.

No, I didn't have those thoughts at seven going on eight years old. Actually, I went to church most of the time because that was the law according to Grandma. Pastor Box, a darker, older lady pastor, seemed to understand that as the only boy in the congregation, it wasn't easy for me to be asked to sit quietly and patiently for all the hours of the long—and I mean *loooonnngg*—services. Grandma didn't just try to keep us in church on Sunday: there was also Wednesdays and Fridays and special holidays when we were expected to go.

Pastor Box, before and after the service, would always check up to see how I was doing. I rarely said much other than that my report card was good and maybe my daddy had taken us out for ice cream as a reward. During the service, the pastor would praise my hard work in school, calling me the church family's little superstar. She'd say, "I have a feeling this boy is going to be something special." I didn't know what that meant really, except that it felt good.

Most of what was said and talked about in church went right over my head. Later, I would find lessons kind of sneaking up on me, almost like the punch line of a joke that takes you years before you can laugh and think—*oh, now I get it*.

Take the solos that Tragil and I used to sing in what I considered to be *our* song—for good reason. It was a spiritual called "Wade in the Water." The chorus was a sort of a riddle that told the children to wade in the water and that God was going to trouble the water. Why? The verses talked about Moses leading the Israelites through the water, helping to get them through. I knew there was a message in there somewhere. Was it that anything that you wanted to do bad enough would make you face your fear? Maybe. As an adult, I learned that Harriet Tubman sang this song as a sort of map for runaway slaves to escape their masters and the dogs chasing them.

One Sunday morning Mom came in to hear us sing and sat in the back alone. I wasn't thinking about the meaning of the words. I was feeling happy to see her smile and feel proud of her children. I was also happy thinking about the epic meal that would happen after the service was over.

That morning, I'd gone upstairs to check in and smell what Grandma was cooking for the later meal. Everything was almost ready: fried chicken, greens, corn bread with butter, and a couple of pies that she would bake and serve hot later, straight from the oven.

It always seemed to me that Pastor Box took the service long past the time that church was supposed to be over. But this day it was almost forever. But at long last, the final prayer was said. When I opened my eyes and looked toward the back, ready to go get Mom and walk her back home to Grandma's, I saw that her seat was empty.

Tragil had spotted her leaving earlier. There was nothing to do but put our focus on what we had in front of us—food. Out of church we flew, sprinting down the street and into our building, up the three flights of stairs, following the unmistakable aroma of fried chicken and the sounds of laughter.

Grandma's house was full of different relatives—her sister, my aunts and uncles, cousins, everybody. Mom wasn't there, but since people would flit in and out all day, maybe she had stopped in earlier or would come later? As usual, I managed to be first in line for the buffet. That way, by the time everyone else was served, I could come back for seconds.

After the seriousness of church, everyone joked, making small talk, catching up with each other and the latest gossip or news. Unless you were me or Tragil, the keepers of family secrets, you would have never guessed that the day before, I was scared almost to death when police held a gun to my head during a drug raid.

DURING THAT SPRING OF 1990, OUR HAPPIER DAYS WERE few and further apart.

My fondest memories were the little things. More and more, basketball was just me going up to the park by myself with Roger's ball and trying to get me a game. Or running my own drills, shooting the ball from every conceivable spot on the court. The dream of being great one day at basketball felt too big for me—like shoes that I couldn't fill. But I liked the feel of the ball in my hands and the way I could forget everything else other than getting it through the hoop.

My favorite pastime that spring was watching *Knight Rider* with Grandma. In syndicated reruns, the show came on in Chicago once a week and that was my time. Everyone in the neighborhood and most of the Southside just about knew how much Willie Mae Morris loved David Hasselhoff and his talking car, KITT. Everyone knew not to mess with me and my grandma when we were up there watching that show. Years later, I actually told David Hasselhoff how he helped me get through tough times in childhood.

The violence with Mom's boyfriend became more dangerous. She was around less and less. One night when they were home and the electricity had been turned off in our apartment there was another police raid. This time, as usual, the boyfriend had slipped out just before the police came pounding—*boom, boom, boom*—at the front door, announcing themselves. I scrambled out the back door and up the steps, hoping that Tragil was right behind me, at the same instant that the police threw on their floodlights, catching me in blinding white light as I got to Grandma's back door. My sister knew they'd snatch both of us if she tried to get out, too, so instead of running she decided to go back inside and hide under her bed. The police came into the dark apartment with flashlights and guns drawn. They found her but couldn't see that she was a young person and put the gun to her head, telling her to come out real slow. Then they interrogated her at length about the person they saw going up the steps—about what drugs I had and who I was.

Tragil was traumatized, sobbing and telling them, "That's my baby brother. He didn't do nuthin'!"

Eventually they accepted she was telling the truth. As always, they didn't find any drugs but took Mom down to the station to question her about her boyfriend. That was a night she didn't come home. Nor did she return the next night.

Tragil tried to reassure me but I was distraught. Those were sleepless nights. Mom wasn't at the jail, so where was she? Nobody could convince me to leave the porch and come inside. No one was going to let harm come to me. I knew that. But my mother was somewhere, not safe, fragile, but trying. I couldn't banish the thought of someone, some man hurting her, and especially my never seeing her again. And those thoughts scared me more than the police, more than anything, enough that when staying awake became impossible, I cried myself to sleep.

Days passed and Mom finally came back, looking tired but more clear-eyed than I'd seen her in a while. Tragil and I didn't say anything, not wanting to jinx any possible improvement, although we were both hopeful. We had to be.

But who were we? Two kids without power to do anything. Just how powerless we were was made very clear one morning when I stumbled upon a sight in an alley not too far from Fifty-Ninth and Prairie. I was on my way back from going to the store for Grandma, getting closer to our place, when I spotted what looked like a pair of sneakers left in a garbage can. Shoes? Free shoes? As I approached, however, I realized there were legs attached to the sneakers. When I looked more closely, I saw the body and the face of a dead boy a few years older than me.

I knew him. Whoever took his life and put him there, nobody would tell.

The most tragic part of the wasted humanity, wasted life, was that the world wasn't crying for the children getting killed in my neighborhood. When I joined Grandma on the porch after that, I couldn't bring myself to tell her what I'd seen. She had enough on her mind.

Mom had fallen so far behind on the rent that the landlord took drastic measures. One afternoon Tragil and I arrived home to find the furniture outside our building in the front yard and our mom sitting on the curb, crying her eyes out. We had been evicted. One of Tragil's friends walked by and asked if she knew whose stuff that was and my sister only shrugged, pretending the people getting evicted were neighbors. Grandma talked the landlord into letting us move back in and Mom swore up and down to start paying off the back rent she owed.

For a short while, there was a noticeable improvement. But selling drugs to make money and get out of a financial hole only led her further into an even darker hole, addiction. My hope was disappearing fast.

One Sunday morning after days of not seeing Mom, Grandma sent me on an errand and I went running down to the store a block away. Just before I went into the store, I paused to see who was hanging out on the corner. There in the group of homeless people, dealers, and addicts—some scavenging for drugs, others in different stages of being high, some leaning against the wall next to the alley—was Mom.

She didn't know me.

On the way out of the store, I looked again to make sure it was her, my mother, Jolinda Wade. That woman was my mother but at the same time not. She didn't see me. Or if she did, she couldn't recognize her youngest child.

The glazed, lost look in her eyes was not something I could ever forget. For all that I'd seen, I was more haunted by that moment than by almost any other from these years. How could I fight whatever it was that had her in its clutches so tight that she didn't know me, her only son?

Back at the house, I remember telling Grandma that I was going to pray for my mother at church that day. My grandmother had been praying all those years and now Tragil had been telling me that we didn't have to be too proud to ask God for what we needed. I didn't know if my prayers were getting through, but I had to try.

A year earlier, Tragil had been losing hope that our lives would ever improve, when a lady at church told her, "You only twelve years old, but you can make a difference at home if you ask for the help you need." Those were the days when Tragil protected me from her tears, turning up the TV loud so I couldn't hear her crying, because, she would later say, "I could take the pain but you were young and I didn't want you to have it. You were no trouble. You were so good. Never complaining. You didn't deserve the pain."

But now the time had come for her to tell me that enough was enough. "You know," Tragil would say, "you can complain, you can ask for whatever you want and say it out loud and God hears you."

Every night, we would close the door and sit on our beds and ask for what we needed. My first prayer was this—*"If you take me and my sister out of this place and you save our mother, I will be someone worthy of your help and I'll be the best dad and take care of my family when I grow up and I'll be good to other people, too, and if I jump out of line or make a mistake, I'll admit it and get back on the right road."*

When my words were hard to form, Tragil would remind me that God knew my heart and my deeds, so there was really no wrong way to pray. That freed me. I talked to Him, I bared my soul, I prayed my heart out. I wanted something different, another life for me and all my family, just for us to have a chance. I wanted the dreams to shine real for me, too, whether it was playing basketball or owning a sports car that could talk to me like KITT, and I connected the prayers to my promises of living up to my word to achieving my dreams.

Tragil and I prayed to get out of there and we were heard.

ON THE RIDE HOME AFTER THE GAME AGAINST THE MEMPHIS Grizzlies, Zaire is the first one to comment on the level of play.

"Daddy," he says, "that was crazy!"

Usually the boys don't watch the whole time. We've made a deal that if they stay for the first two quarters, then they can go to the practice facility upstairs to play for the rest of the game. And sometimes they have trouble waiting until halftime. But not this time. Maybe they picked up on the strong emotions that Tragil and so many others in our circle were having as the game unfolded. Whatever they sensed, Lisa Joseph tells me afterward that the boys didn't want to leave their seats at all except for a couple of bathroom breaks and for snacks. Yeah, they have good appetites!

What can I say? There is no question that out on the floor I felt supercharged with Daddy power and the energy of countless answered prayers. My game was a dance of gratitude.

And that's got to be funny for anyone who knows that dancing has never been my strong suit. But I could have fooled myself with this game. That's why when Zaire makes his comment with a chorus of "That was crazy's" from Dada and Zion, too, I can only say, "I know."

Normally I walk away from a game, win or lose, and prepare for the next one. But in this instance, I had to watch the replays and review the story of what had happened, as reported that night in the Associated Press.

The headline read: "Dwyane Wade turns back Grizzlies as Heat turn up D in romp." The article went on to say that the tone had been set at the start for the 118–85 score when "Wade blocked four shots in a dazzling 55-second span shortly after tip-off" and that we had rolled over Memphis with the largest margin of victory since December 27, 2009.

It wasn't just me. LeBron scored 27 points (sitting out the fourth quarter, too) and Chris Bosh, picking up on our energy, had 18 points and 10 rebounds. Every single one of the twelve active players on the Heat roster put up points.

Whatever they were feeling, I was very proud to be described as the catalyst for the Heat's firepower on the court. And had to laugh in reading, "Wade was playing defense on everybody. All five of his blocks came in the half, and he inadvertently leveled James on a defensive possession just before intermission." This turned out to be the fourth time in my career to have five blocks in a game. I also learned from the AP story that to date that season there had only been three games in which guards blocked five shots in a game—and two of those records were mine.

Zaire was right. That was crazy. The quote that did it for me, though, was this one:

> Wade's final line: 28 points, nine assists, five rebounds and five blocks. The last NBA guard to have numbers like that in a game? Michael Jordan, in 1988.

So I guess that's what I'm trying to say about prayers, promises, and dreams.

And I think that part of the reason for telling the story of where those ideas first came from in childhood is to share the rewards that come from making the commitment to be an involved father. Not because I think it's easy, but because for all the effort required, you will empower and uplift your children, your community, and, most of all, yourself.

CHAPTER THREE

IN THE BACKYARD

SUNDAY MORNING
MARCH 13, 2011
AT HOME IN MIAMI

I WAKE WITH A JOLT.

Normally on a Sunday when the boys have come for their visit, I try to get up early so we can play outside together or have some fun in the pool before they have to fly back to Chicago. By reflex, when I see that it's almost 10 A.M., I'm about to spring out of the bed, but then remember the news that came in less than forty-eight hours earlier.

That's the mental reminder that the boys still don't know yet.

I sill haven't decided exactly how I'm going to raise the subject, other than borrowing from the psychology of one of my favorite movies, *Jerry McGuire,* about a sports agent, played by Tom Cruise, who uses the line with Cuba Gooding Jr.: "Help me help you."

When in doubt, "help me help you" has let me learn from my kids how best to be there for them.

To put it another way, I have to play it by ear and let my sons guide me in determining how to address what's going to be happening and how they feel about it. Judging from the sound of a very unhappy Zaire that's coming from the backyard, this conversation needs to happen soon.

During their last few visits, none of the three boys was eager to go when the time came. But Zaire had started to take our pending separations the hardest. Usually, by the middle of Sunday morning, right about this time, the tears would start to flow.

These Zaire "episodes"—as he and I call them—are also, in my opinion, a healthy way for him to express his feelings. But because he really is a kid who loves life to the utmost—and wakes up every day ready for fun and action—the emotional outbursts do seem out of character.

One obvious explanation for his upsets was the closeness he and I have shared from the time he came into this world. When Zaire was born, I was only twenty years old myself, a college athlete with an uncertain future, not sure how to support a wife and a baby—let alone myself. After the promises that I'd made as a boy that I was going to be different, Zaire was the real test. He was the son I could pledge to be there for, to be around for, in those times when too many fathers aren't. And I wanted to be around for everything—to see him take his first step, to celebrate when his first teeth grew in, to hear him speak his first words. I wanted to be there for everything that was his first. Plus, I wanted him to be there for my firsts.

Zaire and I had adapted together to the reality of my work schedule. Not easy.

After his mom and I broke up, he and Zion both had to adapt to living in two cities, with the time and distances that involves. Hard for all of us.

Zaire always tried to put a tough face on, but I'd hear reports from others that he would count the days on his hands from when the two of us last saw each other and how long it was before we were supposed to have a visit again.

I hadn't forgotten my own countdowns—to the days when my dad was supposed to come. I'd imagine how he would go upstairs to Grandma's with us and tell jokes or take us somewhere else. I hadn't forgotten what it felt like when he didn't show. Not seeing him and not having him around sucked, and his not coming left me feeling unwanted, unloved, angry.

True, as a kid we didn't have a phone so we couldn't get the explanation that something had come up. By the same token, explaining custody arrangements to children doesn't take away the pain they feel when separated from either parent.

All I could do and all I had tried to do from the start was develop those open lines of communication with my sons so they could be free to tell me what they were feeling. I didn't want to be Father Knows Best. In fact, I would tell them that just because I was Daddy and earned the money and paid the bills and made the rules so they could get what they needed and wanted, we could talk about their concerns no matter what. We spoke often about how each of them was different and that I didn't expect them to be alike or just like me. That didn't mean that I was going to have all the answers. But I could still listen and then hopefully together we'd come up with a solution.

"Help me help you" is in my thoughts as I go downstairs to the kitchen to hear from Rich that sure enough, Zaire is having one of his episodes, complete with a temper tantrum.

Out in the backyard, Dada and Zion are on the basketball court, happily engrossed in some kind of game they're playing together. In contrast, Zaire's sitting off on his own, a basketball cradled in his arms, looking sad and lost.

The image takes me back just for a minute to a series of other backyards where I played when I was growing up, sometimes feeling not too different from Zaire on this day.

I COULDN'T COUNT HOW MANY TIMES I REPLAYED THAT afternoon when Tragil and I were supposed to go to the movies on the bus and instead she dropped me off at our dad's girlfriend's place for good.

Eventually, when we did talk about it, my sister recalled that she really did intend to go to the movies and then maybe afterward stop by the apartment where Dad's girlfriend, Bessie McDaniels, lived. Her plan evolved differently when the bus came to a stop right there in that neighborhood and we spotted Donny playing in the back lot of the apartment building. The fact that I was so happy to get out and play with the boys made my sister's efforts easier. Since we didn't have a phone for Tragil to call ahead and clear the possibility with Bessie or Dad, she was playing this whole thing by ear.

Unbeknownst to me until much later, when I was in the alley in the middle of a game with the boys, thirteen-year-old Tragil had gone up to the third-floor apartment and said something to Bessie's mom about me staying. That night, after Tragil left, telling me she'd be back the next day, I went upstairs with Demetrius and Donny and there was no acknowledgment either way about me being there. Like me, everyone else must have assumed this was no different from the other times when Dad had brought us over and we'd stayed.

Those first several nights were a free-for-all! Whatever bedrooms there were in the apartment were occupied and besides the three boys from Bessie's previous relationships, the household included their grandmother, Grandmom Chris (whose place it was), a couple of uncles, and some additional kids and adults. There didn't seem to be any rules, or bedtimes, or anything.

As best I can remember, Dad was already upstairs when Demetrius, Donny, and I came in hungry around suppertime. Flashing me the familiar Dwyane Wade Sr. grin, he lifted his hand up in the air for a high-five as I jumped up and tried unsuccessfully to slap it back. In my mind, my father was a giant who towered above me and I was never going to be able to jump that high.

"How you doin', son?" was all my father said to me. Maybe I nodded or mumbled that I was fine. And that was that.

My soon-to-be stepbrothers and I rummaged around in the kitchen for leftovers, ate what we could find, and then went back outside, where the Chicago summer night air was cooler than inside. When we returned to the apartment late that night, there weren't any beds to be found so the three of us took pillows off the sofa in the living room and put them on the floor, where we crashed out together in a pile.

In that crazy, fun hangout atmosphere, I was just one extra. Not a problem.

Over those first days when I kept expecting to see my sister, I didn't want to admit to hurt or confusion about her not returning. But when I could no longer count on my two hands how long it had been since she dropped me off, I began the painful process of facing the new reality. Not wanting anyone to know that I was sad, I'd sneak down to the back lot and sit under the tree—watching for the same bus that had brought me here, waiting for it to come to the stop and let passengers off, hoping for the outside chance that maybe I'd see my sister among them.

My head pounded with questions.

Was Mom doing all right? Was she sad, too, because I didn't get to come and say good-bye to her? What about Grandma? Who was going to watch *Knight Rider* with her every week? And then there was the issue of my bike, which I was mad about. Earlier that summer I had been lucky enough to be given my first bike, one of the only memorable presents that I'd received in all of my eight and a half years of life.

Where was my bike? I wanted it!

The biggest question was how was I going to look out for myself without Tragil on a daily basis. Come to think of it, I'd always been protected. Oh, no, people would say, you don't wanna mess with him, that's such-and-such's nephew or so-and-so's little brother. Tragil and I always had that sphere of protection because of having relatives high in the drug and gang games. None of that coverage extended to this part of the Southside. How could I keep myself safe?

The only answer that made sense was to be on my guard now more than ever. The rule became that I could have fun and join in the good times but never all the way, never to let go fully as others around me could. Maybe I was scared that letting go would cause me to forget my promises or that I couldn't protect myself if I let go, if I allowed myself to be happy all the way.

But in spite of me being sad and mad and scared, none of that compared to the relief of not living in the war zone that I'd left behind. Being in another neighborhood in an equally poor area of the Southside wasn't like living in another country, but then again, I was able to breathe. The fear and stress of sitting out on a front porch worrying or not knowing when the next police raid might happen was all too much. My worries about my loved ones weren't over, no, but I could be more of a kid in the new setting.

The more relief I felt, the more I was able to understand Tragil's sacrifice: how she put her own happiness and security second to giving me back a part of my childhood. And the hard truth that stayed with me was that I felt guilty. My sister was still in the middle of the madness that I had left behind while I was basically enjoying a kind of summer camp with an element of brotherhood that hadn't existed in my life before.

Fun! That was our job, at least for those waning days and weeks of summer. No curfew or nuthin'! We could be out until midnight or one in the morning. When we weren't shooting hoops in a makeshift basket or throwing a football or playing baseball in the back lot, we were organizing games with the little girls in the neighborhood, from jump rope to chase games to dancing in the street to old-fashioned hide-and-seek. We had some boundaries, of course, that kept us from straying too far away from the house. But until the time came for the school year to begin, we'd run nonstop all day and long into the night

When we couldn't go anymore, we'd crash out and sleep, then wake up the next morning and do it all over again.

All that freedom didn't liberate the part of my mentality that kept me from completely letting go and dropping my guard. But the one thing that allowed me to relax in new ways was that I had a daddy in my life on a daily basis. Not that he was doing anything extra to raise me or anything. Instead of singling me out, Dad saw me as being raised alongside Bessie's three sons—Demetrius, Donny, and the youngest, Kodhamus—which removed the pressure of being always in the spotlight.

By now I was already familiar with the militant side of Dwyane Wade Sr. He was the tough-guy drill sergeant who showed up when it was report card, inspection, cleanup time. A lot of that wasn't going to change. So I was prepared for that military mind-set of Dad, who was tough stuff, who laid down the law, and who would assure you that there was to be no stepping outside the lines and no mouthing off and no doing things halfway. Or else. He was bottom line an army man. I had every reason to respect him and every reason to avoid going outside the box and getting myself into trouble.

At Bessie's house, Dad continued the role of enforcer, holding accountable any of us who did something wrong, and then getting us all back in line—as much as anyone could have in that atmosphere where there weren't many rules. Dad probably held back from instituting boot camp right away, as if he were allowing the two of us to get a feel for each other before he decided what kind of toughening up I needed.

If you ask him, Dad will say that he wanted his life to be an open book, complete with his disappointments and shortcomings and secrets. "I wanted you to know my mistakes and be better than me," he'd remind me later on. "I told you everything. You just forgot!" Maybe so. Or maybe we had selective hearing.

I do remember that my dad's dad had been an excellent athlete in his younger days and went on to make a living as a referee and an umpire for various local leagues. My father did say, "My dad was never at home but I knew where to find him so I could go to his games and ask him questions about why he wasn't around." Sports became their connection and Dwyane Sr. was talented in a multitude of them. In high school he played football and baseball extremely well and also wrestled.

After he got out of the army, the most popular sport around the city of Chicago with the most competitive amateur league was softball—the same league that his dad had umped for. Before basketball came along, softball and baseball dominated Dad's interests. We used to watch him win championships in softball during weekdays and then play in a basketball league on Sundays. Dad's diverse athletic background was his explanation for why he was so loud and wild on the court—running over people or just jumping over them. By his own admission, he was not even playing basketball. His game? Football on a basketball court. What were the fights about? Anything. As he himself put it, "I'm not a bad loser but I like winning."

That may give you some insight into Big Dwayne. He was nothing if not consistent. He worked hard, he drank hard, and he played every sport he ever tried even harder.

Who exactly he was, I wasn't so sure that I knew.

That is, until the school year began and Dad let it be known that he didn't think the free-for-all was good for raising children. So he looked for a place where he and Bessie could raise us with more structure. Eventually, they moved us all in together in an apartment at Sixty-Ninth and Harper. While there, after I missed some chunks of the school year, I enrolled at Fermi Elementary School for the remainder of third grade. Interestingly enough, I didn't suffer too much at the time academically. Maybe that was a function of being forced to adapt to new and changing circumstances. The downside was that there was only so much information I could process and retain. Later this would take a toll when it came to testing, but in the meantime, despite the moves and missed time in the classroom, I continued to do well at school in both the third and fourth grades.

The place where we lived wasn't terrible, but the surrounding area was bad. The atmosphere at home changed. All of sudden, the fun of the free-for-all and running the streets at all hours came to a halt. To create more structure, Dad and Bessie implemented more rules than they had in the past. Needless to say, we hated having our freedom restricted.

Apparently, this was when Dad came up with a compromise. As long as we didn't get into trouble and didn't bring home D's or F's on our report cards, we could get some special coaching on the basketball court from him. On Sundays he'd take a group of us kids to the park to watch him play, and either before or after the game we'd get to go out on the court ourselves to shoot hoops and get some pointers. On other days, he also made time to take us across the street from our apartment to play at the church that had a hoop in the back. We weren't in an official team at that time but Dad was serious business, introducing us to fundamentals and drills; no glory moves whatsoever. And, yeah, he was tough, always pushing us to demand more of ourselves.

This was his program, his way of creating better father-son relationships. He started to think about putting together a real team. To hear him talk about his expectations and what we would need to do to play in the competitive Chicago youth leagues, you would have thought we were being groomed for the NBA. That was Dad, thinking ambitiously.

Once we had a team, there was no doubt Demetrius was going to be our star. He was lanky and fast and could shoot. Donny wasn't bad, either. There was some other good local talent that Dad would consider.

And then there was me. Other than Dad's workouts so far, I had never been coached and had a lot to learn. I likely had a level of natural athletic ability that gave me some potential. Or so Dad would acknowledge on occasion. But he never said a word to the effect that he saw anything special about me. Not his style, unfortunately. No matter how much we improved in our skills, we were never good enough. Never.

That left it to me to decide for myself at age nine that I *did* have something special, that I had found in basketball the love of my life, and that if I worked hard enough, who knew, one day the game really could take me somewhere. Somewhere big.

If I needed any proof that such a feat would ever be achievable, I didn't have to look any farther than my own backyard—where the Chicago Bulls, led by Michael Jordan, now reigned supreme. The whole 1990–91 season had been a fairy tale come true for all of Chi-town. Not only had Jordan been named Most Valuable Player for the season—after the Bulls clinched the division with a franchise record of sixty-one wins—but we had then swept our archrivals and nemesis, the Detroit Pistons, to take the Eastern Conference. With that, the Bulls rolled into the NBA Finals for the first time in franchise history, vying for the championship against the Los Angeles Lakers.

Most of that chaotic year had been a blur, but time stopped for me during that series, which Chicago won decisively, 4 games to 1. Although there were so many electrifying moments, the one that stood above the rest was when Michael Jordan was going up for a dunk on Sam Perkins and was able to avoid a block by—unbelievably—switching the ball from his right to left hand in midair, before laying in a thunderous basket. No living, breathing person of sound mind could fail to see who would win the trophy for MVP in the finals.

Jordan fever caught hold that spring and summer in Chicago like an unprecedented epidemic. Local teams of young hopefuls with dreams like mine flocked madly to basketball courts in parks, school-yards, and gyms.

We all wanted to fly.

EVEN THOUGH IT SEEMED LIKE MONTHS THAT I WAS SEPA-rated from my sister, actually Tragil had come to check up on me within a few weeks of dropping me off at Bessie's. Over the next couple of years, she continued to make regular appearances, always fussing over me to be sure to dress warmly so as not to get a cold or even whipping out some iron-on patches in case recent falls had left rips in my pants or shirts.

When I complained during that first visit about missing Mom, Tragil agreed to come for me on the bus and take me back home to surprise our mother that next weekend. As the days ticked by, all I could think about was how happy Jolinda Wade was going to be when she came back from wherever she might have been and found me sitting on the stoop waiting for her.

On Saturday, we rode the bus together and Tragil asked me questions about the new household, laughing at my stories of our free-for-all. When we arrived at the front yard of 5901 Prairie and saw Grandma up on the porch like always, I could have sworn that in just those three weeks the building had gotten smaller, more neglected, and the neighborhood even more run-down.

After a long hug, the first thing Grandma wanted to know, of course, was, "You children hungry?"

"I'm always hungry!" is what I answered. But before going up to have something to eat, I wanted to go see Mom, who was already inside.

Tragil accompanied me into the apartment but went back to our bedroom, telling me that I'd probably find Mom at the kitchen table.

Nervous, I walked slowly down the hall, afraid of what I was going to see. But I relaxed as soon as I turned the corner and found my pretty mother sitting in a chair at the kitchen table, looking not too different from the last time I'd seen her.

Mom did seem a little sleepy. Still, when she looked up and saw me, a light of joyful recognition came into her eyes and her beautiful, familiar smile spread across her face. "Come on over, baby," she said, gesturing me toward her, as I went to give her a hug and a kiss. Mom went on to say that she knew I was staying with Dad and that she believed that was a good thing.

I sat down next to her as she continued to hold my hands, asking me to tell her how I'd been spending my summer days. As I talked, Mom closed her eyes, the way you would do if you were going to listen closely.

But after a few minutes her hands went limp in mine and her chin fell toward her chest.

"Mom?"

No answer. Bent over in the chair, almost frozen, Mom didn't even seem to be breathing.

"Mom?!" I shook her.

No answer.

"Mom, please wake up," I pleaded, thinking she was dying.

Finally, she stirred, sat up, and smiled, telling me to keep talking. She nodded off again like that a few more times. After an hour or so passed, she said that maybe I should be heading back before anyone started to miss me.

That was my clue that our visit had been as painful for my mother as it had been for me. Another couple of months went by before I went to visit again. The next time I saw her she was staying somewhere else. Dad drove me that time, dropping me off and returning for me later. Mom was more alert than she'd been during our previous visit. She made a point of telling me to mind my father and, with a laugh, warned me to stay away from "all them fast women trying to talk to you" because I was her baby, her only son. When I left, Mom remembered to ask, "Who your favorite girl?" and I hugged her tight, answering as always, "You!" fighting like hell to hold back the tears.

When I left that day, I tried to tell myself that she was getting better. But I didn't know that. There was another visit in there somewhere when she was less alert, nodding out so much that as before I panicked that she was going to die. And when I left that day, the battle within me had begun to rage: fear for her life versus faith that she could find the power to save herself.

No matter what happened, I never believed there was something wrong with Mom at her core, only that she had a sickness that made her need the drugs. The idea occurred to me that she was using them as medicine for some basic hurt in her life—even if I couldn't put that thought into words at the time.

The most heartbreaking visit that I paid to my mother during this period took place one spring weekend day when I decided to go on my own to see her. Tragil had given me an address where Mom was staying and had told me how to get there on foot or by bus. When I arrived in the vicinity of the address, having had no problem getting there, I had a little lift to my step and was kind of proud of my navigational skills.

But as I turned a corner and headed down the block to the exact address, I saw an ambulance parked directly in front of the house. There was no light blazing, no sirens wailing. Everything suddenly became deathly quiet. A crowd gathered outside on the sidewalk in total silence as an emergency crew brought out a yellow stretcher with a person on it. The body and face were covered.

"Please, please, don't let that be my momma!" I started to pray out loud for all to hear, and kept on praying as I raced into the building and found the apartment where she was supposed to be. After I banged on the door while calling her name, a man slowly opened it. I flew inside, out of breath, my chest pounding, eyes wide, and found my mother sitting there clearly unaware of anyone being carried out on a stretcher.

"I thought that was you!"

"No, baby, I'm okay."

"I thought you was taken out dead!"

"No, no, my sweet boy, my little man, I'm not dead. Everything's gone be all right." Mom saw how scared I was and spent the rest of our short visit telling me how I was the best thing that happened to her all day, any day. She motioned to the man in the room there to give me a couple of dollars so I could get some candy on the way home.

That was one of the toughest moments of my young life—the realization that she was too ashamed to have me stick around. As it turned out, because of subsequent events beyond our control, we wouldn't see each other again for close to a year.

In the meantime, whenever Tragil visited me, she avoided giving me too many details about how our mother was doing. Rarely would my sister even complain about her own situation, which in many ways was much tougher than mine. So smart and alive with whatever she was studying in school or at church, Tragil would tell me everything, like a teacher, hoping to get me as excited as she was about academics— reinforcing the idea that education was the way out.

Then she'd laugh and apologize for being a nerd. At fourteen and fifteen years old, Tragil was not a nerd in the least. Because we never had any money for nice clothes and shoes, my sister might not have been one of those fast, flashy women that Mom warned me about, but as a teenager her looks made her appear to be the girl next door— wholesome and pretty at the same time that she could be tough and independent. And the guys were starting to notice. One in particular had been showing lots of interest and Tragil confessed that the attention was flattering. Well, at least at first.

Knowing that I would worry, Tragil would only say that Mom was asking about me; she didn't tell me when our mother first went to the county jail or how that meant my sister had started moving from place to place. Although Grandma and our older sisters had been there to help her out, they all had full households and lives of their own.

At one point, Tragil attempted to come live with us at Sixty-Ninth and Harper. Around that time, Bessie and Dad were in the process of getting married. This coincided with the arrival of their first child to-gether, my baby sister Maryya, as well as my father and stepmother being in the early stages of trying to rein in the four of us rowdy boys. Tragil had a hard enough time adjusting to a new school, where she faced threats because word got around that relatives of hers were in gangs not welcome there. Even tougher was coming home and being expected to look after the baby, just because she was the teenage female in the household. Tragil, raised to be independent, had already been on her own, more or less, and wasn't accustomed to being bossed around, even if she was fourteen. So there came a point when Tragil was so overwhelmed with the drama at the new school and the new rules at the house that she complained under her breath in a way that upset our stepmom.

Well, that didn't go over well with Bessie or Dad. When he came home, the Denzel Washington of *Training Day* erupted out of our father. He said that she was flip-mouthed and needed to be more respectful. Dad then proceeded to wash Tragil's mouth out with soap. And once Grandma heard about that, as well as the gang threats, that was the end of her stay in the household. Dad tried to convince Grandma to let Tragil return but our grandmother was adamant: "She ain't going back."

Meanwhile, Dad had stayed in touch with Mom to make sure she understood why the decision had been made for me to come live with him. Dad said to her, "Jolinda, if it gets to be too much without your son, you know he can come back and stay with you when you get settled somewhere."

Mom later told me and Tragil, "I didn't want to admit that I couldn't take care of my boy. Pride had always kept me from saying before that I was in the midst of a struggle, trying to raise kids but feeling failed. When your dad came to me that day, I could have been angry and said 'bring him back, that's my only son, my child.' I could have gone and gotten you back. I could have done that. And I want people to know that because it's never easy. But I looked around my world and asked myself—what the hell was I going to bring you back to?"

Mom acknowledged that my father's life at that time was better than hers. "One thing about your dad is you always respected him. He had a place to live, a job, and he had sports that the two of you could share." She reminded me, "I was on drugs and had a boyfriend beating me day and night and I didn't want you to learn that this was how it was supposed to be. So that's why I didn't go and take you back. I chose what would be best for you and God helped us all out."

Amen.

• • •

ROBBINS, ILLINOIS, IS ABOUT A HALF-HOUR DRIVE—JUST under fifteen miles southwest of Fifty-Ninth and Prairie—from where I spent my life up until the age of ten. But when Dad purchased a three-bedroom house of our own in Robbins from one of our relatives and then moved us all there toward the end of my fourth-grade year, I went through major culture shock.

Robbins was no mere small suburb of Chicago. In fact, Robbins labeled itself a village and embraced a proud history that went back to 1917. Incorporated in that year, the village had become the first all African American–governed town to exist in the United States above the Mason-Dixon Line. Then, in the 1930s, the village leadership built the nation's first black airport and only flight school at the time where African American pilots could receive training. Many instructors and graduates went on to become heroes of World War II as Tuskegee Airmen.

Wow! To me, Robbins was an amazing wonderland when we arrived there. Talk about movin' on up. I could almost feel an added strut to my step and lift to my chest. I was like, *Dang, this is the Jeffersons!*

Life was normal. Stable. We finally had a place of our own and we were being raised now as a family—the kind of family that my father had worked hard to make. Up until this time, maybe there was a sense that I was more of a guest or an added responsibility. But in Robbins, and probably for the first time since I had been under the watch of the women who had raised me, I was made to feel like a real part of the family, which now included my stepbrothers and our new baby sister.

The first shock came a few nights after we moved into the house. Demetrius and I went out front to see if there were any kids to meet. None in sight.

"Listen," I said, noticing something bizarre.

"What?"

"Do you hear that?"

"No, unh-unh, what?"

"I know." That was my point—there was no sound of gunshots. In the past, gunshots were what used to put us to sleep at night, almost like background noise. Out here in Robbins, where the crime rate was lower in those days, there was only a quiet hum of crickets and cars going down the street, the normal nighttime sounds of a poor, working-class, family-oriented community.

Even though the village itself was still almost completely African American, we went to schools with neighboring districts that were much more mixed. That was another big shock when I started school at Springfield Elementary and got to know classmates who were white.

Weird. Really weird. But in a good way. The multicultural atmosphere was unlike any school situation I had ever experienced. The facility was nicer, cleaner, and safer. No more of all that surrounding stress, either.

Even though Robbins was poor, with more than a third of the population living below the poverty line and the rest barely above it, the move for the Wade/McDaniels household was a huge step up. That's how bad it had been in the city.

There was one other shock that my brothers and I hadn't really expected. Dad and Bessie had decided in the new house that they were going to implement new rules. And they were going to be absolute sticklers about us complying with them! There were chores and homework hours and bedtimes we'd rarely had before. Gone was that lack of structure and freedom that we once had in the city where we could run the streets at all hours. Now we weren't allowed to go beyond our own block! Since there weren't many kids we knew close by, the only way we could go anywhere was by prior arrangement between parents.

We couldn't believe it. We were tough city boys, not babies.

Dad and Bessie were quick to remind us that part of the reason for moving out here was to be able to have a backyard of our own. Why should we be running off anywhere else to play when a safe, nice yard was right behind the house?

My brothers and I exchanged bewildered looks. How were we supposed to make any new friends when we were stuck at home? But Dad shot us enough of a menacing glance that we knew better than to open our mouths.

Structure sucked. A week later, however, we began to see the light. And what had seemed to be a bad thing became a good thing.

Dad woke up early that Saturday morning and took off, returning an hour later with a few of his basketball buddies. We watched as they walked down the driveway that ran alongside the house and toward the detached garage in the back. Dad pointed up right over the garage door as the others nodded their heads in agreement. The next thing we knew, they had unloaded plywood, power tools, a ladder, and an honest-to-God real basketball hoop.

We now had our own court, complete with a wooden backboard and everything that Dad and his friends had made for us from scratch. At first, it was just me and my brothers out there. But soon enough, all the friends we started to make wanted to come to our house. Our basketball hoop in the backyard became something like magic. We became that house on the block where you wanted to be. Instead of being the outsiders who had to fight our way into games, the deal was—*Hey, if you want to get into basketball y'all gotta come play with us.*

The backyard was also a place where I could be alone and put aside all the stories that had preceded our life there, and feel a new kind of release. Playing basketball against myself became an important preparation for the challenges of the game ahead. Then again, everything that had happened so far was preparation for competition at a high level, for developing a mental toughness that life required of me even more than the game did.

Until the age of nine, basketball was something I liked and something that could be a way out. It was a connection to my mom and my dad, something that made me feel good, that made me feel cool, that provided comic relief in a mad, mad world.

What was it exactly? I suppose for a kid who kept so much emotion locked up tight, basketball was my comfort, something that brought a feeling to me that other experiences didn't: a feeling of confidence, of satisfaction, of completion.

At age nine, because of Michael Jordan and the Bulls, because of the skills I started to develop under the guidance of Dad, my first coach, I dared to let myself go, to fall in love with basketball, and invest a solid belief that these dreams could be real.

At age ten, alone in the backyard of our house in Robbins, playing one on one, me against me, I found my wings. Now the challenge was to grow into them.

INSTEAD OF CALLING ZAIRE OUT AND MAKING HIM COME TO me, I walk over in his direction. He looks up, as sad as can be, and rises to meet me.

Zion and Dada are still locked into their game, oblivious to the two of us.

"Zaire," I begin, trusting that he's about to help me help him, "come talk to me." So we find a shady spot and sit down on a bench together and I start in, saying, "I heard you're having a bad day—an episode. What's going on, son?"

Unable to keep from crying, he leans in, buries his head on my chest, and says, "Daddy, I don't want to go . . . I don't want to go home yet."

"Zaire, you don't have to . . . ," I say slowly, searching for words. Then they come as I look directly at him and announce, "You are home."

Still crying, he says, "What . . . what do you mean?"

"Well, I didn't tell you this, but on Friday the judge made a decision. Remember I told you a while back that soon she was going to decide whose house you and Zion are going to live in?"

He nods, listening closely.

"The judge decided on Friday that you and Zion are going to have to live here in Miami with me."

Zaire's eyes blink away the tears in an instant as he starts to smile. But then, his voice anxious, the first question he asks is, "What about Mommy?"

And I say, "Look, this is all new, and your mommy is still gonna be Mommy and you're still gonna go visit her. But you'll live here and we'll work out the details together. I haven't talked to Mommy, but she knows." There isn't much more I can say about my faith that eventually she and I can create an open line of communication to make shared decisions about our boys. Instead, I ask Zaire, "Do you have any problems, or questions about living here now?"

He shakes his head no, adding, "I just hope Mommy's okay."

Then, after that, I watch him just perk back up, Zaire animated-style as he jumps to his feet and says, "So, so, wait, wait, I'm living here and I don't have to go back?" Seeing my nod he asks, "Does everybody know?"

"Yeah, pretty much. I was just waiting to tell you and Zion, but I wanted to tell you first."

"Can I tell Zion and Dada?"

"Sure."

With that, he runs over to Dada, singing out, "Zion and me are living here from now on, we're not going back! You can come visit anytime!" To Zion, he says, "Did you hear that? We get to live with Daddy!"

Zaire is so excited and joyous, his little brother and cousin can't help but be, too. I go to give them both hugs. Zion does one of his running leaps into my arms.

Dada looks like this was a no-brainer. He can see his cousins more often by visiting us in Miami for vacations. Zion nods. If his big brother is happy and his cousin approves, he isn't going to miss out on the fun.

Zaire can't stop smiling and neither can I.

When I suggest that he and I go for a walk to a park down the street, I keep the conversation going as we walk, asking him questions and asking if he has questions for me. There is no rush, no hurry, no tearful good-bye to have to endure, nowhere to go. Just me and my son.

We talk about everything: father and son stuff, everything that he may have been holding inside, anything that I can help address, all kinds of subjects that he knows so much about, surprisingly, also how we were so fortunate to get to build the kind of honest, open relationship that not all dads and their kids get to have, how I don't want him to be afraid to tell me anything and to know that there are always going to be bumps in the road ahead but we'll deal with them together.

And this brings me to the close of the long answer to the question of how, by the end of that weekend after I was granted custody of the kids, I figured out how to tell them.

Zaire and I sat in the park together, talking about everything, talking for so long in fact that eventually I started to get hungry.

Then again, I'm always hungry.

PART TWO

Each warrior wants to leave the mark of his will, his signature, on important acts he touches. This is not the voice of ego but of the human spirit, rising up and declaring that it has something to contribute to the solution of the hardest problems, no matter how vexing.

—Pat Riley
President, Miami Heat
Head coach of five NBA championship teams
NBA player, seven championship titles

CHAPTER FOUR

SANCTUARY

TUESDAY EVENING
MARCH 15, 2011
AT HOME IN MIAMI

WHAT A DIFFERENCE A HOUSE FULL OF BOYS CAN MAKE!

In the matter of a few days, I've been transformed. That's truly how I feel—as if getting that one-line e-mail changed my life on its own. For good.

It's not just the joy of waking up in the mornings to the sound of my sons' voices calling, "Daddy get up!" or having them physically pounce on the bed to wake me. It's the realization that they're my partners in building our new lives together. And I'm so happy to be Daddy/Coach of Team Wade and also just teammate, one of the boys.

Besides the main task of enrolling them in their new schools, by Tuesday afternoon I've drawn up a chart for each of the boys to be able to see their daily and weekly responsibilities at a glance. I explain that this is a game plan for success. The chart has reminders for activities like brushing teeth first thing in the morning, then washing faces, or putting away shoes and changing clothes after school, sitting down for a regular homework time before dinner, and then showering before bed.

"Just the same as I have a game plan for success to win basketball games, you two have your own game plans for success." We talk about all the R words: Rules, Respect, Responsibility, and Rewards. Oh, yeah, and one more that everything can be built on: Routine. Nothing is written in stone, I emphasize. But a routine reinforces respect for house rules and responsibilities and leads to an understanding of order, along with respect for self and others, which in turn leads to major life rewards. "Any questions?"

They appear to be excited. Zion boasts, "My chart's the best!" Zaire is about to take the bait and argue, but then goes along with him, agreeing.

We also have a calendar they put up on the wall in their bedroom so they can both see when important events are coming up. Zion and I make a big X on the date when they'll be going back to Chicago and he'll see his mom.

Whether my ex and I have communication yet or not, I do recognize that my sons are the happiest when they know they're going to see her.

Earlier on this Tuesday morning, I was interviewed on ESPN's PTI. I had anticipated that questions would come up about the resolution of the custody fight. Throughout the divorce and custody proceedings, I avoided interviews that touched on my personal life. However, since detailed reports were being published in the media about the judge's findings—and because this was only the five-minute "Pardon the Interruption" segment on ESPN, which was going to focus on the Heat's rout of the San Antonio Spurs on Monday, I agreed to talk.

After dinner Lisa Joseph stops by with some paperwork for me to review and sign. The boys, already in their pajamas, jog into the den to give Lisa hugs and then run off to enjoy a half hour of play before bedtime. I'm about to go join them when Lisa checks the time and suggests, "Let's watch the PTI interview." She was with me when I did the live interview and wants to see how it plays.

I turn on the TV as she and I prepare to watch it when Zaire, with his superpowered nine-year-old ears, magically reappears back in the den and snuggles up next to me on the sofa. Though I want to shield the boys from the publicity, I also don't want them to ever feel secrets are being kept from them at any level. I know the damage that feelings kept inside can cause. So I let him watch, not sure how he's going to react.

Of course, the initial questions have to do with the fact that a mere ten days earlier, the Spurs crushed the Heat by thirty points and, lo and behold, by March 14, the night before, Miami hosted San Antonio and "returned the favor."

In answer to how we had gotten out of our losing rut and were now back to dominating in three consecutive games, I began by admitting that we had regained some much-needed confidence. After all, for anyone following us this season, most of the country seemed to be cheering for the Heat to crumble.

Well, I was asked, could that have been our fault for having such a high-profile celebration at our arena to kick off the season with James and Bosh now on board? And if we had it to do over again, would we maybe rethink drawing attention to ourselves that way?

"No, sir," I answered. "That celebration was for our fans." If we as a team could do anything to boost spirit in the city, I went on, we should. My point was that although a lot of people think of Miami much like the backdrop behind where I was sitting at the moment—flowers, sunshine, and South Beach—there was great challenge and struggle in many South Florida communities. "So if we can do something to bring the light, we will." The celebration to kick off the season, I continued, was us showing our appreciation for the people of our hometown, and it just happened to be on TV.

"Exactly!" says Zaire, giving me a thumbs-up. I shoot a look at Lisa, who hides her smile. That's my boy, an expert on media relations.

But then the interview shifted gears with the announcement that the long, drawn-out custody battle was decided in my favor.

PTI: How has that changed your life?

ME: Oh, it's changed dramatically . . . Of course, I was preparing for it mentally. I went through a long divorce proceeding and custody battle but today I'm thankful for the judge for seeing that Miami and my home are the best place for my sons in their lives. . . . I'm happy for them to grow up with me in my household with me as a father but I'm happy to nourish a relationship with their mom and to make sure that we as a family continue strong, together or not, that my kids get all they need out of life from both their parents. It's also a good time as father-sons.

PTI: LeBron was asked how your game came alive and he said, "He's got his kids." (Laughter.) But Dwyane I gotta ask, how hard has this been for you?

ME: It's been very hard. I just want to be a father. I just want to be Daddy. That was taken away from me for a while and if anyone knows me, I'm a family man. I am all about my kids and I didn't have them in my life for a while and it took a lot out of me, out of my personality. My mind was clogged up a lot. Friday the eleventh my mind got unclogged and I could focus on everything I care about—which is to focus on teaching my kids everything that I know and I don't know . . . about life. So I'm out there playing with a free mind. Now I don't have a lot to think about. . . . I've been going through it for three years. . . . It's made me a better person, a better man but right now today I'm a happier man.

As the interview wraps up, I turn to Zaire to gauge his reaction and see that a shadow has fallen over his face. Before I can ask him what's wrong he says sadly, "It's longer than three years."

"You know, you're right Zaire," I say.

Then he counts out on his hand exactly how long that it's been since he was a little over five and a half, back in July 2007, when his mom and I started to be apart for good. "That's three years and eight months."

"Three years and eight months," I echo him, glancing over at Lisa, who is as struck by his comment as I am. Somehow, until now, I wasn't aware that he was as involved and affected by the legal, emotional roller-coaster ride of the past several years. And the fact hurts me for him that at his young age he knows specifically how long it has dragged on.

It hurts me that my firstborn son, the same kid who usually wears his heart on his sleeve, who can act out when something is bothering him, has been forced to internalize this stress within himself all this time.

Damn, that was one family trait I never wanted to pass on to my children.

The realization dawns on me, thanks to this lesson from Zaire, that as parents we're always walking that fine line between wanting our children to be protected from difficulties and wanting to give them tools for learning how to be strong and how to grow, how to toughen up without losing their innocence.

Not that I was ready for the toughness lessons when I was growing up. But they were necessary even so.

IF YOU ASKED ME TODAY WHAT MY GREATEST DISAPPOINT-ment in life has been, it wouldn't be a season loss or a game that slipped out of my hands or any one major goal that didn't materialize. My biggest disappointment was in myself for leaving the old neighborhood, for not making my way back after I'd been with my dad for a while and doing more for the women in my family who raised me.

No, it doesn't make sense. Tragil had given me the ultimate gift of saving my life and getting me out of there in time. But still, I was disappointed that I didn't stick around for the people I loved, that I wasn't tough enough to handle the challenges. Not that I could have done anything to change the downward spiral Mom was facing or the danger that Tragil was going to be in. But that was a part of the frustration and disappointment—not being able to help change things that were beyond my control.

Like in the movie *Big,* I wanted to get older fast enough to be able to do more. But in reality, I couldn't do that. I couldn't go buy a ticket and change myself overnight to make a difference. So the only way that I could live with the lasting disappointment was by promising myself that if I ever was successful, I'd go back and make up for lost time by helping out in a major way. Not just my family but other boys and girls and their families growing up in the madness.

Until I had gained the power of being able to do that, my guilt and regret would simmer for years. By the time I had settled into the fifth grade after we moved to Robbins, I had toughened up enough just from learning to block the memories—at least temporarily. But there was one memory that became unblockable.

On one of those gloomy fall days when the daylight is shrinking back and colder winds are starting to whip down the streets, Dad announced after our Saturday chores and backyard basketball drills, "Dwyane, you need to go see your mom. Wash up, get Demetrius, and let's go."

My mother would later stress how much credit she gave Dad for honoring the bond that I had with her. But she would also admit to being angry at him for arranging this particular visit when and how it happened. Almost a year had passed since I'd seen her. That was partly because our visits had only made me worry more and I hadn't pushed to go see her. But mainly it was because during this time she had gone from a series of shorter-term incarcerations to longer stays behind bars at Cook County Jail, where she would be kept a couple of months at a time as her various cases made their way through the court system and she awaited trial.

Until Dad pulled the car up in front of the main entrance to the Cook County Sheriff's Office, where scary guard towers could be seen above a series of so-called dormitories for prisoners, I didn't know that Mom had been arrested again. Saying nothing, Dad parked and nodded for us to get out, soon leading me and Demetrius toward the entry point for visitors.

After going through metal detectors and passing a physical inspection, we were allowed into a waiting room. The smell of institutional cleaning solution came over me in a wave, triggering a sick feeling in my empty stomach. Dad checked in at the scheduling desk and we were told to go through the door, where a security window provided a glimpse into the holding area for inmates.

I caught the first sight of Mom coming down the stairs. Suddenly I didn't care where we were or what any of the reasons were that she was here. All I knew was that she was my mother and she appeared to be healthy.

Strange as it sounds—she looked better. Clear. Tough.

Later Mom would say that the only way God could get her attention was to have her behind the walls where, once she dried out, they could have a conversation. Mom would also describe her memory of our meeting this day. When she saw the name Wade on the visitor log, she assumed that meant just Dad alone. Later I learned she was still unhappy with him about a previous visit that had taken place a short time before we moved to Robbins. At that time Dad had brought papers for her to sign that gave him legal custody of me. Apparently the bank that was helping him finance the purchase of the house required proof of custody for all the kids living with him. The paperwork was also important, he had explained, for getting me into the better schools in the neighboring districts. Mom was more heartbroken than mad. She knew he wasn't doing it to hurt her on purpose or to take me away from her. Besides, by then she expected to be facing jail time. Mom recalled telling Dad that as much as she wanted to see me, "Don't bring our son to me when I go in. Don't."

As an adult, I understood. But as a child, I hadn't seen my mother in nearly a year, so it didn't matter.

"No," Mom would say, "you should have never had to see me behind the glass." So that day when she came down the stairs and looked through the main window that separated her from the visitors, her first reaction at seeing Dad with my stepbrother and me was actually anger. I read it on her face as she shook her head, gesturing for my father to come up and talk to her. She basically asked him, "What are you doing?"

His answer? Her request must have slipped his mind.

Even though I didn't know any of this, I could tell from how my mom was reacting to Dad that she was upset. But she shook it off, pulled herself together, and pointed me down to the last window, where we could sit across from one another, away from Dad and Demetrius, who went back out to the waiting room. Alone, I walked toward the last window, surprised that there was no one else in there to see another inmate at that particular moment on what should have been a busy Saturday afternoon.

Jolinda Wade told me later that God arranged it that way. "He didn't have nobody in the visiting room that day except me and you," she reminded me.

I sat down and leaned in, hurt not to be able to hug her or be held by her. I put my hands up on the glass, hands bigger than a scrawny ten-year-old boy would normally have.

Mom held strong. She didn't cry when she asked, "Who's your favorite girl?"

"You, Mom . . ." My voice cracked. But I held back the tears.

My mother raised her index finger, telling me, "I need you to do one thing for me, okay?" She didn't wait for me to answer but continued: "Don't ever think I don't love you. You understand?"

I always understood that. What else we talked about, I don't remember. Maybe we promised to see each other as soon as she got out and was back in a place of her own. I knew she was fighting. I never stopped believing that day was coming.

Almost numb, I kept my face stone cold all the way out into the dark afternoon, following Dad and Demetrius. But sitting next to my father in the front passenger seat, I lost it. He reached out his arm and pulled me closer. For most of the ride home, I stayed there, leaning on his shoulder, sobbing harder than I probably had ever cried.

Before or since.

OUR BACKYARD BASKETBALL COURT TAUGHT ONGOING LES- sons in toughness.

Even though Dad had started to lighten up and let some of his humor and fun personality shine through every now and then, he continued to coach us boys, as usual, like a drill sergeant getting his troops battle ready. No messing around.

As in: blasting a wake-up call early on a frosty morning just for drills. Left hand, right hand. Dribble with the right. Dribble with the left. We'd stay in the back for hours, until I would actually wonder if I wanted to play this game at all.

As in: just when you think you've impressed him or conquered a challenge—*bam!*—he'd raise the bar and set up another series of obstacles.

Thinking ambitiously, Dad used our backyard basketball court as his one-man campaign to keep us out of the gangs that we soon learned were as prevalent in the nearby projects as they had been in the city. His crazy vision was that the team of players he assembled from Robbins could actually be competitive with city kids. But to do that, his game plan was to train us to be able to take on older players—including adults. Like him.

Out on that court, I mean, he would beat us up. You had to become a man at a young age. Not just that. The thing with Dwyane Tyrone Wade Sr. that was most unnerving was his tear-your-ass-to-pieces mouth.

He was not, let me repeat *not*, abusive to us kids physically. But that wasn't the end of the story. Let's just say he could get abusive verbally. In certain situations he could become a verbal monster, a tyrant with words. When he was on the basketball court, that kind of set him apart. Or so I used to think (almost proudly) when I was young and we'd watch him slay his on-the-court opponents with an endless spew of cutting comments, all while slashing his way wildly to the basket. Once Dad started to coach us, however, that side of him became much less entertaining.

But maybe there was a method to the madness, on the court and elsewhere, to constantly being on us about our lack of discipline or determination, our lazy, slovenly ways, or whatever it was. My brothers and I bonded around that. Who knows? That may have been the point.

Otherwise, with the competition as fierce as it was, I couldn't have put up with the relentless taunting from Demetrius, Donny, and eventually Kodhamus. Dad instituted a "no foul" zone for us in the backyard. If you went up for a shot and someone came out there and cleaned your clock, you had to take it. Body to body.

Whatever it took to get the ball away from anyone else was fair game. So I went quickly from those years of getting teased by all my sisters for tripping myself up to being teased by all my brothers for getting tripped up by them. Fortunately, I'd learned how to fall without seriously hurting myself. But Dad and my brothers were brutal. No matter how flagrant the push or shove, the slam or kick that put me on the ground, Dad wouldn't call a foul. Complaining didn't help, either.

Like I learned fast, ain't no crying in basketball.

I got so used to smackdowns that I had to teach myself how to shoot the ball while falling.

Some of those shots may have earned the most admiration Dad ever showed me, especially when I'd shoot the ball over the head of my attackers from a position of being almost laid out on my butt—and then the ball would go in!

"Naw," my father said one day after a series of such awkward but successful baskets, "nobody can do that on purpose. You just lucky."

And so Lucky became my nickname.

I liked it. I liked being called Lucky even though it was Big Dwyane's way of making me raise my sights, of telling me, in so many words, that I'd never really be any good—unless I was willing to work harder than anyone else. In other households, reality could wait. But in ours, even before middle school, we were taught that luck without a supersized will to excel, to continually sharpen your work ethic and surpass limitations, well, just being lucky was close to worthless.

Those lessons not only toughened me up, they came to define my battle with any forces that wanted to tell me I'd never be nuthin'. Dad was just giving me a taste of much more to come from others. So proving that assumption wrong became everything to me. Everything. Whether Dad did that on purpose or not, he would never admit. But clearly, it worked.

I wanted to be more than Lucky. For quite a while, there was no secret about it: I wanted to be Michael Jordan. That meant catching every free moment out in the back to practice the latest Jordan play. I watched him so closely, before long I couldn't help but start to imitate him off the court, too—his mannerisms, his quiet power, his smooth, gliding way of moving across the floor.

During one of the few times Tragil was able to come visit me during these years, the first thing she said as I sauntered up to give her a hug was "Why you walkin' like that? That's not how you walk!"

Proud, I'm like—"Hey, that's my Jordan stroll."

My sister cracked up. As she always did, Tragil came bearing gifts—clothes, doughnuts, a little money for anything I needed. When I asked how Mom was doing, she didn't know the latest. And when I asked if everything was cool with her, Tragil only shrugged. Something was wrong, I could tell, but she didn't want me to worry. Instead, my sister focused on how well I was doing and urged me to continue to make her proud.

"So Michael Jordan, huh?"

"Or Scotty Pippen." In the backyard, I'd been practicing both of their moves. Sometimes at the same time!

"You just be you, Dwyane," she said, starting to leave. When I asked her if she wanted to come to a game, she promised to try. In the meantime, she urged me to mind Dad and not let his militant style get to me too much.

We both said "See ya' soon," when Tragil left that day. Like déjà vu all over again, I had this feeling like she was going somewhere and I wouldn't see her again for a while. Or maybe that was my guilt talking, I silently wondered.

In any case, I forgot my worry about her and focused on the day-to-day in front of me. The fact that Dad was never satisfied did get old. Naturally, some of his criticism was justified. After all, we were rowdy boys and we wanted to have fun. We were normal. We didn't want to have to come in from playing outside all day with our "stanking feet," as Dad called them—and, ooh, trust me, they were—and have to shower or do more chores. We wanted to kick back for a little while. At least. You know, catch our breath.

No. Unh-unh. Not in Dad and Bessie's house. Dad didn't play no body odor, no hint of the house not being clean. That was his drill sergeant boot-camp approach and we were not ever going to go against him and have to face his verbal wrath. In the army, when he was stationed out in the field in Panama, my father's job had been supervising the cleanliness of latrines, basically the portable toilets used away from the base. He was tasked with making sure soldiers weren't exposed to any diseases from lack of hygiene. That was the mentality he used when insisting that we followed protocol. An equal-opportunity enforcer, Dad's rule was that if one guy got in trouble, we all got in trouble.

There was the time, for example, when an issue came up about taking the trash out to the backyard at night. My brothers and I hated this particular chore because the garbage cans were all the way at the far, dark end of the yard. In my imagination, hauling trash bags after dinner could turn into some Robbins horror movie with us being attacked by rabid raccoons, wild coyotes, or demonic werewolves. Or worse, birds. (Seriously. To this day, birds freak me out and so do horror movies.) And Donny was as scared as me.

Donny and I came up with what seemed to be a reasonable solution. After dinner, we walked out the side doors with the trash, then snuck across the well-lit street and left the bags in a ditch. Then, in the morning, once Dad went to work, we'd move it to the backyard. There was not a damn thing wrong with this strategy. Well, except for that day when Donny and I either got lazy or forgot to move the garbage in the morning.

Wouldn't you know it. That was the same day that Dad happened to go across the street after work and happened to see all our garbage in the ditch where we'd left it. We didn't know this until he marched into the house and blasted all of us with an order: "Get naked."

That was all he said. "Get naked."

If Dad didn't kill us, I was sure that Demetrius would. There was nothing I could do but start to cry immediately.

To prolong the fear, Dad said, "Wait." Then he escorted the four of us boys across the street and pointed to the garbage in the ditch and asked, "Who did this?"

Donny and I raised our hands instantly, saying, "We did it, yep, that was us."

Breathing fire, Dad went on to explain why it was wrong and disrespectful of the community and the family and made us all look like worthless riffraff. Or something to that effect.

With that, he nodded in the direction of the house and when we got back inside, he hissed, "*Now* get naked."

We all had to go into one of the bedrooms, even though I was pretty sure that only Donny and I were in danger of getting our bare butts whooped. Oh, the terror of waiting for him to come in with the extension cord for the electric piano keyboard that he only used as punishment for serious offenses. I contemplated running away.

"Donny," I whispered, as the two of us stood there without any drawers on, "I'm gonna jump out the window and leave for a while. You wanna come? Get your pants."

The thought of getting caught and whupped after running away suddenly seemed scarier than just staying to face our medicine. Instead, we prepared for punishment, all four of us on our stomachs with bare butts waiting for the inevitable three swats of the cord. No more, no less. But that cord was so painful!

Dad walked in and announced we could put our clothes back on. No spanking. Talk about Lucky! Obviously, he had taught us the intended lesson without having to put his hands on us. From that moment on, we braved the backyard each night when we took out the garbage. And lived to tell.

Those experiences were behind my conscious decision later on not to spank my kids—because (a) I don't believe in whippings and (b) Dad showed he could get his point across without resorting to putting his hands on us. Of lasting importance was the idea that our behavior and demeanor would reflect, bad or good, on the whole family.

Under that heading, Dwyane Wade Sr. scared my brothers and me far away from everything that he considered to be vices that he himself occasionally indulged in. Not just drinking, drugs, and smoking. Dad didn't tolerate earrings, hats, baggy jeans, none of that. The suggestion of getting a tattoo would bring on a tongue-lashing like you'd never forget.

The rules were rigid but, as he would say, he wanted us to be better than him. And he had another factor in mind: sometimes all it took to get shot was a hat turned the wrong way, or a tattoo or a certain earring, and so he'd rather be a stickler about those things. He'd tell us, "I don't want to see you dead."

Interestingly enough, to this day I don't do drugs, smoke, or drink. Once I could afford nicer clothes (much later) I made up for lost time on the style front. But even when most of the NBA was covered in tatts, I couldn't go that way. I could admire them on others but I just never wanted to wake up one day down the road after doing something permanent and wonder what I'd been thinking.

Obviously, I grew up seeing many examples of the toll that substance abuse takes. My brothers and I also saw in our household reasons why *not* to drink and get high. Dad didn't need alcohol to set his vicious tongue free but with a couple of drinks in him, the fireworks flew.

During the entire time that I'd been with my father and stepmom, I saw how hard they tried to give us kids stability and a family life many others didn't have. Bessie was always very sweet and loving toward me, so all I could feel toward her and Dad was appreciation for the tough task they'd taken on of raising five kids the best they knew how. At the same time, when there was drama and loud, epic arguments and problems with paying bills or keeping food in the house because of the reality of our situation, I didn't necessarily want to be there.

As time went on, the atmosphere became increasingly uncomfortable and I'd stay out in the backyard even longer, playing alone or with the guys. When we weren't in our regular season, with Dad coaching, as time went on I'd sometimes find excuses to stay over at friends' houses. I just needed a break.

Nobody really missed me or had to worry. Maybe that went back to Grandma telling Tragil and me not to be no trouble to anyone. In any case, at school I was known as one of the best-behaved students in the classroom. Rarely did I act out or misbehave.

Oh, occasionally I'd see kids getting attention for being bad and being sent to detention, as if that made them cool, and I'd join in. So every now and again I'd try to get my bad-boy rep going. But once I was sitting there bored out of my mind in detention, thinking about everything else that I could be doing—at a practice or game I was missing—I'd realize that this wasn't who I was.

School otherwise continued to be a place where I could let loose and temporarily not think about the daily struggles at home and for other family members. In my middle school years, I definitely started to become known for being good in sports. But in academics I went through different stages. The move away from the city to the better schools challenged me at first. Not wanting to look dumb, I wouldn't readily ask questions if a subject wasn't being explained in a way that seemed simple or interesting enough for me to grasp basic concepts. Then I'd try to make up for what I'd missed by studying, but I continued to have a hard time retaining too much information at one sitting. With test anxiety on top of that, I would not do well on the exams that mainly determined my grade. But fortunately, I was able to recall an early lesson that had been reinforced by my mother and sister: when in doubt, *ask*.

Those first instances were so *embarrassing* when I had to overcome shyness and lack of confidence in certain subject matter to raise my hand. And yet I discovered that teachers actually welcomed the chance to help. If I had the nerve to say, "I didn't get that, could you go over that again?" a lot of the time I'd see other students nodding their heads. Or if I stayed after class or came back at the end of school to talk to a teacher to address the sections I couldn't get, that would improve my understanding of the information and my grade in the class.

The truth, as I know now, is that all kids learn differently and at different rates. Without knowing it then, I was practicing a form of helping my teachers to help me—by not being afraid to ask, "Could you dumb it down?"

But it was maybe not so much about making things dumb as it was about helping an adolescent put something into context in the real world. Take math. As one very wise algebra teacher pointed out to me, in following basketball so closely I was already doing high-level statistics—percentages, fractions, probability—without even realizing it. After that, I'd look for ways to convert problems into familiar scenarios and often conquered material faster than many other students. The approach was so successful that even nowadays when sitting down with my business advisers, if I don't understand all the variables, I'll have them explain the situation as if I have x amount of points and we're going to be banking on y shooting average. And so on. All variations of me helping them help me.

School also continued to give me a social outlet, somewhere that I could be free to express myself and not feel judged. Though I was still that kid who watched and observed more than I talked, my goofy sense of humor was able to come to the surface more. Once I got to know someone, that is. In the process of doing so, I developed great, lasting friendships. In fact, my closest friends today are the same core guys who have been with me from the time I moved to Robbins.

Of course, Demetrius and Donny became part of my inner circle once we were living under the same roof. Then there was Wug, as in my cousin Antoine Wade, who at different points lived in the same Englewood neighborhood as me and then in Woodlawn, also on the Southside. Laid-back, easygoing, and a people person, Wug came to visit periodically and soon became part of the crew. As time went on, I started to call us guys "the fellas." We all hooped together at different stages but mostly we laughed and hung out. One of the original fellas was Vincent Holmes, the first friend I made in Robbins. Back in the day, Vinny was more of the leader of the crew, someone who was naturally outgoing and vocal. A year or so later, after getting to know Vinny, I met Marcus Andrews, whose family moved to Robbins when he and I were both in the sixth grade. The two of us clicked from the moment we met. Always someone who looked much younger than he was, Marcus was kind of soft-spoken, like me, but he just came across as really cool. Hip. Underneath that laid-back demeanor, though, he had big dreams and recognized that I did, too. Although Marcus wasn't sure exactly where his would take him, he seemed to believe from the start of our friendship that one day I was going somewhere special. The only other person who really believed that in those early years was probably me!

But not because I definitely had all that it would take. Not in the least.

First of all, when I graduated from the eighth grade and prepared to go to high school, I barely topped five foot five. My long-awaited growth spurt, which was supposed to coincide with hitting puberty, was nowhere to be seen. Second, there was this little flirtation I'd been having with organized football. The thrill that came along with scoring touchdowns was something that could easily become habit-forming. Plus I liked being the kid you didn't see coming—not big, no, but wiry and speedy, with a knack for catching passes that seemed close to un-catchable.

The main reason I saw no hard evidence that basketball was a viable path for my future was that my only coach through eighth grade—that is, my dad—never indicated that that was even a possibility. Maybe he did have high expectations and was just testing me to see what I was really made of. Another lesson in toughness? Probably. There was no winning, though. Once Demetrius got to high school, two years ahead of me, I was hands-down the best player on our team. If we scored 36 points and I scored 30 of them, according to Dad, I was slacking and should have scored more. Like I said, Denzel in *Training Day*.

And that may be the secret of why I had to make myself keep be-lieving in a golden future—simply because I had so much to prove.

So toughness became not just about being able to take everything that was thrown at me but also about finding that seam right through the center of the madness, that path through the defenders to the basket. Life, being what it was and what it had been, made that sometimes im-possible. But on the court, I found my sanctuary, my place of escape, where problems didn't exist.

When I was playing basketball, everything was thrilling. Every-thing was defined. I didn't have to worry about where my next meal was coming from, how far the budget was stretched in the Wade household, where my loved ones were, why there were so many like us having to struggle. Basketball didn't tax my mind or my heart. It was all this ball and this rim and this court.

I didn't know how far the game could take me. My hope was to follow Demetrius's footsteps and do well in high school. But I knew this was my home and my haven for as long as I wanted, a place where no one had to know what was going on in my life. Including me.

Basketball was never going to disappoint me. It was going to be the one thing in my life to never let me down.

WHENEVER MY MOTHER TALKS ABOUT THESE YEARS, SHE gives thanks to Dad for always making sure she was included in important news and events of our lives. Then again, Mom was never easy to locate. In the past, Tragil had brought us news of Jolinda Wade, either from direct contact or updates from the grapevine that included my grandma. Suddenly the person we couldn't locate was my sister. None of us fully knew until much later why Tragil had first been forced into hiding.

The boyfriend whose attentions were flattering at first had quickly turned out to be not so nice. As tough, independent, and smart as my sister had always been, what had happened? Tragil's explanation was that for most of her life she has been a caretaker, and he had come across as a knight in shining armor—Tragil's romantic idea of someone to watch over *her* for a change. So he found her vulnerable side and exploited it.

My sister wasn't clueless. Once he began wanting to control how she dressed, where she went, who she knew, Tragil wasn't going to stand for that and tried to break things off. He didn't take that well, and he begged for forgiveness, promised to change, and pleaded for her to take him back.

Tragil desperately wanted to get away from him. But that was going to mean dropping out of high school and not being able to work. Dropping out of school? Tragil was beside herself. Back in our younger days of telling each other our dreams, she and I had pledged to go on to graduate from high school and college. The solution in this case was to send Tragil to San Diego, where an aunt had been living for a while.

And that was how Tragil's prayers were answered and she was given a way out of the madness and the streets that had only gotten worse in the years after she got me out. At age seventeen, in a completely different world and school setting, she began to re-create herself and her dreams. From time to time, she would call Dad at work from her job, asking if I needed anything. Whatever it was, she'd manage to send me money for it, often going without something she might have needed, and never complaining about her circumstances.

Nobody needed to tell me that she was a hero for her sacrifices. Yet Tragil didn't see her role that way. In her mind, continuing to take responsibility for me, even when she was thousands of miles away, was what she was supposed to do—because of how our mother raised us from the beginning.

Mom also checked in on me through Dad. At her request, however, he didn't always report back to me. As she would explain when I was older, "In my sanity or not, I didn't want you to know I was behind the walls again."

Though the details are somewhat hazy, it seems that when I had last seen Mom at Cook County Jail, she had sat there for four months, from November to February, awaiting judgment and sentencing—not expecting leniency. After delays and postponements, however, when she went before the judge finally, she was given a reprieve.

What happened?

"The judge in God's mercy gave me probation. The judge said out his mouth, 'Ms. Wade, if you come back in front of me, I'll send you to Dwight Penitentiary.'" This was a high-security prison for women out in the middle of nowhere, about an hour southwest of Robbins. Mom remembered, "I got out that February and do you know what? I didn't give that man a month before I was back in front of him again and he sentenced me to three years for the case and four years for violating his probation. He ran it concurrent."

With time served, my mother was at Dwight for under two years and released in 1995. Behind the walls, sober, she had begun to find a little peace of mind, a sense of self-forgiveness and self-love that had been missing. That was because, as she would say, "The one thing that I got in prison was that God did talk to me." Out in the world though, Mom lost that connection and her sense of purpose. She put it this way: "I got out thinking—what am I gonna do now? Tragil wasn't in Chicago. Your dad had custody of you. Wanting to be a mother was all I knew. I wanted to start over and do it right. But it was too late. So I went and found churches, looking for the feeling that I had behind the walls."

Fairly soon after getting out, Mom paid a visit to the old neighborhood, both to visit Grandma and to attend the church down the block. Although she heard a small voice warning her to be careful, on the way back to where she was staying, she stopped off at the stretch of the block where she used to hang. Fatefully, she wound up running into the same guy who'd been beating up on her all those years. Mom admitted, "My life went right back to the same abuse and pain that it had been before. He was the same nut. Maybe worse. And I went right back on the dope."

After unsuccessful attempts to kick her habit, Mom decided to try one more time, around her birthday in November 1995. To wean herself off dope without becoming violently ill, she bought enough to "get my sick off" and was going to sell the rest for money to live. But after completing the transaction, she was arrested. The charges were such that Mom was kept out of county jail but had to turn herself in when the time came for sentencing. With delays and heavy backlog in the courts, that left her out on the streets until the following summer, when she anticipated being sent back to Dwight.

During the interim, Mom fell into the depths of despair. Still using. Still feeling that the big *F* of failure was controlling her life, feeling that she had failed us. Of course, this wasn't being reported to me as it was happening. The only news I heard from Dad—which came toward the end of eighth grade—was that he had been to see her.

She was doing all right, Dad said with a shrug, which was not very encouraging. When I asked where Mom was staying and how to go visit her, Dad predicted, "You'll see her soon."

Careful not to get my hopes up, he didn't tell me that he had gotten a ticket for her to attend my graduation plus a ticket for my sister Deanna to join her.

In later years Dad recalled doing that but said it wasn't a big deal. "I mean, that was your mother. She deserved to be there." (And Deanna had paid the fees for my diploma, when Dad didn't have the money.)

But to Mom it was a big deal. Not only was she able to surprise me that afternoon by showing up before the ceremony—looking very thin yet bright-eyed—but she also presented me with a watch she had bought and passed me a handful of singles to put in my pocket. All that must have cost her everything she had at that time.

"I love it! You didn't have to . . . ," I tried to tell her, just after she flagged me down as my friends and I, in our caps and gowns, made our way into the auditorium where the ceremony would take place.

"Yes, I did," she insisted, making sure I put on the watch and held up my wrist for her to see. Mom stood there admiring her choice, nodding in approval at the suburban setting of the school—even though it must have seemed like we'd landed in Oz. She now probably understood why Dad and Bessie had felt that we'd get a better education and be in safer classrooms by avoiding Robbins schools—even though my stepsiblings and I were a definite minority here.

There was a pained expression in my mother's eyes that pained *me* to see. I figured she was hurting for the time we had missed together but was unaware, as she would later admit, that she felt awkward and out of place, ashamed that she hadn't been there on a daily basis.

I wanted to reassure her but didn't have the words. All I could do was reach up and hug her. Almost shyly, Mom turned to Deanna and said, "Isn't he the most handsome thing?"

We both stood for another moment, not saying anything. Then it was time for me to go catch up with friends and take my place in the auditorium. We hugged again quickly and she said we'd see each other after the ceremony. As I turned to go, she asked suddenly, "You want me to walk you in there?" No sooner had my mother spoken those words than she broke out in a big smile, obviously aware she was talking to a much younger boy than I was by then.

"Naw, Mom, I'm all right."

As I bolted and ran toward the auditorium, I knew she would stand and watch until I vanished from sight. Sure enough she did, as she would recall years later, telling me also, "That was when it dawned on me my baby grew up."

1 A.M.
MARCH 16
AT HOME IN MIAMI

I'M STANDING AT THE DOORWAY, CHECKING IN ON THE TWO boys asleep in their beds. Still thinking about this question of teaching toughness. This is no small challenge for me or for most fathers, I have to say.

Maybe this is one of those parental responsibilities that has to become an overtime kind of thing. Certainly it has to begin with striving to be the example of tough—in terms of teaching that it's possible to overcome anything. With Zaire and Zion, I want to be able to talk about little difficulties they can overcome, as well as bigger things. Those need to be ongoing conversations, too.

But thankfully we'll have time for those conversations and also for the next item on my daddy agenda: having fun!

CHAPTER FIVE

HOOPIN'

On the Road
March 29–30, 2011
Cleveland, Ohio
Washington, D.C.

"How was your day?"

As a parent, I love that question. It gives permission for everyone in the family to share feelings—like taking a snapshot of the moment. With my kids, I always want to know how the school day went or how a playdate was enjoyed.

Oh yeah, in the Wade household we are big on setting up playdates.

There are a few reasons for that. First of all, I believe that relationships are central to happiness and success. In terms of career building blocks, I've learned as an adult that *who* you know is often more important than *what* you know. Also, experiencing joy is no doubt a great human endeavor.

Whenever we have our "How was your day?" talks, I'm always interested to know something that was learned or some new aspect of fun that was experienced. Or, if the day had disappointments, grades were bad, lessons were challenging, or problems got in the way of playing well with others, I want to know about that, too.

During the first weeks of our new life together, I established the lasting priority of having a daily check-in—either after school on the days when I picked the kids up or at dinner together. Honestly, this was as important for my adjustment process to full-time single-dad status as it was for Zaire and Zion. I needed to really pay attention to how they were feeling as well as doing.

Zion, initially, hadn't slept well and had cried about missing his mom. My message to him was just to let him cry and be there for him. Tragil also stayed close to the boys, continuing as loving aunt and pitching in as nanny during the transition. I had already reached out to Brenda Larson, the nanny the boys adored and whom I'd hired to care for them whenever I was in Chicago. I'd interviewed many candidates but she was the one the boys immediately loved, especially Zion. The blessing for us was that Brenda had agreed to move to Miami to take care of the boys full time and would arrive before summer.

Zaire's issues were tougher. Since he never wanted to feel or say anything negative about his mom, he seemed to have almost a sense of guilt about allowing himself to be happy. So we had work to do on that. He had been so overly drawn into the divorce drama that I knew we should continue to seek the resources of therapy together, both for Zaire and me with him.

In the meantime, what appeared to be working was just keeping the conversation going. In the mornings at breakfast, we could talk about what was on our agenda for the day and then continue in the car on to other subjects. Because I happened to be one of the few dads doing drop-offs at the elementary school and at preschool, first walking the boys to their classrooms and then staying to chat with some of the other parents (all females) doing the same, I soon earned a new nickname: Mr. Mom.

Maybe not as catchy as Flash, but just as meaningful.

Game-wise the month of March was at first a light travel month, thankfully. However, by the end of the month, the Heat's schedule had us on the road for four away games. That meant my boys and I planned to have our "How was your day?" conversations via Skype. The rest of the time we could text, call, and e-mail, too. But we like the video chats. Though it's never the same as being together in person, being able to see and hear each other through our computers does make the time go faster and easier.

After all of our traumatic separations earlier on, waking up in a hotel room without the sound of their voices nearby is a shock. Less than a day away from home, after returning from the shoot-around at the arena, I log into my Skype account early, unable to wait for our check-in.

Right on time, Zaire's face lights up the screen. Zion tries to squeeze in, bringing his face up closer to the camera. Not much is going on, Zaire says. Zion shrugs as well, saying, "Nothing new." We go over the daily schedule, which includes their regular check-in with their mom. Then, before we sign off, they wish me well for the game. We say good-bye as we always do with a group "I love you!" and promise to talk the next day.

About twenty-four hours later, during our check in on Wednesday, Zaire has lots of news for me. School is very hard, he says. "Way too much homework. I mean, I never had to work this hard in Chicago!" As it turns out, this is leading up to the explanation about how he didn't do an assignment. We'll take a closer look at that later. On an up note, he reports having lots of fun entertaining some friends from school at the house.

Before Zion answers my question about how his day was, he squints his eyes and again comes in very close to the screen. Like he's trying to read my mood. So true to his Gemini astrological sign, Zion can go hot or cold. When he is happy and having fun, no one is happier. When he is down, he doesn't want to be cheered up or babied.

The fact that Zion isn't even four yet is something even I keep forgetting.

As a case in point, when I ask again if he had a good day at his preschool, he gives me a look like that is a silly question—then goes on to tell me about someone having a birthday in class and having a cake and party favors. How was that? "Fun!"

Prodded by his brother, Zion innocently asks me how I am. The two then squeeze their little faces onto the screen to check out my reaction and to offer cheerful smiles.

The truth is that the Heat's loss the previous night to the Cleveland Cavaliers was rough. I've trained myself over the years not to linger too long on victories or losses but to learn from them and move on. As I've told the boys, the test is always to look at mistakes, see where there is room for improvement, and to be able to ask, "Did I give my all?" Then gear up for the next game. Because win or lose, there's always going to be a next game.

The Cleveland game wasn't the first time the Heat had been back to play on LeBron's home turf during this first year after his coming to Miami. We expected the cool welcome—to say the least—although not perhaps the extreme level of anger expressed by the crowd. Not as intense as when we'd been there in December, however, when we won by eighteen points. This time, though, we let the noise get to our heads and lost by twelve.

What made the loss tough for me was the expectation I put on myself to deliver for the team, to set an example for how to stay calm in the midst of a storm. That was something that I should have been able to do, I felt. But given the wrath of the crowd, the loss might have been the best thing for us in the end, to give the city a win.

So as I gear up for the game with the Washington Wizards in D.C. and talk on Skype with the boys, I try to explain my disappointment in myself for not doing more to help my team keep our heads in the game. "And what else did I forget?" I ask my sons.

Bad question.

Next thing I know, the two of them are coming up with a slew of ridiculous answers—everything from forgetting to change my socks to not doing my pregame ritual of grabbing the hoop and doing the three pull-ups.

Now we're all laughing about who has the stankiest feet and so on. On that note, I remind them to go take care of business and help out the home team and that I'll see them soon.

The answer I was trying to have the boys remember was about the importance of playing for the love of the game. Certainly in the past there have been times when I've played angry and hurt and with a chip on my shoulder and managed to score points and help win. Sometimes those emotions are needed to power up a team, too. Spo, as we call Coach Spoelstra, has said that I can play mad probably better than any player he knows.

But in the end, without joy, the game just becomes a slugfest powered by testosterone and ego. Without heart, teams can become little more than a set of stats and basketball runs the risk of not really mattering. Without heart and without the choice to embrace joy even in the midst of fear and uncertainties, life is just a series of events that don't connect to each other and don't connect us to the purpose that we're all given.

And those are only some of the conversations that can be inspired by the question "How was your day?"

NOT LONG AGO, I HEARD A STORY MY FATHER HAD NEVER told me before. He recalled an evening in spring 1998 at the end of the basketball season for my alma matter, Harold L. Richards High School in Oak Lawn, Illinois. As Dad tells this tale, a very emotional head coach, Jack Fitzgerald, approached him after the awards ceremony that night to confess how broken up he was that my brother was going to be graduating soon.

"I'll never have another player like Demetrius," Coach Fitzgerald told Dad, tears in his eyes. "Never."

Without question, when Demetrius McDaniel finished playing his last season of varsity basketball for Richards, he already had earned himself a page in the history books for breaking almost every school record. At the time, he claimed the all-time number-one spot in points scored (1,432)—a record broken by only one other player eight years later, Cody Yelder. Demetrius also held the all-time high for rebounds (504), surpassed only by two others: Cody Yelder in 2006 (516) for the number-two spot, and yours truly in 2000 for the current all-time record of 539.

What Demetrius had done for the basketball program itself was just as impressive. When he arrived at Harold L. Richards, boys basketball was a far cry from the powerhouse football program. In those days, when you walked down the halls of the school, most of the banners and trophies on display were for Bulldog victories in football. Photos hanging in the gym showed the famous Richards graduates who had won all-state and gone on to play football at Division 1 colleges and even in the NFL. Demetrius had this ambitious belief that he could be a contributor in changing the perception of basketball at our school. He did so as a varsity starter for three years and as a senior by becoming the first all-state player in school history and by leading the Bulldogs to a 28–2 record, which included winning our conference championship, our regional division, and sectionals.

So it was no surprise that Coach Fitzgerald would tell my father that he would never have a player as good as Demetrius again. The surprise to me was that Dad then told Coach not to worry. "You'll be all right," said Mr. Dwyane Tyrone Wade Sr., with a shrug. "You've got Dwyane."

"Dwyane? You think Dwyane could be as good as Demetrius?"

Dad had to pause to think about it. Up until that moment, as he himself would admit, he had not been so confident. But something told him I was going to be coming on. Even maybe better than Demetrius. Good enough for college basketball? No, nobody was looking that far down the road. The NBA was like winning a lottery. That was something you never talked about seriously anyway. Except in your dreams. But the question Coach Fitzgerald put to my father, my first coach, was whether I could do on the court for my high school everything my stepbrother had done. Finally, my old man just laughed and said, "Sure."

Whether or not I could be as good or better was definitely yet to be seen. But Dad did know that I certainly aspired to follow in Demetrius's footsteps. From the start, that was why I'd gone to Richards instead of other area high schools. Oh, yeah, and the football program. No, I hadn't gotten that out of my system yet. That actually turned out to be to my benefit because I could use my position as cornerback and wide receiver in football to work on toughness, just as track let me work on quickness and the high jump helped develop my jumping and all-around athletic abilities. All of that served basketball in the end.

If you asked me what was my favorite sport back then, I would have answered whatever it was for the season we happened to be in. A form of "love the one you're with." But when it came time to choosing which sport I loved most, basketball would inevitably win out—especially once junior year rolled around.

The irony was that even though I had followed Demetrius to Richards, the timing didn't work out exactly for us to be the daring duo on the court that I had originally expected. That said, coming in as Demetrius's little brother got me early attention. I remember the first day of freshman tryouts when the sophomore coach recognized me from all the weekend practices I used to attend with Demetrius. When the team was doing drills, I'd be down at the other end of the court shooting on my own. Not being no trouble to anyone, as my beloved Grandma used to advise.

When we started freshman tryouts that day I was clearly above the skill level of the rest of the players. They couldn't make left-hand lay-ups and other basic moves; but, to me, a left-hand lay-up was easy. Chalk that up to the backyard court and my dad. So when the sophomore coach spotted me, the first thing he said was "What are you doing down here with the freshmen?"

Before I could answer, he waved me over to sophomore tryouts. In essence, that meant I had made the team and was being moved up to play at the next level. That first season I started on the sophomore team and went on to be a top scorer for us, leading also in rebounds and steals. The only problem was that at a young fifteen I was still small—five foot six, closing in on five seven.

The varsity team that year, which included Demetrius, a junior, was having a great season. He was the man—outgoing, popular, putting Harold L. Richards High School on the map—the guy you loved to cheer for. As one of his coaches, John Chappetto, later said about Demetrius, "I've never seen anyone that loves basketball like he loves it. Basketball makes him happy and, because of that, everyone around him gets a piece of that happiness."

Part of my brother's influence was teaching me to take that joy onto the court and combine it with the work ethic Dad had drilled into us, along with the direction that Coach Fitzgerald and his assistant, Gary Adams, provided. Could I put all those elements together as well as Demetrius? The answer began to be revealed over the summer between my ninth and tenth grade, when he and I played together, side by side, in a local league that had some of the top high school players in the state of Illinois.

The Chicago summer league is well known to college and pro scouts as being one of the most competitive in the nation. And even if I only grew about an inch that summer, my confidence soared. What's more, I think Demetrius sensed me starting to elevate my game. With nothing to lose, at the end of the league competition he and I entered a two-on-two contest. In the early rounds of the contest, my brother kind of messed around in one game and we lost. To make it out of the losing bracket at that stage and then make it to the championship game, we had to win two grueling games in a row.

So adrenaline at a certain point takes over and now he and I are suddenly unstoppable. I'm like, wow, we ballin'—both of us, going against seniors, older guys, all the best players in the area. Holding my own, I start to score above twenty and then in the final, I kicked into a higher gear that didn't seem like it had been there before—hoopin', ballin', going crazy scoring thirty points on my own.

Then there was the moment, as we closed in on the win, when I saw Demetrius take a step back and really look at me. The expression on his face was something—as if to say, oh, my God, this is my little brother. Soon after he must have come to the conclusion that little bro was growing up and ready to come back to school and win side by side with him for the school in what would be for him his senior year.

Well, it didn't go quite like that. When basketball season got under way, Coach Fitzgerald did bring me up to play on varsity. Coach did let me play the first three games, but he didn't play me a lot. He had a tight rotation developed with a team that had been together since the guys were freshmen, and here I was, a sophomore, trying to get playing time—at least as the sixth man off the bench. But he didn't seem to feel that I was ready yet. After a few games, I asked him, basically, that if I am not going to play much, rather than sit me on the bench the whole year, could you send me down back to sophomore so I could at least play with my friends?

When I'd been to the sophomore games, I'd felt baaaaaad. They were down there struggling and I'm like—*Dang, my boys losing, they getting killed! Let me go try to help!*

So I went down to that team again and I murdered sophomore level. Coach Fitzgerald then moved me back up to varsity for the playoffs and I had an okay first game, scoring six points, and then something like two points for the next game. Demetrius did indeed lead the team to the finals, coming within two points of winning the state championship. I remember sitting on the bench watching the clock ticking down and being able to visualize how I would have brought the ball in and shot to make it at the buzzer. But maybe only in my dreams. Or maybe not.

And it was a few nights later, after we came within a basket of winning the state championship, that my father made his comment to Coach Fitzgerald. Dad distinctly remembered repeating the fact that he didn't have to worry about losing Demetrius—who was going to go play for a junior college in New Mexico—and again saying, "You'll see. Dwyane could be as good. Maybe better."

That may have been my father's last bold prediction about my career that he made. The truth is that I would have loved to have heard such confidence from Dad back in those days. But the good news was that he got Coach Fitzgerald's attention. Even so, I don't think he or anyone was really expecting much from me.

That is, until after that summer between sophomore and junior year, and I returned to school in the fall a drastically changed young man.

TRAGIL HAD GONE THROUGH EXTREME CULTURE SHOCK OUT there in San Diego. After having been one of the best students in her classes throughout her schooling in the Southside of Chicago, she found out that at the suburban California high school she attended, most students in her grade were close to a year ahead of her academically. In that more affluent, mostly white and Asian population, Tragil said she would have flunked out if it hadn't been for an assignment given to her by an English teacher.

When she was assigned to write a paper about her life, my sister sat down and began to pour her heart onto the page. Tragil wrote as if possessed, she said, about everything that had happened from as far back as she could remember. The teacher not only gave her an A but she broke down crying after class, telling Tragil how much she admired and respected her ability to survive and hold on to her faith. That teacher went on to help her graduate, which allowed her to attend college afterward.

If she had been anyone else, Tragil could have stayed in the sunny, safer world of Southern California, working a few jobs to put herself through college and finishing up her degree in education. But as she would explain, Tragil felt that her family needed her back in Chicago.

Interrupting her education, she returned to the Southside but moved into a different, more secure neighborhood. My sister, T.J., as I started calling her, was forging a new path. With the middle name of Jolinda, Tragil had made sure to put her full name on her diploma to honor our mom. T.J. was coming into her own, hoopin' in her way. Not just because she was holding down a job that allowed her to afford her own apartment and buy her own car. Tragil also continued college part-time, made sure Grandma was doing all right, and started a youth services program at our same church on Prairie Avenue. Oh yeah, and led the youth choir, kept the financial books for the church, and brought in new members so that the seats were full every Sunday. A one-woman force of nature.

Between her activities and mine, we didn't see each other much. But every time she checked in, her questions were all about what I needed: could she bring me clothes or some spending money, whatever it was. Tragil knew that times were lean at home and that the chaotic atmosphere at Dad's house was causing me to spend more time at my friends' houses.

One day she came to see me and wanted to talk about not rushing into anything serious with the opposite sex. I had my first girlfriend at the time and we were nowhere near serious. Tragil started to go into a whole conversation about not doing anything rash and becoming a dad in my teens.

The embarrassed look on my face must have told my sister every-thing. She then proceeded to try to tell me about the birds and the bees. I stopped her right there. "No, that's okay. I'm playing ball right now. No serious girlfriends." As far as becoming a father in my teens, I knew all too well what happens when kids themselves start having babies. Now, as far as being eager to lose my virginity, that was another story. But even after having a first girlfriend, I was still pretty clueless.

The next young lady I dated was someone I'd known since the move to Robbins. Her name? Siohvaughn Funches. We had been friends from the neighborhood and school all this time, never with any hint of romantic interest. Siohvaughn was one grade ahead of me. She was very smart, very cute, outgoing, talkative, a go-getter. Around the time when she was sixteen and I was fifteen and a half, we started spending more time together and soon were more than just friends.

Part of that was built on my needing Siohvaughn; at the very least I had come to depend on the support and affection we shared. Siohvaughn was sensitive to the trials and tribulations of my background. Raised by a single mom, she had recently gone through the loss of a sister in a tragic car accident. Our different struggles became a bond for the two of us.

At Siohvaughn's house I could do homework or just hang without the arguing and drama of being at the Wade household at the time. Not that I was always over at the Siohvaughns'. But as the weeks and months passed, I'd be staying over one night and then maybe another, until it would be a few days at a time and so on. Eventually the Funches women became almost a second family, giving me a place to stay, a shower after a long practice, and a hot meal. And I liked that a lot. I enjoyed that treatment. Who wouldn't?

Unfortunately, I now know that being drawn into a relationship so young wasn't the way to build toward a lifelong commitment like marriage. Neither of us knew who we were and what we ultimately might want from a life partner. Certainly I didn't. Of course, I wasn't thinking long term. There was a moment or two when I realized, as a popular athlete in school, that this was the time to enjoy the perks of being the big man on campus. That said, in those days, I was more focused on basketball and seeing where it could take me. In hindsight, I should have definitely played the field more when it came to the opposite sex.

Then again, I thought the concept of being high school sweethearts was cool. Siohvaughn had qualities I'd been raised to value: church-oriented, an excellent student, and not one of those "fast women" my mother always warned me about. As more of an introvert, I was impressed by her ability to express herself forcefully, to get loud and free at times with her sense of humor, too; yet she had insecurities and wasn't stuck-up. All of that led to a comfort factor. Besides, I felt a commitment to what was the right and honorable thing to do. After all, I was being given the safe haven I needed (and wanted) a lot in those days. And because of the huge sense of responsibility that's at my core—this belief that if someone does something for me, I want to do something for them *times ten*—I fell easily into the role that was presented to me, of boyfriend. But our relationship was built on that flawed foundation of my needing her, a dynamic that would reverse and come back to haunt us later on.

Darlene Funches was a very caring mother figure. Here, too, a void was being filled. As my future mother-in-law, she would soon take an active role in helping guide some of the decisions that would alter the course of my career. And that brought with it mixed blessings—as only time would tell.

"IS THAT MY GRANDSON?" MY GRANDMOTHER CRIED, CALLing down to me from her spot up on the porch at 5901 Prairie.

Early in the summer of 1998, I managed to take breaks between practices and games in the city to go see how Grandma, at almost eighty years old, was doing. Anything to hear her laugh, to sit up on the stoop next to her outside in the thick Chicago humidity and watch the world around us.

Willie Mae Morris hadn't aged a minute. She still had her full pretty head of white hair, her tough pride, and constant concern for all of her loved ones. Everything else around, except for her, seemed to have changed. The corners nearby had been mostly shut down, much of the action moved on to other blocks, leaving this stretch of the Southside to look kind of barren. Almost a ghost town.

As a younger kid, I had never understood how communities like mine could be allowed to fall through the cracks, how people in a country as rich and powerful as the great United States of America could be left to scrounge for the most basic of needs. Yes, I had made an early vow to be different and not continue the cycle of poverty and the cycle of fatherless families that lay heavy like a suffocating blanket on my streets. But now at sixteen, I started to do the math—and to grasp the reality that becoming successful enough to make a difference for my family and community was going to take money and influence far beyond the reach of anyone I'd ever met.

How? How to do that? Was I crazy to think that I could have money and influence to do big things for others one day? Probably. I knew the odds. The odds were as close to unheard-of as me growing four and a half inches over one summer. That wasn't even in my dreams.

A much more realistic dream was fulfilled right there on the porch with my grandma when she finally asked, "You hungry, chile?" She told me to go on up to the kitchen and help myself. And you know I did!

When I returned, my stomach full, I sat back down on the steps, waiting for Grandma to bring up news of Mom. But she said nothing, other than to ask God to continue to watch over me and my cousins and to spare her grown-up kids from too many more troubles.

I could have asked more specifically about Mom but didn't. This was at that stage where you didn't ask for fear of hearing worse than you knew before. Grandma and I communicated on that level where you didn't have to say anything anyway. No news of Mom was bad news.

One of the last times most people knew what had happened with Jolinda Morris Wade was in August 1996 when she appeared in court, as per the terms of her last arrest, and was sentenced to another four years at Dwight Penitentiary, effective immediately. With time served and her prior record of good behavior, the sentence was reduced to eighteen months.

Once again I would have to wait years until my mother could recount the dramatic events that followed. As in the past, after Mom went behind the walls, getting sober was no problem. She'd say with a laugh, "You know, as before, God was in there waiting, telling me, 'Jolinda, this is the only place I can talk to you!' " Four months at the penitentiary and she was doing so well that she became a candidate for work release, a program that helps inmates find jobs in the real world and gives support for eventually transitioning into an independent life. After she put in for the program, Mom recalled, "I got accepted November 1996 and shipped out to the Work Release Center on the Westside of Chicago. While I'm in there, God had me favored. I didn't drink, I didn't smoke cigarettes."

Her first job was in telemarketing, and as long as she was given supervision and structure, Mom thrived. She felt like her life could have meaning—that maybe she had finally battled her demons. The big area of discomfort, however, was meeting other people. That was how, in March 1997, when she started attending classes as well as working her telemarketing job, with free time to independently get from the center to work and to school, she had her first slip, walking unsupervised to class with enough money for something to eat in her pocket.

An inner warning told her not to stop off at the liquor store for a sandwich, she admitted. But the nervousness about connecting to others blocked out her better judgment. "I remember going into that store and asking for a pack of Newport," she would say, explaining her rationalization, reminding me that she never smoked menthol cigarettes. And then she bought something other than her old standby of red wine, telling herself that anything else wouldn't tip her off. She made it to school without incident and then went back to the Work Release Center, thinking she could camouflage any telltale signs. "When I got in, the lady called me over and asked if I had been drinking, and that's enough to send me back to the penitentiary. And I said, 'Yes ma'am.' "

The woman thought about it and told Mom, "I know how hard you've been working. I don't want to send you back." Instead, she recommended that my mom go on to work that afternoon and then come back in to see her afterward and they would discuss getting her into a new program and class.

If there was a lesson there, that one slip didn't have to ruin all the progress she had made, Mom hadn't reached that understanding yet. She still hadn't overcome the *F* of failure she had branded on herself. So what did she do?

"When I left up out of there, I was supposed to take the train going north to work. Instead I took the train south, right back to the old neighborhood. And I had money in my pocket." As it happened, Mom had run into Dad on her way back to the Work Release Center and he had given her money, hoping she was turning her life around with school and work. But there she was, back on the same block with all the familiar triggers and temptations.

The rest of the day did not go according to plan, as Mom told the tale: "First thing, I ran into a friend of mine and he was sick. Dope sick. And he asked if I had any change, and I gave him ten dollars. I'd decided to ditch work and then get back to the center in time." That went awry when she stopped over to see her brother, one of my uncles, and sat talking to him and some friends. "Well, by that point, I stayed too late and couldn't get a ride. Nobody."

It was never easy for me to listen to how my mother made her decisions at different crossroads when she was in her madness. But that difficulty is nuthin' compared to her effort to look back and recollect the numerous ways that she fell down without ever fully giving up. So I have tried never to judge her or blame anyone else for where her decisions took her. I admire her even more for being able to tell others the truth of her actions without self-pity or excuse, but by owning her actions.

The thing that I understand better now about Jolinda Wade is that her true nature is all love, all heart, all joy. Obviously, her temptation out on this work furlough program wasn't the result of wanting to go back to the old life of dope and addiction. The temptation in those moments when nobody could give her a ride back to the Work Release Center, where she was about to be sent back to the penitentiary, was more primal: the desire for freedom.

Mom said it more simply: "That night, I made up my mind. I wasn't going back in." Her sentence by now was whittled down to only eight months to go. "Eight months and . . . I left. On my mind was where to go next. I tried the guy who asked for money earlier but he wasn't answering his door. That was unusual. But I had to go somewhere because I was now an escapee. I wasn't sure what was about to happen—whether they were gonna send the police after me or how they would track me wherever."

Months passed before I even heard about my mother's situation. Eventually I learned that she went to a friend's place and was able to stay there that first night, not saying that she was on the run. When she left there the next morning she was for all intents and purposes a fugitive, basically moving to different neighborhoods incognito.

"The first thing that happened that next day was that I found out the guy who had asked me for the ten dollars had OD'd that night. He was a dear friend of mine and I couldn't believe I had given him the money. What if I hadn't? He could be alive. If, if, if. When I'd gone to his place and he didn't answer, he was up there OD'd."

My mom never told me how long she managed to stay off dope in this time. I do know that she blamed herself for the misery and desperation of her existence. I do know that she blamed herself for the misery of others. After a few days of her not having anywhere to go, another friend let Mom stay in an extra room at her house. The downward spiral happened faster than ever. Mom recalled that she was truly scared. "Now I feel like death is following me, that anyone I'm around is gonna die. I felt like God was telling me, 'You ain't gonna be able to be out here and take all this stuff I'm giving you and throw it in my face.'"

For almost five years that was going to be her life: running from the law, dealing and using, getting beat up. She couldn't be legal or have an ID on her in case she did get arrested. Of course, she couldn't work or rent a place to live in. Finding her was tougher than ever.

In the summer between sophomore and junior year, a month or so after I had a good visit with Grandma, Dad heard of the address where

Mom was staying and gave me a ride to see her. My father had apparently given her a heads up, enough for my mother to pull herself together and not look too bad.

Or maybe that was just because I hadn't seen her in so long. Still, I wasn't encouraged when I glanced around that room—where the air was thick with smoke and the smell of burnt chemicals and there were ripped sofas, piles of cigarette butts in ashtrays, and people in the shadows either with the glazed-over expression of a dope fiend or the edgy glare of a crackhead. I thought my mother had landed in hell. She would tell me later that after all the years of being abused, she had become abusive, beating up the men around her who were in that same hell.

No matter what, Mom was going to see to it that I didn't leave without something she could give. So after she asked who was my favorite girl and I told her, like always, "You mom," my mother turned to the others in the room and said sharply, "Who got money up in here?" She waited a beat and then insisted, "Put it on the table."

Mom scooped up twenty dollars lying there and said, "This is going into my baby's pocket," as I took the money from her.

That was my cue to go. I tried to stay longer, hoping that my mother could see through the haze to notice something about me that was starting to change, hoping that she would give me a sign that she was not too far gone. That's what some of the members of the extended family had been saying—that she was a lost cause. I refused to accept that. But some kind of sign would have helped ease my soul.

All she said, was, "See ya later, baby."

I KNEW FROM LOOKING IN THE MIRROR AND NOT FITTING INTO my clothes or shoes that over the summer of 1998 I had experienced an actual growth spurt. Finally. But only when I returned to high school in the fall did I find out the actual measurement.

Four and a half inches! I grew from five foot seven and a half to six foot two! Improbable odds for a kid just wanting to play high school varsity basketball. But apparently not impossible.

The basketball coaches suddenly wanted to know my name. The year before, they knew me as the stepbrother of Demetrius McDaniel and that I had done well at the sophomore level. But the only sense they were given that I had varsity talent was from my dad's prediction to Coach Fitzgerald. They were still not expecting much other than that I was taller and that I might have grown into my feet and hands.

Once the season kicked in, everything suddenly seemed effortless. Like magic. In our first few games, I came roaring out of the gates early and the transformation was like superhero time. Those first few games, I'm ballin', I mean like *ballin'*, putting up close to thirty points a game, blocking, stealing, making crazy shots, and even dunking like I've been doing it all my life. The tougher the competition the better I would play.

Coach Fitzgerald must have been thinking that Dwyane Wade Sr. was a prophet. Or, at any rate, he might have been thinking that Junior maybe could be getting ready to deliver for the team that year.

Jack Fitzgerald was the ideal coach, mentor, and surrogate father figure to come into my life and my basketball training at that time. On the short side, Coach Fitzgerald was Irish to the T, a red-faced pit bull when he needed to be, tough as nails, willing to get in anybody's face. Nice-looking, too, Fitzgerald had a great head of hair he always had combed just so and was also what I thought of as a sweater coach. At games he always wore these dapper sweaters and confused the competition with his preppy attire. They had only to wait until the game was under way to find out he was a classic tough Irish guy through and through.

The most important lesson I learned from him over the next two years was really this: how to be a teammate. Even though I was the best on the team, Coach Fitzgerald would never let me go out in a game and score 40 points—even though I might have already scored 24 in the first half. He wouldn't let me take bad shots or show off the fact that now and then those bad shots of mine had a good chance of falling in. Coach encouraged leadership but wouldn't let me outshine my teammates. That was new because I'd been raised up in the backyard, where it was every man for himself. That wasn't the Fitzgerald way. He wanted me to know—Dwyane, this isn't about *you*, it's about *us*.

While this may sound like the basic message given to all younger players, it's all too often lost as ballers ascend to higher levels. Jack Fitzgerald really drove the idea of team into me and today it's a big reason why I'm able to play with stars like LeBron James and Chris Bosh—because I believe in team and don't believe in self.

For his part, Coach Fitzgerald would later say that what he most valued in me was an ability to be fearless. He liked how I, too, would confuse the competition by being the quiet guy on the bench and becoming someone who could tear up the floor and kick ass on the court. He came to the conclusion that I liked challenge, something I was learning about myself. The bigger the game, the bigger the crowd, the tougher the opponent, I used the uneven matchup to prove that I couldn't be intimidated.

Every now and then, especially in playoffs, Jack Fitzgerald would unleash the hounds in me and tell me just to go out and let loose. On one such occasion I went into the history books for a tournament by scoring 48 points in the morning game and 41 points in the afternoon.

As this development was unfolding during my junior year, out in New Mexico at college, Demetrius started hearing how the team and I were doing. Somewhat skeptical, he let it be known that he would have to come home and see for himself. And so that next summer as soon as he arrived back in Robbins, he offered Donny and me a prime opportunity to win back the pride he'd stolen from us all those years when he used to beat us both together.

We took the battle out into the backyard. The three of us started going at it like in the old days. Demetrius had gotten even stronger. What was different now, besides my height, was that I'd reached another level of confidence. And I was pretty good, too.

So there we were playing in the backyard, going at it full throttle, hoopin' like madmen, and I just felt that an important rite of passage was before me, a big moment. We were matching each other basket for basket, steal for steal, when at last everything came down to a final push from us, the underdogs. I had the ball in my hands and I took it at Demetrius and went up for the basket and he jumped and before I knew it, I went *higher* than him, elevated out of nowhere and I just dunked on him!

The incredible feeling of disbelief and belief and joy was like— Holy you-know-what!?

Donny's eyes just about popped out of his head, as if he'd never seen anything like that. We'd just climbed Mount Everest. Dunking on Demetrius was that high of a bar.

And Demetrius pulled back, sweat flowing off him, with the strangest mix of joy and sadness in his eyes. As if this story had been written long ago and was now being enacted. The torch had been passed.

I fell down on the ground and sat there on the grass catching my breath. All these years I never thought that I'd ever get to be as tall as my father. Well, I was about to do that and would grow another two inches by the end of senior year. But dunking on Demetrius meant something much more telling.

Oh, yeah, I thought, it's time.

WEDNESDAY NIGHT
MARCH 30, 2011
ON THE AIRPLANE

AFTER A GREAT WIN AGAINST THE WIZARDS, I'M IN MY SEAT on the plane to Minnesota, chuckling to myself over the earlier conversation with the boys. Once again, those little moments of laughter are big reminders of why the fight to have them in my life mattered so much and should matter to all of us dads and moms. Also, two realizations about fatherhood and parenting in general have come at me over the last few hours that are worth noting.

First, of course, is the fact that as dads we sometimes make our own jobs harder than they really should be by insisting that our kids conform to our idea of what makes for their joy. In my various households where I grew up, we may have all wanted similar things but had to find our own paths to what we were good at, as well as what we loved. Demetrius and I are a prime example.

After that day in the backyard, I went on to my senior year and followed down the path of playing ball at the high school and college level, later as a pro. Demetrius returned to play college ball for another year but by then had completed that ride as far as it was going to take him. Then something amazing happened. He returned to Harold L. Richards High School as an assistant varsity coach under John Chappetto—and in 2008 helped guide the Bulldogs to their first state championship. To bring everything full circle at one point, our youngest brother, Kodhamus, was on the team, being coached by Demetrius.

Each of us has our own path. Dads and moms, whether together or not, can support every child's ability to believe in himself or herself.

And here's the second thought. Sometimes, in helping our kids pursue their dreams and joys and interests, we don't have all the tools and skills needed to assist them. At such times, we shouldn't feel like we have to be the ultimate experts on all aspects of parenting.

As I learned in many different ways over the years, there are always resources for vital information as long as we're willing to admit we don't have all the answers.

That's a lesson, by the way, that you can take to the bank.

CHAPTER SIX

MARQUETTE

TUESDAY AFTERNOON
APRIL 5, 2011
AT HOME IN MIAMI

"WE CAN'T ALWAYS DO EVERYTHING WE WANT TO DO," IS THE answer I offer to Zaire about why I've said no to him playing in an actual basketball league this spring.

This has come up in one of our "How was your day?" conversations. Most of our talks since my return have centered on my reassuring them that the road-trip injury sustained in the game against the Nets, a killer inner thigh bruise, was going to get better.

No, I wasn't going to be able to play in our next game, as the regular season entered its last week. I was going to go for rehab and hope that I'd be back in the game after that. There was a lot of pressure on the team to finish strong in these last games before the playoff. Without getting too worried or too confident, I was just trying to keep an even keel.

And that's the balance I'm trying to find in this situation with Zaire. Telling my kid no about something that matters so much to him is something I don't enjoy. I'm still hurting for him that he was prevented from playing or watching me play at my games or even on TV. Whatever he loves, I want to encourage it as motivation. But, then again, since we've been talking about setting goals and having a work ethic in general, we have to find the balance together.

When Zaire first asked about joining a basketball team, I told him we would wait and see how he applied himself in school. If all went well, we agreed, he could play on the condition that he had to go out and play for fun. I knew the pressure that would be on him to live up to some expectations because of being my son. He didn't mind, he said—almost with a bring-it-on attitude. Like father like son? Oh, no, I thought, he's only nine!

All in all, Zaire and Zion are both adjusting well at home and in their schools. Zion sometimes doesn't listen to his teachers (or to anyone else for that matter) when he comes up with something he wants to do. Zaire is better at listening and he does want to do the right thing, but between basketball, video games, and girls—yeah, girls, even at his age—he sometimes doesn't focus on priorities. Or then there are his occasional outbursts when he's not getting to have the fun, fun, fun that he likes.

Often his schoolwork reflects focus or lack of it.

Hmmm. I'm trying to figure this out. On one day in a particular subject he has an A; and three days later, same subject, same material, he flunks the test. In the instances where he didn't do well, I know for a fact that he studied.

"Zaire, you are much smarter than me. So your grades should be much better than mine." My question is whether he has test anxiety like I used to have or trouble retaining information, also one of my own challenges.

He thinks about this and realizes that, no, he is just in too much of a hurry. And on one test he was thinking about a friend of his in class who had a family member that died. He was feeling sad about that.

"Anything else?"

Well, he admits, sometimes the class work is not fun.

Our goal then is to get the focus back on the things we call important—our daily responsibilities, schoolwork, respect, how little steps build habits that lead to success. I just have to be a stickler on those things, I explain to him, pointing out that the daily structure is important because if you wake up in the morning and can't maintain focus on what's on the chart, I can see why you might forget to write your assignment down in class. If you're rushing to go out and play at recess, no mystery that you skipped questions on your test.

Here comes the refrain: "We can't always do everything we want to do."

"I understand," he says, shaking off the disappointment that he'll have to wait until the fall to join the local basketball team.

"But I can compromise," I say, proposing that if he wants to work out with a trainer and improve his fundamentals, that can be arranged.

That changes everything. All of a sudden the boy who can't sit still anyway starts running happy victory laps around the room. Zion soon joins in, racing at top speed to keep up with his brother.

I'm glad, as well, that we have a plan in place. All of this requires patience and paying attention as we move forward. Whether or not it's all we'll need, I'm not so sure. But one thing I know absolutely is that Zaire and Zion want more than anything to please me and make me proud. That goes for their desire to make their mother proud, too.

I know the power of the desire that most kids have to make their parents, teachers, coaches, and communities proud of them. I know it well.

COACHES MADE A TREMENDOUS DIFFERENCE IN MY LIFE ON and off the court. I give lasting credit to all my coaches—starting with Dad, and stretching to my high school and college coaches and beyond—for helping me become the man I am today. Though I had the will to grow as a player and person, I certainly didn't have all the answers. That made me coachable. And as a result, these mentors helped to mold me, influencing my beliefs and values—though not without high expectations and demands.

At Harold L. Richards High School, our assistant varsity coach, Gary Adams, raised the stakes for my game without drama or hype. Basketball through and through, Gary stood at about six foot four or five and wasn't a yeller or a whip-cracker. He knew the X's and O's of the sport and believed that the young Jedi in training had to pass through many tests to attain mastery. To do that, Coach Adams was all about having a work ethic. He picked up where Coach Wade Sr. had left off. Hard work by itself was no longer enough. Now what mattered was also the important element of focus.

Around the beginning of our junior season, Coach Adams approached me after practice and asked if I wanted to get in extra workouts.

"Yeah," I shrugged. As in: who wouldn't?

"Fine," he said, before asking for the address of our house in Robbins. Then he told me, "I'll be at your house at eight A.M. this Saturday. I'll hit the horn one time. That's it. It's your responsibility to come out, ready to go." He went on to say that after he picked me up in the car, the two of us would go to the gym and practice for two hours. If I wasn't ready or didn't show, the offer was off the table.

Excited, I was outside waiting for him that next Saturday. Besides the workout—at a Chicago gym that was nicer than what our high school had at the time—Gary talked to me during the ride there and back about how far I saw myself going in the sport.

Not used to that question, I laughed and sort of mumbled, "As far as I can, I guess."

"Good," Gary told me. "Good that you want that. Because if you do, if you want to play after you leave high school, you will have to become so much better than the players who are already in front of you. You will have to work five times as hard as them. You'll have to work when they're not working. When they're sleeping, you'll have to be working. If you think you've got that drive in you and you're willing to work that hard, I can help. But you need to show me that's what you want."

His version of "help me help you" was for me to take the initiative and he'd be there to egg me on. This work ethic brought with it the lesson that if you really want to do something you have to invest yourself in it 100 percent.

Almost every weekend for the rest of the school year, then every day over the course of the summer between junior and senior year, and back on the weekends during my last year at Richards, Coach Adams continued our practices. He also took me to watch games at the college level and would point out specific players whose style was similar to mine. Part of his coaching approach was to emphasize the visual component of player development. As someone who grew up watching basketball long before I played, I was a visual learner and athlete anyway.

One of the first games we attended was at DePaul University, where Gary wanted me to observe the technique of Quentin Richardson. Today Quentin plays for the Orlando Magic and is one of my best friends. In those days, I knew him only as the star of Chicago's Whitney Young High School team, which he led to a state championship; as a freshman at DePaul he was already a phenom, too.

Coach Adams kept leaning over to me as we watched Q give a master class. "Look at that, see the dribble, you can do that." Gary nodded to emphasize the point. See it and do it were all part of his coaching style. Show, not tell. He wanted to show me things that others did well and that I could choose to add to my own game.

This wasn't so much scouting the opposition. I wasn't going to be playing against that team. Instead Gary was taking me to another world, to see how the game was being played at that level and learn it. Learn their moves? Why the hell not? At DePaul, Q was doing things that big guys do, putting up 20 points and pulling down 12 rebounds a game. His technique was about precision, not just combat. So I watched and refined what he did and brought over some of his stuff to my high school game.

In fact, the next varsity match I played for Richards, I tried my version of that precision technique and scored 27 points and 12 rebounds—because I saw how effective small adjustments and improvements could be. Not long ago one of my high school teammates reminded me of how I'd played after that visit to DePaul. "D," he said, "do you remember how you won that game? You did a tip dunk off the free-throw line! I knew then you were going to the NBA." He said his dad had told him the same thing after the game.

Well, that made me proud. Because it wasn't by accident. Coach Adams worked on it with me after watching Q. We worked on how to get to the ball before an opponent as it came off the rim, something as simple as a quick move then a quicker reverse. Technique. Finesse. And very effective. Just from going to games. The power of the visual.

Another layer to these lessons was not to be so cool that you couldn't borrow and adapt from the best. For me to play smart, I couldn't expect to develop my own game just from imagination and originality. And I do like to think of myself as being creative and resourceful. Many of my moves over time I've borrowed from others and then put my own spin on them. That means I always watch players. Oh, if I'm guarding someone and they do something that worked on me, of course I'm gonna go work on it! If it worked on me, it should still work with me doing it.

Later, when we were training for the Olympics in 2008, I saw Kobe Bryant make a move I thought was amazing. Not too proud to ask, on the next break, I turned to Kobe and said, "Show me how you just did that." He didn't mind showing me, any more than I mind when someone asks me to show them one of my moves.

In the middle of junior year, as the recruitment wave began to be felt, Gary Adams took me to my first ever Marquette game, across the river in Milwaukee, Wisconsin. Up until now, I'd barely heard of Marquette University. But with my name starting to get out there, he thought I should watch their team play, check out what was distinctive about them, and just generally get the environment of college basketball—again, to show me what it takes to be successful at that level. The player at Marquette he wanted me to know about was Cordell Henry, a point guard who at five foot seven compensated for his height disadvantage with grit and speed. He was something—fast as shit and tough as shit. Cordell had played with Quentin Richardson at Whitney Young—one of the best basketball high schools in Illinois.

Gary Adams was strategic in showing me that players not too different from me had made it to college and were thriving there. These excursions prepared me in a practical sense by showing what was going to be expected of any contender at the next level, but they also gave me something just as important, hope and belief.

I feasted on that hope. Soon I convinced myself maybe I could be out on that floor. Maybe I could do what they were doing.

And finally, I was pumped and ready: C'mon, recruit me!

THESE LAST BASKETBALL SEASONS IN HIGH SCHOOL GAVE me a small taste of glory. As far as the eye could see—that being *my* eye, of course—the future looked golden.

My athletic identity was now being forged from a focus on putting team first and hard work, the dual mantras from Coach Fitzgerald and Coach Adams. In making a name for myself—"D-Wade" was out there early and fit the bill—I was aware of not initially being on many colleges' radar. I wasn't the kid necessarily being groomed with all-expense-paid trips to big sponsors' training camps or any of the other special perks given to the more obvious college-bound candidates.

Much of that at first had to do with my height and the reality that I was what recruiters would later label a " 'tweener." Was I a point guard or a shooting guard? What was that one thing I did so well that college coaches would spot and need me to deliver for their team?

Those were questions I couldn't answer in words. But whenever I hit the floor, during practice and especially during games, I was going to answer with *actions*. In my increasingly confident mind-set, why not try to do it all? That became my own mantra: Let my game show you; let the score speak for itself.

Where I did gain additional experience and attention was in playing for the Illinois Warriors, an AAU (Amateur Athletic Union) team. In the summer before junior year, my goal was to be remembered. Sure enough, by the time school began that fall, and with Coach Adams getting me out to see the college possibilities, I started to get letters and inquiries.

My dream school? No question. The University of Michigan. When the scout came to my workout, I didn't hesitate to say that's where I wanted to go. The reason was clear: Michigan had been the home of the Fab Five. Led by Chris Webber, that 1991 team captured my imagination right along with Michael Jordan and the Chicago Bulls.

Michigan was where I'd dreamed about going since I was a kid. When they began to show interest in Darius Miles, who played with me at the AAU (and ended up skipping college to go to the pros), he told a scout, "Yo, D-Wade wants to come to Michigan," to see how much they wanted him. Darius was told, "Oh, yeah, we'll recruit D-Wade, too."

Other than hoping to play for a top school, I mainly wanted to go where they wanted me the most and to a good university. Many suitors came knocking. Nice! But by the end of junior year my first round of ACT scores became cause for concern and next thing I knew, the crowd thinned. Michigan moved on. Interest started to wane on the part of all those recruiters who'd been sending letters and watching me on the AAU circuit.

My first set of scores wasn't bad. They were disastrous. They sucked.

My grades were right on target for a college-bound athlete, if not better than expected. But my ACTs were below passing. My coaches and the recruiters assured me that there was plenty of time to retake the test and bring up my scores. You could take it up to a total of three times. All that was required was to achieve a composite score of 17 out of 36. To do that, you were allowed to take the best score for each section from any of the different sittings.

Right away I signed up for prep sessions, speed-reading classes, special tutors for the different subjects. Using that same work ethic that I brought to the court, I convinced myself that I could do this. I *had* to do this.

Once the dust had settled, about a dozen schools were still in the mix. Ultimately, four stayed in the hunt: DePaul, Illinois State, Bradley, and Marquette. There were pluses and minuses with each of the programs. Marquette was a top choice from the start, because of something that happened on the day when their recruitment calls were scheduled to begin.

On that day, June 25, at 11:01 A.M., one minute after the calls were to begin, I was over at Siohvaughn's house, where I'd been hanging out regularly, and the phone rang with a hopeful sound. As I recall, Siohvaughn's mom, Darlene, told me to pick up. Soon I heard the warm, strong voice of Tom Crean, head coach of men's basketball at Marquette University. Instead of waiting to contact me later in the day, he said, "I wanted to be your first call. And I want to be your first call because this is how important you are to Marquette and our future." The conversation was even better from there. Coach Crean had just arrived at Marquette. He had come from Michigan State, where he was the assistant coach. So, to know that for his first order of business he would make the call to me—wow. That carried weight with me; it meant a lot.

Even so, I held off making any kind of decisions until the rest of the calls came in, the other suitors had a chance and the official visits took place over the coming months . . . and until I saw my next set of scores. Bradley University in Peoria, Illinois, was the one program I could see wasn't a fit for me and didn't take the visit; I wanted to play at a more competitive level than where the team was at the time. But the visits to DePaul and Illinois State were amazing. At DePaul I had a ball—hanging out with Quentin Richardson, who was now my homey, getting to see him in his school and social setting, and imagining myself being able to finally have the big-man-on-campus experience. Being able to stay in Chicago was also a plus.

Pretty much all the boxes at DePaul earned check marks from me. That is, until the end of the interview with the coach when I had an opportunity to ask questions myself. The one question I asked him, as I did at every school, was simple but significant: "If I don't pass my ACT will that change things?"

A pause followed. The coach said that if I couldn't pass the ACT, that would mean that I wouldn't be eligible to play until my junior year. But, he explained, they didn't think with their roster that I'd be ready until then anyway. They had Q and another guy who was more seasoned.

I sat in the coach's office and tried to maintain composure. That was not what I wanted to hear. What I was looking for was a belief in me no matter what happened, a sense of "we want you and we'll work with you and do whatever it takes." DePaul wasn't making that offer.

So then came the visit to Illinois State. Talk about rolling out the red carpet. First off, I loved the head coach, Tom Richardson—great person, great knowledge of the game. He later went to coach at Vanderbilt. When he came to high school to see me play, after our interview, Coach Richardson challenged me to a shoot-off. And proceeded to beat me! Well, not by much.

Then came the visit, starting with the helicopter that was sent to pick me up and bring me to campus and then return me after the weekend was over. My eyes were wide open. When I walked into the gym, there was a full-on presentation with my own jersey and my name in the starting lineup, and music, pomp, and circumstance. The players were cool, too. They immediately made me feel at home and escorted me from one fun activity to the next. There was a big college football game and a memorable party. I'd never been to anything like those events in my life before. Needless to say, after all that royal treatment, Illinois State clearly had the most appeal.

The main hitch was that I wanted to play basketball at a higher level than where they were. And again there was no assurance about what would happen if I didn't pass my ACT.

Ironically, the visit to Marquette was boring. Oh yeah—and cold. *Very* cold. If Milwaukee could get that chilly in October, I could only imagine what it was going to be like in January. They assigned me to be shown around by Cordell Henry, the player that Coach Adams had brought me to watch previously, and the two of us didn't do much. No going out to parties the first night. No big fuss. The main event, Midnight Madness, was fun. This was my first time to participate in this traditional kickoff of the official collegiate basketball season, falling usually in mid-October. As it so happened, in an effort to rebuild the program, Tom Crean had only just instituted this as a Marquette tradition, making it a first for the university as well. During the pep rally before the clock struck midnight and ushered in Marquette's season, I was shown a lot of love and felt the genuine Golden Eagle spirit. But if fun was going to be the criteria, Illinois State had my vote in the bag.

The moment of truth for me occurred during my parting interview with Coach Crean. In his early thirties, Tom Crean wasn't a bad-looking guy, with his great head of dark hair and hip glasses. Smart and energetic, he was physically fit and notably tan in an athletic, outdoorsy way—even though, frankly, I saw that he was terrible as an actual player. Not his calling. Coach Crean was married to Joani Harbaugh, San Francisco 49ers coach Jim Harbaugh's sister, and, as a member of that extended family, could have been mistaken for any of the good-looking Harbaugh guys. His most noticeable trait, however, was an intense power of observation. Like he was capable of reading your mind.

Known as a keen evaluator of talent and for his top-notch recruiting abilities, he asked me questions that showed depth in my view. I liked that. Besides, he had already shown interest by making me his first call and by being my first call. Most of my questions had been answered already over the course of the visit. Then, finally, I looked straight at him and asked, "If I don't pass my ACT, if I'm in trouble when the last scores come in, what happens then? Are you guys prepared to stick with me?"

Without hesitation, Tom Crean nodded and said, "Absolutely. We are committed to you as a person first, even more so than you as an athlete. We believe in you."

Later, I found out that Coach C probably didn't have the right to say that and he had to go back to the school to make sure that he could stand by that. No matter, I was sold all the same.

Overall, the values of the Jesuit Catholic school appealed to me, especially the emphasis on being of service to others. Also meaningful was the Marquette motto, *Cura Personalis,* or "care for the whole person." Here was a college where I could flourish on the court *and* in the classroom.

Marquette had my vote. But the excitement and relief that should have accompanied my decision wasn't there. In spite of Tom Crean's assurance that they would stand by me no matter what, I was so disappointed when I learned midway through my last basketball season at Richards that my second ACT scores had only shown modest improvement from the first time. Not enough to pass.

I had one more shot. Everyone was counting on me. Failure wasn't an option.

ONE OF THE SECRETS TO GREAT COACHING, AS WELL AS PARenting, goes back to the old song about accentuating the positive and eliminating the negative. That was a guiding philosophy for Coach Fitzgerald and Coach Adams. With me they might have played good cop/bad cop now and then. But once senior season was off and running, they placed full trust in my own process of self-evaluation. They saw me as a leader, a player-coach, and encouraged me to be the expert on the ground, responsible not only for decisions on the court but for motivating the rest of the team to play smart as well as hard.

Individually, I knew how to turn up the dial on the court and was able to put a page or two in the high school history books that year. Ending up with an average of 27 points and 11 rebounds per game, I set school records as a senior for the most points and steals in a season.

In my personal life, I tried to accentuate the positive and, because I had no power to eliminate some of the negatives, I trained myself to ignore them. Not so healthy in the long run. Maybe not so healthy in the short run, either.

Be that as it may, I continued to avoid the ruckus going on at our house by spending more time at Siohvaughn's. When I was a high school senior, she had already left for her freshman year at Eastern Illinois University. But her mom generously extended the invitation for me to come by, study over there, and enjoy the quiet, as well as the meals and supportive conversation, and stay over.

Darlene genuinely wanted to help, I thought. She would ask me to do odd jobs, anything from changing lightbulbs to taking out the trash, and then would pay me for it. That was a way to put a little money in my pocket without making me a charity case.

The choice to spend more time at Siohvaughn's house, even without her there, was simpler than others might have thought. That was an opportunity for me to not have the worry of the phone or the electricity being turned off or the tension of being in an unstable environment. And perhaps because I knew that the next year I'd be leaving home anyway, Darlene's house felt like a place where I could begin to make the transition to the big life just around the corner in my dreams.

As I've thought about this in recent times, I've come to recognize that relationships matter in your life at certain stages and may be exactly what you need at the time. But often those relationships can run their course or you can outgrow them. In the same way, I felt that Dad had been there in my life when I needed him and had given me the lasting tools to survive in this world. In fact, my dad had probably helped to push me out the door without even having that as a conscious goal. I had a vision for getting out of that life of hardship, as far away as I could, and I don't think he would have wanted anything different for me in the end.

To the best of my knowledge, Dad didn't take offense that I wasn't around as much as in the past. He and I were never estranged or anything. His home with Bessie remained my official place of residence. But once I graduated from high school, I was more or less out of there.

Later on, he admitted to feeling left out of some discussions about the direction of my life. In being honest, he did recall being confused about why my girlfriend's mother would be more involved than him and my stepmom. But Dad did want the best for me and never said anything.

TRAGIL WAS EXCITED ABOUT MY CELEBRITY STATUS IN THIS last basketball season at Richards and had been to some games. The biggest excitement for her, though, was the fact that I was college-bound. Every bit of news was validating to her that her tag-along baby brother, the kid who used to trip over his own shoelaces, could be good enough at basketball to attend a private university as prestigious as Marquette.

Teasing, 'cause that's how we are, T.J. would say, "You sure they didn't make a mistake? I mean, you play good but . . ."

Come to think of it, she might not have been teasing! All I know is that the only person more concerned than me about my passing the ACT was my sister Tragil.

The true believers, not worried at all, were my same core group of guys: Marcus, Vinny, Wug, and my brothers, who came to most of our games, home as well as away, and became superstars as fans cheering up in the stands. Early PR!

Teachers and students I'd never met would pass me in the halls, high-fiving and congratulating me on the latest victory. Toward the end of the season, one of my teachers saw me to the door after class to tell me, "Dwyane, you're going to make all of us here at Richards proud. You're a shining example to other students."

Maybe now, I thought to myself. But what if I bomb on the test? What if I've raised everybody's hopes only to let them down?

Blocking out those pesky, defeating ideas, I thanked her and started to leave.

Then she added, "I know your parents must be so proud."

Again, I thanked her and walked out down the hall by myself, letting myself feel just a twinge of regret that we didn't have the kind of situation she must have been imagining. We weren't the *Cosby Show* version of a family gathered around the dinner table, sifting through college pamphlets and recruitment offers. We didn't have coaches coming or calling to talk to parents to persuade them why their team would be the best for their son.

We didn't love each other any less than those families, however.

With all the issues going on with Dad, in fact, he came through for me a short time later, one freezing cold night in early 2000, by making sure that Mom was able to see one of my high school games.

The weird thing about my father was that he seldom came to high school games for Demetrius or me. We never knew why. Maybe he didn't want to run the risk of trying to coach us from the stands.

Oh yeah, there were a lot of those dads out there. The bleachers at Harold L. Richards High School were full of them. I already had made a promise to myself never to become one of those fathers.

During this game, Dad and Bessie sat down near the front, both of them cheering loudly with the rest of the crowd at all the right moments. Mom wasn't sitting with them, but from the instant the team and I entered the gym, dribbling onto the court, I could feel her presence.

She was way up in the back by herself, trying to look inconspicuous in her coat and hat. From down on the floor, I couldn't see at first that this was the worst shape she'd ever been in. The fugitive life, on top of the drug use, was robbing what was left of her fight, her beauty, and spirit. My mother would recall this low point by saying, "I wasn't me no more. Staying wherever I can stay, abandoned buildings, cheap rooming houses, all over the place. I was more disgusted with myself than those disgusting places."

Seeing her set off in me a chain reaction of emotions: relief and gratitude at just being able to see her, worry that she was so far gone, fear that this wasn't the worst and that she could decline more, joy that she could see me in my element.

Throughout the game, I'd sneak looks up at Mom to make sure she was still there and check out her reaction. She seemed incredulous in the beginning. Awestruck. And then her eyes had the light in them again and she was Jolinda Wade again, sitting there puffed up, her troubles gone, like she wanted to lean over to someone and say, "Wow, that's my boy!"

Her memory of that night: "I couldn't believe it. They right, you did show off when your momma was in the building. I looked at your dad and he looked up at me and we were both so proud! I was thankful. I was thankful your dad was your first coach and me your first cheerleader. And I was so proud that your dad was behind you. And I was looking up to God asking if there was any possibility that I hadn't missed out on everything? I wanted the best for you so I let your father and stepmom and all of the other people who had a part in your life do for you what I couldn't. Had I made the right decision? Only God could say. So I sat in the back and cheered on my own for my baby. You were on your way."

FOCUS. OR LACK THEREOF. THAT WAS MY PROBLEM. WITH all my classes to prepare me for passing the test, I never felt confident when walking out of any of those sessions that my brain could retain everything we had just studied.

Another problem was that much of the ACT drew from knowledge retained over many years. Wait, geometry? I knew it but hadn't retained all of it. Worse, nobody knew what exactly was going to be on the test. So how do you study for that? My test anxiety had improved during high school because I figured out that if you ask for help ahead of time, teachers will generally let you know what's going to be on the test and how to focus on the important material. Since that was not possible with the ACT, the anxiety crept back in.

Even so, at the last sitting I went in with positive energy and support from everyone who was close to me and who had helped. I felt better than before on some of the subjects but not all. With the ability to take the top scores from each subject no matter which of the three tests, I was optimistic. Some of the questions were tough but maybe there I'd get lucky. Why not feel hopeful?

For the next several weeks, I tried to stay positive and focused on ending high school on a high note. And in that mind-set, I was called out of class to come to the office. The hall pass indicated that the results were in.

Many high-pressure moments had happened to me before that day and many more would come later. But for the rest of my life, I will never forget how long that walk was when I went down to get my scores. I remember the level of humidity in the air inside that hallway, leftover smells of lunch from the teacher's lounge, the dim institutional lighting, and the sounds of muffled voices behind closed classroom doors.

I remember my heart beating, the hesitation of my footsteps. "Hope for the best but prepare for the worst" was another mantra that had served me well so I reverted to that. The weight of the moment was how many people I cared about were counting on me. For that reason, before I even got to the office and was handed the envelope, I was teary-eyed.

Envelope in hand, I left the office and took a few steps down the hallway, then stopped, leaned against the wall, and opened it up. Pulling out the paperwork, I scanned down to where the different scores

At five years old, even though I didn't talk a lot, I was already cooking up big plans. No matter how hard times were, that smile tells you that I believed one day my dreams could become real.

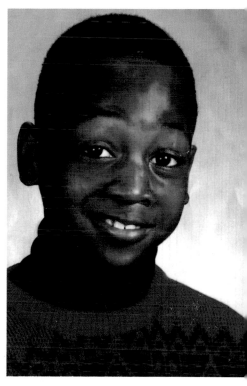

At age nine, around the time that my fourth-grade picture was taken (*above*), and before the move to Robbins, I fell in love with basketball. By eighth-grade graduation (*pictured with cap and gown*), despite a height disadvantage, with toughening up from Dad's coaching and hooping with my brothers, I was skilled enough to make shots in the middle of being thrown on my butt. That's when my father nicknamed me Lucky.

At Harold L. Richards High School, under the mentorship of Coach Jack Fitzgerald and Assistant Coach Gary Adams, I was taught the power of teamwork and the importance of continually pushing myself if I really wanted to go further with my game.

Just ten years ago, at the age of twenty, I was already a new father and finishing up my sophomore year at Marquette University. In this shot, I'm joined by my oldest sister, Deanna (*far left*), my youngest sister, Maryya (*in front*), and my closest sister, Tragil (*far right*).

High school senior prom feels like a few lifetimes ago. I'm with my favorite girl and Big Dwyane. No matter what was going on with my parents, long after they divorced, they always made the effort to get past their differences to be there for us on special occasions.

Hoopin' on home court for the Marquette Golden Eagles, on a fast break, and ready to slash to the basket. In my sanctuary!

A tense moment during a game as my Marquette teammates Travis Diener (#34), Robert Jackson (#55), and I get an earful from Coach Tom Crean. He used every opportunity to point out how we could do better—whether we were on the floor or not!

NBA draft day 2003. Until moments before the announcement that I'd been selected as the number five pick to go to the Miami Heat, I'd had no earthly idea that's where I'd be headed. At twenty-one years old, with one-year-old Zaire in Pat Riley's arms, I couldn't wait to put on the jersey and get to work. It was the realization of prayers, promises, and dreams.

November 2008. Grateful to celebrate Mom's fifty-fourth birthday (*shown here with her on right and Tragil on left*). But you can see on my face that being separated from my sons during the early stages of the divorce/custody battle was taking its toll. This was the season that I took out my anguish on the court, becoming the first player in NBA history to accumulate at least 2,000 points, 500 assists, and 100 blocks within one season.

Mom was right— I get crazy giddy when I'm happy. And this is one of my happiest days, after the Miami Heat won the 2006 NBA championship and I won MVP.

The thrill of competing on behalf of my country at the 2008 Olympics in Beijing and helping Team USA reclaim the gold medal will always be a highlight of my career.

Me and my mini-me at the Central Park Zoo in New York City. No matter what city we're in, visiting local zoos and museums is one of my favorite father-son activities—or as we call it, "Man Time."

(*Left to right:*) Tragil, me, Mom, and my niece Myanna Lockhart. We're holding up our hands to show five and five because we're having a big party in honor of Mom's fifty-fifth birthday. Every year in November, my mother flies out from Chicago to Miami for her birthday and every year she looks younger!

Like I always say, if I could live my childhood over, I'd be Zaire Wade. At his tenth birthday party, we pause for a family portrait. (*Left to right:*) Zaire, me, Grandmama Jolinda, Zion, Dada, Grandpa Dwyane Sr., and TT, a.k.a. Aunt Tragil.

With my hero, Pastor Jolinda Wade, at the 2010 launch of her book, *Divine Grace Behind the Walls,* a collection of letters she wrote to God and other writings she did on her road to redemption during her incarceration. One of my mother's earliest dreams was to be a writer!

Zaire made me so proud when he chose to wear #3 as his basketball number. Zion and I came to cheer as usual and surprised Zaire by bringing along his favorite player. Yep, that's LeBron James.

At Hublot's launch of the Dwyane Wade Signature Watch, I'm joined by the family that raised me—Dwyane Wade Sr. (*far left*), Jolinda Wade, and my sister Tragil Wade (*far right*). After our separate struggles and the different paths we've walked, it means so much that we can be together as a family.

Returning to Marquette University always makes me feel right at home. This visit in 2010 was extraspecial because I was able to host a Youth Basketball Clinic there. Whenever my foundation, Wade's World, sponsors camps and clinics like this with kids, I am humbled to be able to tell them that I never gave up on my dreams and that they shouldn't give up on theirs.

Zion never fails to put a smile on my face—even with the sprained ankle I got during the All-Star Game in Los Angeles in February 2011.

Wow! Look at all the hands giving me high-fives at the Overtown Youth Center event, sponsored by the Wade's World Foundation! I see my younger self in so many of their faces.

My thirtieth birthday weekend in January 2012 was filled with multiple surprises, each more touching than the last. But the moment that stood out the most was when I felt a hand on my shoulder during a family brunch, and I turned around to see Grandma. Willie Mae Morris had just celebrated her ninety-first birthday. For nine years I'd been trying to get her to come visit, but she'd refused to board a plane. But for my thirtieth, she overcame her fear and brought my life full circle.

6/21/2012. On top of Mount Everest again! Later that night, I thought I'd dreamed it, got out of bed, and convinced myself to go back to sleep. That's when it hit me: OMG! It wasn't a dream. A world champion once again! The first time, it had taken three years, and now it had been six long, hard years. Wow!

Celebrating the NBA championship together and LeBron's MVP win.

After all the nay-saying, adversity, falling short, falling down, getting back up again, here we are, laughing our heads off about something someone just said. Nuthin' in the world beats the feeling of knowing you did it together as a team.

I wanted to share every moment of the weeklong festivities with my boys. Looking at their faces, I can see they know they helped make this day possible for me. (*Left to right:*) Zaire, Dada, Zion, and me.

Three generations of Wades, all together on top of the world! (*Left to right:*) Mom, Zaire, Dad, me *(top)*, Zion, and Tragil, surrounded by the support of Team Wade, the Heat family, and the great city of Miami. Who could write a better ending to our story so far?

This picture says it all: Pure joy!

After all of the parades, celebrations, and attention, the best part of all is getting to come home to be with my boys, who are the lights of my life, forever and always.

were listed and even lower to the previous scores. At that moment, I calculated what I would have needed to get and what I had gotten.

A second or two ticked by before I realized that I didn't get the scores that I needed to pass. Now with the envelope in my jeans pocket, I went into the bathroom and cried like a baby.

With a deep breath, I threw water on my face, pulled myself together, and finished the rest of the school day. Later in the afternoon, I went over to Darlene's house and used the phone to do what would become natural as time went on: I called Coach Crean at Marquette.

"My scores came in today," I began, with tears starting. "I . . . uh . . . I didn't pass."

"Oh, Dwyane, I'm sorry . . ." Coach C paused, and then he started crying too. "I'm sorry . . . ," he repeated. He knew how much doing well mattered to me. His disappointment wasn't so much in me as it was with the situation.

"I'm sorry," I wept. "I'm sorry."

He told me I had nothing to apologize for, that I'd worked hard. But then he broke down again. A long silence followed as we both fought for composure.

At last I heard him take a determined breath. His energy and tone changed. Now he was the coach, making a call after a tough loss. "Look, here's what we're going to do. You're coming here and we'll stay with everything as planned. The only difference is you won't be able to play in the games or travel. But you'll do everything else. You're on the team."

"I am?"

"Marquette needs you. I'll see you when school starts."

As I listened to a few more details of the plan, the weight of the world lifted off me. My gratitude to Tom Crean was boundless, my thanks even greater to God for blessing me and giving me this chance.

Coach C believed that much in me. And I swore to myself, on my life, that come the next few years, I would prove him right for doing so.

• • •

A LIFE-AND-DEATH QUESTION WAS RARELY FAR FROM MY thoughts. It had to do with my fear that time was running out for my mom.

Over the summer before taking off to Marquette for my first year there, I woke up from a bad dream that left me with a dark feeling. Mom appeared in my dreams periodically, mostly as the way I saw her in my heart: beautiful, strong, a loving figure. But in this dream, she was in a terrible place—a dark, burned-out abandoned building—like she was trapped, struggling to get to a door that didn't exist.

I awoke with a jolt.

No point telling myself this was only a dream. We were connected; this was her reality now. Three and a half years as a fugitive. Because she couldn't risk having identification, she had no access to resources or help for her addiction. She was out there alone—everything I'd worried about as a little boy sitting up on the stoop waiting for her.

A part of me wondered if the dream was picking up on her needing to see me. That was a strange thought, because the last I'd heard from Dad and Tragil was that she was avoiding us.

Why? Mom clarified her reasons later, saying, "I didn't want you all to see me because I had lost so much weight, my head was the biggest thing on my body. I was down to a size five. My arms were scarred up. I was with a man with no dreams who had beat me so bad he had knocked my teeth out of my mouth."

In our last encounters, I saw her embarrassment. But she usually put herself together, kept her hand over her mouth, or wore long sleeves even in the summer. Dad agreed to help contact her and after a week or so a meeting was arranged.

We didn't talk about where she was staying the rest of the time. No, she didn't look good. There was no denying that. Still, she was fighting. Jolinda Wade was always a fighter.

There were two things that had been weighing on her, as it turned out, and she wanted to talk to me about them. I couldn't tell if she was high or not, but her words were chosen carefully. Mom began by saying she was concerned about what she had done to me and Tragil.

"You didn't—" I started to interrupt, but she wouldn't let me.

"No, no, I did. I went to God first on this and now I'm talking to you and your sister next. One thing is I don't want you kids to have to bury what I did to you and not get that off of you. I can't and won't allow you to suffer like that. So . . . I need . . . I need to know how you feel—how do you feel about me leaving your life all this time?"

I just looked at her, shrugged, and said, "What do you mean, Mom?"

In her husky, smoky voice, she cried, "I wasn't there!" Then she paused, ready for me to come at her, it seemed, to beat up on her with something worse than she was already beating up on herself with.

None of it mattered in this moment except what I told her: "I still love you."

Mom looked back at me and shook her head. She leaned back and turned her eyes up to heaven and asked, "What type of kid is this that I have?" Then she let me give her a hug and I repeated what I had said.

By staying positive, I wanted to show my belief in her. That's all I could do.

My burden was my burden. Tragil and my older sisters responded as I did when Mom talked to them, too. We understood that our mother didn't want us to be burdened. The day would come for us to deal with what we'd been through. But that was work for another day.

Before we said good-bye, Mom told me again how proud she was that I was on my way to college. She was starting to get shaky, shivering on that hot summer afternoon as she lit herself a cigarette. I got up to go and Mom continued to talk about destiny and making the most of the opportunities that basketball had brought me. That was when, for the second time in my eighteen years, Mom made sure I didn't forget that my life was bigger than basketball.

At the time, I couldn't see that far down the road. Besides, what could be bigger than the chance to finally make our lives easier and get my mother the help she needed before it was too late?

TOM CREAN, AS I LIKE TO SAY, WAS A COMBINATION OF ALL my coaches put together, with his own spin as well. Like my dad, he was tough, harping on fundamentals and tireless preparation. At times he used tough love, like Dad, seeing how far my limits could be pushed. Like Gary Adams, Coach C went the extra mile after team practices to take me to the gym and work with me; if I called late at night or during his off hours, he was right there. For a head coach, he was unusually hands-on. And like Coach Fitzgerald, Coach C put his focus on team and team success. He drove home for me the truth that if a coach doesn't say anything to you, then you're not working as hard as you should—whereas if he's always on you, then he sees something that shows he believes in you.

Coach Crean stayed on me from the moment I set foot on the Marquette University campus. That first year, in spite of the fact that I had to redshirt and sit out that season, I practiced and trained at the same level of intensity as everyone else. In our practices, he clearly saw strengths in me, but he also could see that I needed a lot of work. There was no question that I was ready to be pushed even though the constraints of not being able to compete in actual games was sometimes maddening. Still, what was the most motivating aspect of Tom Crean's approach with me—and why we became so close—was that he emerged as the father figure I needed at the time. He would hug me and let me know he loved me and offer genuine approval of me as a person, aside from my efforts as an athlete.

By the same token, in treating me like a son Coach C placed me in a leadership position with unbelievably high expectations that went along with that role. In effect, that first season he made me practically an assistant coach. Since I couldn't dress out and play, I would be on the bench in my suit watching and taking notes. When the team won or did well, Tom Crean would give all the credit to me— like I was responsible. Oh, but when they lost, he could tear into me like nobody's business, as though I was the reason for the failure.

Brutal!

Nothing had prepared me for this trial by fire. Early in the season at a home game, for example, we were down by at least fifteen points at halftime and as soon as we all marched into the locker room, Coach C turned to me and said, "Dwyane?"

Meaning . . . I had to stand in front of the team and identify what they were doing wrong on the basketball court. Me? The quiet newcomer and redshirt they only knew from what I could do in practice?

"Well," I began, glancing down at my notes, "you guys are playing soft."

Coach Crean nodded and gestured for me to continue.

Then I went on, telling them how many missed shot opportunities I'd counted and where the defense was crumbling and why weren't they passing the ball to their open men instead of taking bad or contestable shots. "Make those adjustments, go hard, and you got this," I said with a shrug. Not harsh but direct. Inside, I was cringing. My powers of observation weren't bad. But giving criticism wasn't in keeping with my personality and wasn't where I normally came from.

Tom Crean had found a way to cultivate my leadership skills and teach me a different kind of toughness. Once I found a comfort zone in talking to the guys, he pushed me further, requiring me to come to his office and watch game films and work with the guys on that. In hindsight, I can see that he wanted everything to be ready when I hopefully met the academic requirement that would allow me to play the next year. Then I would not have to struggle to get up to speed on the court. Smart plan, but I didn't always see that. In fact, there were plenty of times when I was convinced of one thing—*This man is crazy!*

At different points, he pushed so hard I was seriously ready to go home. Then, of course, I realized there was nuthin' to go home to. But that didn't change the backing vocal track inside my head—*This man is crazy!*

There was, no doubt, a method to the madness. Coach C wanted me to shed some skin, even to let go of beliefs about myself that weren't necessarily true. Pretty soon, I came to my own conclusion that if I could retain masses of basketball stats and information being thrown at me and then handle the discomfort of standing up and speaking, there was no reason that I couldn't retain material for my academic classes or confront my test anxiety.

I'm not saying that the transformation was overnight. For most of that year I felt the stigma of not being good enough and of letting the team down by not being out there. No matter how hard I threw myself into my studies, I had to wait until most of the reporting periods were in to be told if I would play that next year.

Fortunately, per the terms of my redshirt status, I didn't have to worry about taking the ACT again or passing it. What I had to do to be eligible to play my sophomore year was attain a GPA of 2.5 or higher for the year. There were encouraging grades in individual classes and I had reason to be optimistic. But it wasn't until the day near the end of the season when our athletic director came to address the team that the official verdict came in. At the first reporting period, I had surpassed the minimum with a 2.67. By the second report I had a 2.8 and then a 3.0 with the next. (And my GPA continued to rise from there.)

Once the athletic director concluded his comments and announced that I was cleared to play that next season, a loud cheer went up in the gym. Coach C and the rest of the coaching staff, along with my team-mates, went nuts, cheering, applauding, hugging me, backslapping and high-fiving each other, like we had won a tournament or something! Everyone knew how hard it had been and how the uncertainty had weighed on me. So to see them all celebrating and taking pride over something I had done—off the court no less—was unforgettable.

That first year at Marquette certainly taught me the importance of patience and reinforced lessons about focus. But more than anything the experience opened my eyes to what Mom had been trying to tell me as I came to understand that, yes, there was more to life than basketball. What had seemed like a postponement of my dreams actually helped me become better and stronger—a better student, a better person. Because I didn't have basketball as my outlet or as the one thing that I did well and that made me cool or heroic, the year changed how I looked at *everything*.

The process was painful, like being separated from the love of my life, such that when I was reunited with the game, that is, able to play again, I was fiercely in control, in charge of everything that happened on the court. Win, lose, or draw. But more than that, I now saw the possibilities beyond the game, at least enough to realize that my world wasn't just about basketball.

Oddly enough, that made me lethal as a competitor. A warrior at age nineteen.

The transformation was powerful. Coach Crean, with laser-sharp instincts, had helped me to help myself in tapping the emotional pressure cooker that up until now had controlled me. Whatever happened, I'd figured out how to put all of the anger, hurt, confusion, and uncertainty that arose from circumstances beyond my control and throw it all into the burner. As for the naysayers, I now had great use for their disregard.

Fuel for the fire.

Aside from that growth, I look back today at all the steps of the journey to make the team at Marquette and can see how each challenge served a purpose as a test of faith. Not that I ever fully doubted that God had a plan. But there had been lows, I confess, when I couldn't see the grand design or the possibility that what had seemed like the worst thing that could ever happen turned out to be the best. And that strengthened my faith, making me believe that if I could overcome and make it this far, so, too, could my loved ones—especially my mother, who at that time was being overwhelmed by her struggle.

Being at Marquette, a private Catholic institution, reinforced the importance of being connected to my faith. That was part of my thinking in choosing to wear the number *3*, to symbolize the Holy Trinity—the Father, the Son, and the Holy Ghost.

With a heart full of gratitude and a mind-set ready for every possibility that the university and life itself had to offer, I savored the rest of my freshman year and took advantage of any opportunity extended to me over the summer to advance myself as a student and athlete. The icing on the cake was that at the end of that summer of 2001, I qualified for an all-expense-paid trip to Europe to train with some of my teammates and other top collegiate players. Talk about life rolling out the red carpet for me!

Foolishly, so foolishly, I imagined that all the major struggles were soon to be over, that the toughest tests and trials were all behind me.

Not so. Most of the tests so far had only been a warm-up. And besides, with my fatherhood journey about to begin, the stakes were soon to become that much higher.

TUESDAY EVENING
APRIL 5, 2011
AT HOME IN MIAMI

IN OUR HOUSEHOLD, ZAIRE IS THE KING OF ALL MEDIA. VIDEO games, music, funny YouTube videos, all of it that's suitable for his age. After homework, before the boys' nightly routine of getting ready for bed, we take some lessons from Zaire, who is pretending to give me some pointers while also kicking my butt at our favorite video game, NBA2K

When the video music comes on, the three of us start laughing for no reason and kind of nodding to the groove. Then Zion starts to dance. Aw, yeah, he's doin' the Dougie!

"Go Zion go!" I tell him as his dance gets more and more wild. If Dada was here, he'd be the master. But Zion is really good. In fact, a short time later he'll ask to take hip-hop dance classes. "You know you probably get your dance talent from me," I say, still losing badly to Zaire.

The boys crack up. They think I'm a terrible dancer. I can't imagine what makes them say that.

Zaire pauses his game controller and he starts to Dougie as only my nine-year-old son can, adding in comic moves and faces that make me want to fall on the floor.

"Hey, if I didn't have my injury I'd get up and we'd have a contest." They can see that the thigh contusion is still wrapped and I do have a solid excuse.

Again, sitting here just appreciating the gift of time that we have to spend together, I'm reminded of the insight that has been helpful to me as a dad—the fact that kids really do thrive when parents, coaches, and teachers take the time to key into what's special about them and what they can use by way of help and interest. With encouragement, as I've seen consistently, kids really want to please. It's true of my boys and it was always true of me as a kid.

This may sound too basic but after I took a couple of parenting classes and after reading up on the issue of how best to help our children to succeed, I think it's empowering to start with two principles: (1) That kids want to make their parents proud and (2) that we, as fathers and mothers, want to be good stewards of the lives that we've been blessed to nurture.

Yes, it can be hard. Parenting requires focus, establishing boundaries and priorities, and can sometimes be thankless and demand sacrifices. I also am aware that my situation, resource-wise and with our family support system, puts me at an advantage. But the bottom line for me is that there is no more important job in life than that of being a parent. So it's all worth it. I promise.

Zaire and Zion have always made me feel proud to be their father. I know my children are also very proud of my role as Daddy.

But am I their favorite basketball player? Well, I thought so, until a day or so later when I heard both kids out on the basketball court name-checking their favorite player. What a flashback to my days in the backyard of my family's house, when I was playing with my brothers, taunting them with "Whoa, look at me, I'm Michael Jordan!"

Who was the favorite player's name my kids were calling? Was it their dear old dad? Nope. It was their basketball idol: "Whoa, look at me, I'm LeBron James!"

CHAPTER SEVEN

MIRACLES

Sunday evening
April 15, 2011
At home in Miami

Over the past five weeks since being given full custody of the boys, Sunday dinner has become one of the highlights of our week. Well, since we're making up for lost time, being with the kids makes every day—morning, noon, and night—a highlight. That's as far as I'm concerned, and I'm always looking for ways to make every day special and celebrate just being together.

But Sunday dinner is like a holiday unto itself. I love listening to Zaire and his knowledge of so many subjects and to Zion's unique, creative contribution to the conversation. I love answering their questions and coming up with new discoveries—thanks to seeing life through their eyes.

Earlier in the mornings on Sundays, the boys sometimes go with Tragil to the church she has belonged to since moving to Miami and where they have a youth service the boys are able to enjoy. As long as I don't have a game, I try to plan a low-key family outing, like going to the park or to a movie. On certain occasions when we just really need some together time, I've created what we call Man Time, where the three of us do something cool that men enjoy doing. Like once we went to a wrestling match. Another time, because it was raining too much we stayed inside, got out a small table, and had fresh-baked cookies with ice cream in my room. The other thing I like to do during our Man Time is have our Man Talks. Sometimes we get into serious questions that can go well or not so well. There are even lists on the Internet of important questions for parents and kids to ask each other. Our Man Talks are great opportunities for me to talk about how I grew up and some of the challenges of my life that are different from theirs.

Sundays and Man Time can also offer the opportunity for my sons to join me in any of the events that are connected to Wade's World, my foundation, which mainly benefits underserved communities in the three states that have helped to feed me—Florida, Illinois, and Wisconsin. The boys get a chance not only to appreciate how blessed they are but also to see opportunities for giving even at their age. Or sometimes we will just get in the car and go for a drive to neighborhoods not so far from where we live where people are living hard lives. Gotta say, Zaire and Zion are men with big hearts who want other children and their families to have what they do.

Our main Sunday theme is pretty simple: appreciation.

We all come to expressing and feeling gratitude differently, I know. But I also think that like anything else, you can practice the habit of being appreciative and become better at it over time. In my parenting research, I've read that one of the common complaints of divorced or single parents is a concern that their children might prefer living with the parent who gives them more things or can afford a nicer lifestyle. These parents worry further that kids being raised in those tug-of-war contests will become spoiled or feel entitled to special treatment. Ironically, that same research shows that what's really wanted by children of divorce, as well as children being raised by single or surrogate parents, like all children, are the fundamentals: love, security, encouragement, structure, and involvement by their parents.

The best approach I've learned to encourage the habit of expressing appreciation—the attitude of gratitude—is by modeling that behavior myself. A little goes a long way. Even just the use of "thank you" and "please" and "you're welcome" can help set an appreciative tone in a household.

Can you overdo it? Not unless you're phony or forced. Most of our kids do have a built-in BS monitor. Timing can be important, too. I have to be mindful that my boys have had their share of turmoil and uncertainties.

After all, it's hard trying to feel grateful when the world feels like it's crashing down. At the same time, I've also found that in those dark times nothing shines a light more than paying attention to the miracles.

My life has been blessed with more than a few.

FOR MOST OF THE TWO WEEKS OF THE 2001 SUMMER TRAIN-ing camp I attended in none other than Florence, Italy, I had a chance to live a dream that surpassed my own fantasies. Though we didn't stay in a fancy hotel or have much time for sightseeing, I was enchanted. For a student athlete on scholarship, training-table meals were already manna from heaven. Add to that all kinds of pasta and delicious Italian specialties. And the people in Florence could not have been friendlier. Everywhere we went, we were treated as celebrities.

Then there was the architecture, like nothing I'd seen in the United States, as well as all the paintings and statues, and my first real exposure to the Italian sense of style. At nineteen, I knew something about exotic sports cars made in Italy. And I'd heard the names of Italian designers—as part of what hip-hop culture embraced. What was new was seeing the designs firsthand and appreciating, say, the fine cut of men's suits or fabric and color. Being able to afford that level of style was not yet tangible.

But why not dream?

Oh, and then there were the beautiful Italian women. Okay, so I'm speaking of appreciation. Yes, Siohvaughn and I were still together, still serious and seeing each other during college breaks and on holidays when we stayed at her house. But I should repeat: I was nineteen and getting ready to come into my own as a college athlete; not to mention a red-blooded male who was raised to value and admire women in general.

Anyone would have agreed that I was nowhere near ready to be in a long-term committed relationship. I did care deeply for Siohvaughn. We'd grown up together and had the romance of first love that no one else could ever replace. Her home had become my second home, her mother a motherly figure in my life. None of that was in question. Maybe I assumed that we'd break things off naturally with her at Eastern Illinois and me at Marquette.

That assumption showed how naïve I was—and also how much I didn't want to have a confrontation. Siohvaughn's energy could be exciting and entertaining. She was a strong young woman and I had grown up around strong women so I liked that about her. But I was also seeing that she could be unpredictable; her temperamental, mean side came out every now and then, when she felt jealous or insecure, and that concerned me. Besides that, I could feel the dynamics of the relationship changing. Where I had been the one who needed her, once I arrived at Marquette that was no longer the case, and she was the one who was in the position of needing me more. As time went on, she would begin to grab for more control—especially the more I grew and wanted independence.

The changing balance of control had become clearer to me early in the summer before I left for training camp. To complicate matters, Siohvaughn's last months at college hadn't gone well and she was not returning. So I put thoughts of breaking up on the back burner and stayed put as the quiet, loyal boyfriend. By avoiding drama—yeah, she had a dramatic side—and deferring to her, my attitude became one of "why rock the boat?" Instead I focused on her loving, fun, exciting side.

Toward the end of my training camp in Florence, I woke up in the middle of the night after a dream that recalled some of our fun. In the dream, Siohvaughn reminded me of that night of pleasure by announcing she was pregnant. Unable to get back to sleep, all I thought about was—what if it is true? There had been that night after school let out when we decided against using birth control because the timing was safe. There was no way that I could be a dad at my age! Everything that I'd just spent the last year working toward would be in jeopardy. Again. I'd have to quit school and get a job to support a child and that would be the end of college, not to mention basketball.

By morning, without much sleep at all, I calmed down, finally convincing myself that this was only a dream and my worry was ridiculous.

A couple of days later, I went to a pay phone in the residence hall to call her at a prearranged time.

When Siohvaughn picked up, she sounded nervous and excited at the same time as she greeted me by saying something like, "I wanted to tell you before you got home . . ."

I stopped her there, saying, "I already know. You're pregnant."

She was mystified. How could I have possibly known?

I told her about the dream and admitted my fear that a baby in our lives at our ages, nineteen and twenty, was as bad as the timing could get. Not just for me. Siohvaughn had decided to transfer to Marquette and had her education to complete, her career goals to explore. We both cried, resolving to figure things out once I returned.

During the trip home, I kept to myself, trying to come up with solutions in my head. To little avail. All my years of vowing to break the cycle of babies having babies, one that ran in my family and community, had gone down the drain. So, too, were all those promises to myself to be different as a father and to be able to welcome my children into a life less uncertain than mine had been.

Yet, with all of those thoughts tearing me up inside, I was still also in awe. Nothing could have prepared me for that moment of revelation, of knowing—*Oh, my God, me a father!*

As soon as I returned, I had to report to Marquette for preseason training with the team and with Coach Crean.

After about an hour of watching us go through drills, Coach C blew his whistle and called for a break. "Let's go, Wade," he barked, pointing toward the exit, meaning he was not happy with me.

I was a mess. Whatever he'd been yelling at us for the last half hour, I hadn't heard. My mind was racing, my heart slamming against my chest, my stomach tied up in knots, as it had been for days. I had so much respect for Tom Crean and he had risked so much to have me on the team. How could I tell him that my days on the court were about to be numbered?

Coach C answered that question as he led me out into the hallway next to the gym. Looking much more concerned than mad, he peered through his glasses into my eyes, asking, "What the hell's going on, Dwyane?"

In broken thoughts and half sentences, I told him everything: that I wasn't ready, that my girlfriend and I were high school sweethearts, how I'd made a promise to be different from fathers who bring children into the world and then aren't there to raise them, how having a baby now would make it impossible for me to play basketball at the level the team deserved and still be able to support a family.

Coach Crean let me go on without saying a word. Then finally, when I finished spilling my guts, he took a deep breath and just said, "Whatever happens, whatever you decide, I'm here and we'll get through this together." Didn't tell me what to do or how to do it. Just that he'd be there to go through it with me.

Coach C hugged me, felt for me, helped me weather the storm of uncertainty, and provided the steadying hand of belief in me that I would come to the right decision on my own. After that, I accepted that God had a plan and that my job was to live up to it as a man and a father first.

Since that moment, not a day goes by that I don't look at both my sons and say silent words of gratitude for Tom Crean and the leap of faith he helped me to take that day in the college preseason of 2001.

"YOU HAVE THE SPIRIT OF MIRIAM ON YOU" WAS A COMMENT made to Tragil by a stranger who approached her following a church service in Florida. This was not long ago, years after many of our family struggles. Tragil wasn't sure what he meant until the stranger reminded her that Miriam was one of the most well-known women of the Old Testament. Being the curious person that she is, my sister immediately decided to find out more about why someone who had never met her or knew her life would have made that remark.

Her reading then took her to Exodus, where she found the story of Miriam, who saved her brother at the request of their mother, Jochebed, at a time when the Pharaoh had decreed that all male children of Israelites be killed. Miriam took Moses and put him in a hand-woven basket their mother had made and placed it in the river Nile—where the water was shallow and the baby could be hidden in the reeds. The Bible story tells of how Miriam stayed with the basket until the daughter of the Pharaoh discovered the basket and decided to adopt the baby. Miriam stepped forward from where she had been hiding and volunteered to bring a wet nurse, their mother, for him.

Tragil more or less knew that part of the story of one of the Bible's most famous sisters. There was more that she didn't know, however. In the main events of Exodus, when Moses is placed in the unlikely role of leading the Israelites out of bondage and toward the Promised Land, Miriam helps give him counsel and rises to become a leader in her own right. Together, sister and brother famously develop a model for leadership that is radically different from the way rulers had led back then. The three guiding principles: to lead by example, to serve the people rather than command them, and to act upon what they believe is being asked of them by the Lord, rather than for their own ambition.

I would never draw too many parallels from those stories to ours. Even so, I could only think that the stranger's observations about Tragil were right on the mark. There was no way he could have known about the bus ride she had taken me on at age eight to deliver me to safety or the other times when my sister played a role in the deliverance of others.

Actually, one of those times had to do with another instance of taking a family member for "the ride"—as my mother would eventually refer to it. This event happened to coincide with my trip to Italy, around the same time when I had learned from Siohvaughn of our news.

Before I'd left for Italy, Tragil and I had a conversation we had avoided up until that point. To even express our fears in words or admit to losing hope for the possibility of Mom being saved would have been to question Jesus. We never doubted that. But we now had to ask ourselves, out loud, whether she wanted to be saved.

This was in a period when we learned that Mom had resorted to working as a tester in return for free drugs. The tester gets paid to take the drugs to make sure they're pure and they're what the dealer claims they are. If they're not pure, a terrible reaction to the drug could occur. If they're not mixed right or bad, the tester can die. As we understood it, Mom had injected herself with what she thought was heroin but turned out to be PCP. An ambulance was called and she was rushed to the hospital before she started having potentially life-threatening sei-zures and hallucinations. Tragil said that God pulled her through but it had been touch and go.

At the same tiny storefront church at 5921½ Prairie where T.J. and I had grown up and where she continued to volunteer, Pastor Darryl Gibson had taken over after Pastor Box passed away. He and the small group of members there had been praying all this time for our mother. Mom still came to church when she could, either by herself or some-times bringing in her group of friends. With the encouragement of Pastor Darryl, she had gone through a series of rehab programs that had gotten her through detox. But time and again, once back on the outside, she'd start using within a couple of days.

The latest effort had been a halfway house that was less about getting Mom drug-free and more about protecting her from living in the abandoned buildings that smelled of human waste and were overrun by rats the size of cats. The program at the halfway house offered classes to educate users about what the drugs they were using actually were and about the long-term effects. Tragil went though classes offered to family members, becoming informed about what heroin did to the brain and the body over time.

When my sister and I had our conversation before I'd left for Italy, Mom hadn't been seen in a while at church, by the people at the halfway house, or by our older sisters. Even Dad didn't know where to find her.

My sister thought Mom was ready to get sober. Her reason? Too many of Mom's friends were dying. She herself had said that death seemed to be following her. Tragil suggested that this could be a sign that Mom was scared enough to find the strength to change. T.J. calmed me down with those thoughts and reassured me that nothing terrible was going to happen over the next two weeks while I was out of the country.

That was Tragil's firm belief. Or it was, until a late August day in Chicago while I was away and she got a call from a friend who alerted her to a news report of a body being pulled out of the abandoned buildings where Mom had been known to stay. The body was said to be that of a woman bearing a description horrifyingly close to Jolinda Wade.

In a panic, Tragil jumped into her car and drove to the building, where she spotted police cars next to a transport van sent from the county morgue. A group of people had gathered around so she couldn't see anything. Sure now that this was our mother, Tragil pushed her way to the front and still couldn't get any answers.

Almost an hour passed before she was able to speak to someone in authority who then connected her to someone else who was able to verify that the woman in the body bag was *not* Jolinda Morris Wade.

By then, Tragil, twenty-four years old that summer, decided the time had come. As she told me later, she watched the van from the morgue cart away the body that wasn't Mom—that was somebody else's loved one, somebody else whose life was cut short—and started to breathe fire. Tragil marched back to her Toyota Tercel, the same little trusty steed that had brought her back to Chicago from San Diego, and she went and searched every known location where our mother might have been.

Tragil found her on the street not far from a park. Though the August day was warm and humid, Mom was shivering when Tragil approached. She even told my sister, "I'm so cold." Then Mom asked my sister if she had any money. She was trying to get a bus to our aunt Bebe's.

Tragil gave her some cash and told Mom, "I'll drive you."

That's when "the ride" took place. As it was later revealed, that afternoon our mother was dope sick—needing a fix not just to battle withdrawal from the drug but in fact to live. Addicts can die from dope sickness as easily as from overdosing.

Tragil might have postponed the conversation she had been need-ing to have for all these years. But not after being at the abandoned building and watching a body bag pulled out and believing our worst fears had been confirmed. Once behind the wheel, still shaking and crying as she spoke, Tragil began, "We have to talk about death. That's what the result is of how you been living. That's what it's going to be. But do you know what that means?" Before Mom could answer, my sister went on, "It means the pressure's on me to bury you and I don't have any money."

Mom recalled that Tragil was crying uncontrollably by the time they got to Aunt Bebe's place. She parked the car and the two sat there outside, with Tragil continuing. What more could she say? Well, she had saved so much up inside her, as she would tell me and others who don't know how to speak to a loved one, that "the ride" led to "the talk." And because Mom had come to us before to say she didn't want us to be burdened with keeping our feelings inside, Tragil gave the oration of her life.

"I'm fed up! And you don't get it," she said. "You don't understand. You want to keep doing what you are, stay like you've been living, blaming yourself for what you doing to *us*? No, that time has passed. Right now, I'm grown. Dwyane's grown. All your children are grown and you can't do anything for us or to hurt us. You can do something to help yourself. You can get yourself together so you can *live*. No longer is this fight for me or for Dwyane. You can't fight this for nobody but yourself if you don't love yourself enough to fight. This is *big*, this is *everything*. Because other than that, you fixing to be as dead as that lady in that abandoned building. We all love you, we all want you to stop. But that's on you now. Let's just talk about it. You say death is following you? You see your friends dropping dead? You is next and I don't have a dime to bury you."

Those were the precise words that Tragil remembered telling Mom, who recalled them much the same way. My mother added in her account to me, "Your sister cried and I cried. Before I got out of the car, she told me again, 'I love you,' and I said, 'I love you, too.' And I went upstairs and told Bebe, 'I'm just messing up everyone's life, I'm hurting everyone. That was my baby and I'm hurting her so bad and I just wanna die.' "

Mom also remembered the sickness getting worse that day and having to walk down to the old neighborhood. She explained, "I had to buy a bag of dope. And I needed to think, to clear my head. To find a reason to live. I had gotten to the point where I didn't want to be around anymore."

No self-destructive act of desperation nor miraculous overnight transformation took place. As time would tell, however, Mom was still fighting. Or as Tragil put it, "Something began to work."

On the heels of that day, just after I'd returned to Marquette for training and had my heart-to-heart with Coach Crean, came the attacks of September 11, 2001. Aside from the fear that seized most of the world, I know that the day was also a reminder of how fragile life is and how suddenly everything can be taken way. Now that I'd made a commitment to fatherhood, I thought harder than ever about the responsibility of making sure any child I brought into the world would be kept safe. How to do that? No clue. At least not yet.

As for Mom, my impression is that after "the ride" and during that period of soul-searching after 9/11 that many were going through, a kind of awakening was taking place inside her that was different.

Tragil was right. Something had begun to work. But what exactly that "something" was didn't come clear until a month or so later—October 14, to be exact. A Sunday. Mom was in church that morning, probably high on something, maybe a little inebriated. But even so she was in search of the light, in a place of praise and worship. She was alone, sitting in the back by herself, when Pastor Darryl called her name and told her to read aloud from 2 Timothy 3:5: "Having a form of godliness denying the power thereof."

My sisters and I had prayed for this to happen for so long but only Mom could feel the truth. She understood. She had already been experiencing God but had been denying His power to change her.

At long last, the madness had come to an end. But the fight was just beginning.

ON SUNDAY, OCTOBER 14, 2001, I IMAGINED FEELING A boulder lift off my chest that had been sitting there for most of my nearly twenty years of life. No one had to tell me about the specifics of what happened back in Chicago. Mom and I had been connected through time and space for all this time so that shouldn't have been too surprising.

This next series of challenges with her trying to get sober was primed for pitfall and traps. But I believed she could do it, as much as I had always believed this day would come.

And having my faith confirmed in that area helped to reassure me in other areas—especially with the new challenges as Siohvaughn and I stepped into unfamiliar, sudden roles of being expectant parents. Any suggestion of getting married right away was out of the question. The baby was due on the second day of February and basketball season wouldn't be over until the beginning of March. Or later, depending on how well we did.

There were other sources of stress. Siohvaughn was only just getting settled in as a transfer student, with both of us determined to focus on our studies. Besides the demands of my basketball schedule, I was against rushing to the altar, for many reasons. For one, we couldn't afford a wedding. What we did do, rather than setting a date, was to make arrangements to take a class on marriage and parenting with Pastor Darryl over the Christmas break.

Given my history and the examples set for me, my sense of responsibility as a parent and spouse was already well developed. The area that required work was on communication, probably the key to all great relationships. Von (as I called Siohvaughn) and I had a ways to go on that front. Then there was the very real source of marital strife that came from our financial struggle. In preparation for the baby's arrival, we moved off campus into a very modest studio apartment. The rent used most of the funds provided by my athletic scholarship stipend. So getting us fed—and the baby before long—would require taking on part-time jobs when our academic schedules allowed.

Siohvaughn had a lot of fear and that was understandable. Her main worry: how were we going to do all these things not just in college but out in the real world?

My main answer: "I can't tell you how but I know we will. I will find a way."

Worry was always in the background, always questioning if I had what it would take to get us into a better place, always pushing me to prove that I could, until the engine that I was driving inside myself was running on: *I'm gonna find a way, I'm a find a way, find a way. FIND. A. WAY.*

All our concerns about bringing a child into the world right then could be seen as normal in a situation like ours. I knew that; Von must have, too. We were babies. From Robbins, Illinois. None of this was going to be easy. Plus, there was a new dynamic in our relationship that meant we had to deal with a different kind of celebrity status that comes from being an up-and-coming name athlete, even on the college level. No guidelines existed for navigating those changes. Even Tragil was shocked when she saw the attention firsthand. Four or five games into the season, I already had whole cheering sections and guys with my name painted on their bare chests.

Success on the court was exciting to share with Siohvaughn. She was definitely proud and knew how much I had overcome to be where I was, especially after a year of not being able to play. At the same time, during that sophomore year while I was proving myself, leading the team to one of the best overall records achieved in years, I could feel tension stirring at home. Again, now that she needed me more and with her welfare based on mine, for worse and for better, neither one of us knew how to adapt. She was used to control, wanting things her way, a certain way, and I pushed back.

However, rocky as the relationship was at the start, one thing we were unified about was the responsibility we shared in becoming parents together. That was not in question. We were both as committed to the baby on the way as any two young college students thrust into our situation could have been.

When doubts set in, all I needed for inspiration was to think of Mom and the reports I'd been hearing. The word *miracle* doesn't even come close to describing the transformation that was set into motion on that day, October 14, 2001, when Jolinda Morris Wade allowed the light in so she could understand what was meant by having God but denying the power thereof. When she left church that day, Mom understood that she needed to prepare to do battle with the Devil as she had never battled in her life before. With full knowledge of what stood in front of her, she went out and bought her last bag of dope, the last time she would allow the poison of it inside her.

She then called a very close friend who lived in Indiana, saying to her, "I got to get up off of this stuff." My mother told her friend, "I have to die so that Christ in me can live." After her friend came to pick her up, Mom was given a place out of state, away from familiar triggers, where she could stay and go through withdrawal from heroin and alcohol.

Anyone who has ever been through the physical agony of withdrawal or has watched someone go through it knows or can tell that the process feels like you are dying. After the substance that a person has been taking has blocked pain and given them that high, the cravings for some more of it is a given. Then there is the depression, agitation, anxiety, a feeling people talk about of having everything hurt, even to where your hair stands on end. Other symptoms of withdrawal are nausea, vomiting, diarrhea, fever, feelings of your skin crawling, stomach spasms, running nose, tears, sweats, not being able to sleep or stay still.

Detox is only the first step, though. The next step is to combat the much tougher withdrawal from the habits of addiction that have become a way of life over many years. The concern, according to experts, is that because drugs change your brain, the mental battle of getting and staying clean is much more brutal than the physical one.

Mom would later say that instead of being afraid, instead of waiting for the Devil to come to her, she stormed into that confrontation as the aggressor, fighting for salvation, drawing from Romans 1:13, praying in the name of Jesus Christ to be saved. At every stage, when she was most weary, she went to Proverbs 3:5–6: "Trust in the LORD with all thine heart; and lean not unto thine own understanding. In all thy ways acknowledge him, and he shall direct thy paths." After a life of saying that the big F had followed her, she shook that off, telling herself that no matter how disappointed life had left her, she would remain obedient to the Holy Spirit.

Within a week, Mom returned to Chicago. God had delivered her in three days from heroin, wine, and alcohol. She came back home sober and, as she said, "with a ready mind."

Tragil kept me posted, telling me that I wouldn't recognize her. She said that the dark purple color of her skin was starting to get back to a youthful, healthy, coffee-and-cream complexion. Her hair was growing. She had fingernails and a sparkle in her eyes.

Then again, my sister reminded me, we had been down this road before. In the past, Mom had never asked Tragil to put her up when she was on drugs, but now she needed the healing environment my sister offered. Since Mom's legal status as a fugitive prevented her from going out to get a job, the long-term plan was hazy. But in the short run, Tragil was focused on feeding Mom, putting some weight back on her, and making sure that she didn't get out too much—to avoid the old traps. The better Mom felt, the more she tried to do around the apartment, straightening up and cleaning while Tragil was at work. She had her Bible with her most of the day and pretty soon she was helping out at the church, going out on walks, reclaiming herself and her life. The next thing we knew, Mom had kicked cigarettes.

What? How does anyone overcome an addiction to coke and heroin and alcohol in one week and quit a lifetime nicotine habit not long after that?

Hearing of my mother's miraculous progress must have given me extra octane on the court from the moment we roared into our 2001–2002 season. Not only did we win the first ten consecutive games that November, but I quickly became a leading contributor—on both ends of the court. Right before Thanksgiving, in a game against Indiana, I scored 21 points to give the Golden Eagles a 50–49 victory. With that we went on to win the next night and take the title of the Great Alaska Shootout tournament, for which I was named MVP.

For me, the feeling was not surprise. Instead, it was exhilaration. And that magic feeling of *appreciation*. I loved finally having a chance to show my stuff, to do my dance, to sing my praise, all while dribbling and posting up and dunking.

There were plenty of naysayers who hadn't seen me coming and still weren't calling my name by any means. Some of the "who's who" out in college basketball even took to referring to me as "the little guy."

I could choose to let it mess with my head or use it as motivation.

So, with Coach Crean driving us, we were off and running, eventually setting multiple records. For the season we would earn a 26–7 record, coming in third in Marquette's history for most season wins. By making an appearance later on in the NCAA tournament, we achieved the best showing for the team since 1997. We would go on to be ranked ninth in the Associated Press's top 25, the first time since the 1970s, and would stay in the rankings for an unprecedented twelve weeks.

In short, by Christmas we were already having a Cinderella season that was only going to get better as we soared to the end. As Siohvaughn and I got closer to our due date, we had grown closer to each other. We were both on pins and needles waiting to meet this little person who we had come together to usher into the world. No matter what hardships lay ahead, my mother was my living proof that difficulties could always be overcome.

When we returned to Chicago from Milwaukee over the break, we arranged to have one of our private classes with Pastor Darryl at our church. And afterward, I'd finally get to see Mom—who was, as ever, still my favorite girl.

Compared to the arctic winds that had been blasting us in Milwaukee, Chicago felt almost mild by comparison. With less than an inch of snow on the ground, the city was all dressed up in Christmas colors, the lights of the season more beautiful and special than I could ever remember seeing them.

In thinking back over my childhood, I couldn't remember many Christmas presents or birthday parties or memorable gifts that helped mark the occasion and the year in question. Now I was being given the only gift I'd ever wanted: my momma in her sanity, the person Jolinda Morris Wade was meant to be. That had to be every Christmas, birthday, special occasion gift rolled into one. In my creative imagination, I kept seeing her with our new baby, being Grandmama and making up for lost time. And that day was right around the corner, too.

During our session with Pastor Darryl, I was pretty much giddy with anticipation and could hardly concentrate. As soon as we finished, I started to grab my coat and help Siohvaughn into hers, when I turned and saw Mom entering the main hall from the kitchen, where she had been waiting for us to finish. She looked amazing, better than anything I could have dreamt. We hugged and hugged. In the past year or so, we had seen each other at different points and prior to that Mom and Siohvaughn had met once before. But this was a reunion unlike any other I've ever known. I may have been about to turn twenty years old, but in those moments I was eight again, back home in her arms after being separated for far, far too long from the real mother she truly was.

None of that pain of separation could touch us anymore. Or so I thought. Then I saw a shadow fall over Mom's face and knew right away something was wrong. Sure enough, my mother gestured back to the kitchen and asked me to follow her, saying she needed to talk to me.

All kinds of worry flooded my mind. Was she sick? Was she having a relapse into drug use?

Mom began by confessing that for the last two hours she had been trying to find the right way to tell me of a decision she had made. There was another step past sobriety that she needed to take. "And I don't want to. But I have to."

"What do you mean?"

"You know I love you. I know you might not understand . . ." She paused.

Everything slowed. I fought the clock, not wanting to hear, wanting to keep us in the time before whatever was coming next. Quiet, I braced myself.

Mom then stated calmly that she had decided to turn herself in. She admitted, "I'm scared to go back. I don't want to go back. It's seven or eight years waiting on me. Maybe longer. Maybe shorter. I don't know." She was going to turn herself in, back to Cook County Jail, and would have her case heard at the courthouse on New Year's Day. All she could do was pray for the strength to accept her fate. For the first time, she was going behind the walls clean and sober. "No drinking, no dope, nuthin'," she said with a loving smile, "just courage and God to go in."

I wanted to understand. I knew on some level that she was right. And noble. But in those moments my heart felt broken. Shattered. This wasn't fair. Was I being selfish? Yes! And, no, I didn't understand. We had just gotten her back. To lose her again, at a time when I wanted her to be able to share in the joys and the challenges of my life, to make up for lost time—oh, God, it crushed me.

Jolinda Wade, my beautiful mother, took both of my hands in hers and, speaking softly, put it this way: "In order to be the mother that you need in life and the grandmamma you deserve for your kids, I *have* to turn myself back in . . . so I can be *free*."

Tears began to stream down my face as I leaned down to give my mother a hug, lifting her up off the ground, letting her know without the need for words that I had faith in her. Even if I still didn't understand. If there were anything I could have done to change her mind or have her postpone the act of turning herself in, I'd have been the first to do so.

But this was not in my hands.

After Jolinda Morris Wade went to turn herself in, ending four years, nine months, and six days of being on the run from the law, we had no idea what to expect on the day of her hearing. Her original sentence had left three years, approximately, not served, even though that time had been reduced with only eight months remaining when she became an escapee.

Though I wasn't able to attend Mom's hearing that took place on January 1, 2002, a Tuesday, Tragil gave me a full report soon afterward. She described how many of our family members made their way down to the county courthouse and crowded into one of the smaller, colder hearing rooms. Dressed in their winter Sunday best, they took up every seat in a long row in the courtroom. Grandma was there, along with aunties, uncles, nieces, nephews, cousins, and our two older sisters, too.

T.J. said that everyone rose when the judge came in. They stayed standing until he called for the bailiff to bring in the defendant. At that moment, they turned to see Mom in her prison jumpsuit as she came shuffling into the courtroom, chains draped on her arms and legs.

When Tragil told me that, I could believe it. She said that everyone started to cry. They were thinking the same thing: Mom had turned herself in and put herself at the mercy of the court. Why did she have to be shackled? Obviously, she had been an escapee and those were the rules. But hadn't her own suffering been punishment enough?

At first, Tragil hoped that maybe the judge agreed. Mom was amazing, my sister told me, as she sat in the front with her back to everyone and stood when the judge addressed her. She wasn't crying or scared. She stood there, tall and poised, in spite of the chains on her, saying, "Yes, sir, I understood what I did, sir."

T.J. recalled that she had never seen strength in that form before. Her attitude was humbling, everyone would later say. Everyone was inspired by her courage to stand there, unafraid, letting the court know— *Whatever you want to do, I'm here before you and I ain't going nowhere.*

In reading out the facts of the case, the judge initially noted that Mrs. Wade had voluntarily turned herself in and was there with the support of numerous loved ones. The judge had only one question for the prosecutor: "Why shouldn't I let her go today?"

Right about then, one of our aunts couldn't hold back from saying, "Praise Jesus!" Everybody was praying, holding their breath, Tragil told me. These were the days of miracles. Anything was possible.

The prosecutor objected and stated sharply that the reason for not letting Mrs. Wade go was that she owed the time. How much? Eight years.

We had been warned before the hearing that the court seldom showed leniency to fugitives and could give her a sentence of as much as sixteen years or more. Tragil recalled that you could hear a pin drop in the courtroom as they waited for the judge to look back over the papers and then at Mom. After a lengthy silence, the judge asked her to stand.

The sentence was fourteen months. Eighteen months with four taken off. The court had favored her with that leniency.

Tragil reassured me that Mom didn't cry or weaken. She turned to look at the family, not for long, but showing only love, and then she turned away and was led out.

That report from my sister was all I had to take with me into the future.

What does a young man about to turn twenty years old and become a father do with any of this? I would love to tell you that I had some major revelation that could convince me of all of the good and great things that were yet to come for all of us.

I couldn't. I wasn't ready. In fact, I was angry. Not at anyone or any identifiable source. Somewhere deep inside was one pissed-off little kid who'd been waiting on those steps too damn long for Mom to come home—and was told to wait just a little longer.

Hell no. Enough with that bullshit. Oh, I wasn't just angry. I was furious. I had rage. Of course, I wasn't ready to admit it. But sure enough, the first day back at Marquette, Coach Crean figured out right away after I'd gotten into some heated arguments on the court with my own teammates that something was up. Again, as he had once before, he called me into the hallway to talk.

What was wrong with me? I almost asked him back, "Well, how long you got?" But I loved and respected Coach C too much for that. Instead, I told him an abbreviated story of Mom's journey. As I talked, just having him listen and allow me to unload, at least in part, helped me to make sense of all the struggles and sacrifices on the part of everyone who knew and loved me. That allowed me to have my revelation and find a release.

A short while later, I sat down and wrote a long letter to my mother. Strangely enough, even though she and I both liked to write on our own, we had rarely written to each other in all of our years of separation. But Mom had specifically requested that instead of visiting her we all write her.

My letter was the beginning of an important correspondence back and forth. First off, I admitted that I hadn't understood why she had to go back in. But now I did. On the brink of becoming a parent, I now understood that without going in, she couldn't become the woman and the mother she wanted to be. I wrote to her that she was my inspiration. In the past she had told me that I was her hero—being steadfast, going off to college, working hard as an athlete. The truth was, as I wrote to her, "Mom, you are *my* hero."

Later, she would repeat that part of the letter to anyone who would listen. Somehow it helped clean her slate and kept her going during the long months of solitary confinement that she was given in prison. Tragil and I were beside ourselves when we found out that the decision to segregate her from other inmates had been made at the start. Nonetheless, Jolinda Wade, my hero, used that time to write a book of prayers and praise.

Once she was back in the general prison population, Mom also started a ministry behind the walls, setting off on the path toward becoming an ordained pastor after she was released.

Early on in our letters, I also enclosed a picture of myself that she'd asked for. On the back, I promised her that great things were in store for all of us and that we were going to have a fabulous life.

How did I know? Or, what made me so sure? The answer isn't a *what* but a *who*.

He made his dazzling stage debut in life on February 4, 2002—when I stood by as Siohvaughn gave birth to the first of our two children. The connection between me and Von during labor and delivery was the most thrilling experience of being in love. I was in awe of her! And then, oh my God, when I beheld this tiny human being in the doctor's arms and saw that we had a son who was so beautiful and healthy, I was in an altered state of being. There was no more important moment in our lives than the birth of our child, as far as I was concerned. When I was given the job of cutting his umbilical cord, I had never felt so humbled. A son! We named him Zaire Blessing Dwyane Wade and welcomed him into the world with joy and devotion. And more love than I had even imagined was possible, just as I would feel for Zion when he arrived.

Zaire was perfect. He was a miracle. And I was a father.

I was the happiest young man in the world on that day when I held my child in my arms and he gave me that knowing Zaire look. He smiled! Newborns aren't supposed to smile. Some say it's actually gas. No, this baby was Zaire—ready for fun.

Pure happiness. And this was before the fabulous life of basketball stardom, the NBA, and being able to help kids and families who struggled as mine had, and having the ability to make a difference off the court. In my mind, at that point in time, I felt triumphant as a son and brother, and as a family. Dad still had work to do on himself but was starting to come around. Mom had been saved, resurrected, and was on a mission to heal others, even behind the walls. And Tragil could finally focus on her dreams and aspirations, instead of looking after everyone else.

We had never lost faith, even through mighty tests. At last I could let down my guard, confident in the knowledge that the toughest battles and hurdles and struggles for all of the Wade family were behind us.

But they weren't. Not for me. Not by a long shot.

Sunday night
April 15, 2011
At home in Miami

It's late on Sunday after dinner and the boys are all asleep.

I'm outside walking through the backyard, checking out the balmy breezes and the starry sky, appreciating being here and now.

The journey into single-parenthood that started a little over a month ago, one I've been piecing together with lessons from the past, has done that for me. These are the stories that have been important for me to revisit to understand the choices that I made to fight to be in my sons' lives.

As much as I tend to block out the most painful memories, I've found that they're valuable just the same. There are the times in our lives when all of us need to go back and revisit a place in the past to fully take stock of where we are in the present. I have to do that a lot in my career. The process keeps me grounded and reconnects me to who I am and what matters to me.

My preference, naturally, is to try to relive only the good and to take the best of what's been given to me by parents, coaches, and mentors. That said, there are great lessons from the painful moments that get lost unless we have the courage to go back and dig them up.

The effort is worth it. It's definitely helped me to know that everything along the way has happened for a reason—a truth that I embrace and hope to pass on to my kids.

And to you.

PART THREE

In the end, that's what being a parent is all about—those precious moments with our children that fill us with pride and excitement for their future; the chances we have to set an example or offer a piece of advice; the opportunities to just be there and show them that we love them.

—President Barack Obama,
on being an assistant coach for
his daughter's basketball team

CHAPTER EIGHT

ROOKIE SEASON

October 27, 2011
Thursday afternoon
Miami

"Daddy, what are you doing here?"

Zion hits a high note of surprise when I go to pick him up outside the door of his classroom. Since he passed his fourth birthday back in May, the school promoted him to a pre-K/kindergarten classroom and he clearly rules the roost.

The funny part is that he is so attached to Brenda, the boys' nanny who moved to Florida in May to be with us full time, that instead of thinking it's cool that I'm there to pick him up, he wants to know, "Where's Brenda?" As in, is everything okay?

"Brenda's at home," I say, and reassure him that nothing is wrong. "I had the day off so that means just you and Daddy get to spend some time together. Whatever you feel like doing. Sound good?"

He nods and shrugs as we walk side by side to the car.

As we head out together, I think back to how much has happened during the eight months since getting that one-line e-mail back on March 11 that changed my life.

The entire last season and the current one (such as it is) could serve as a master class for Team Wade on the ebb and flow that life and sports can bring. How to stay centered between those highs and lows? During a Man Talk, the boys and I had even discussed how to stay centered, a mature concept for all of us, including the challenge of how to look at a disappointment or a struggle and maybe see the upside.

Honestly, nobody likes somebody else trying to tell them how their lemons should be lemonade. Definitely not me. And nobody likes other people trying to say they even have lemons in the first place.

My sons helped me appreciate that fine lesson in those days following the 2011 playoffs. They refused to let me hold on too long to the disappointment. How did I feel? You know, most of the time I'm with my dad, who said it well about himself: "I'm not a bad loser but I like winning."

Still, when the Heat went all the way to the finals against the Dallas Mavericks and fell short of winning the championship, by two games, how could that defeat not be crushing? For what we had gone through as a team, the target that had been on our backs all season, the scrutiny and the haters hating us for believing that we could win, I don't see how the loss could have been any less than heartbreaking.

There was another way to look at the story, however. Most teams take multiple seasons to develop all the requirements and cohesion needed to win a championship. To go as far as the Heat did, almost all of us playing together for the first time in that same season, was practically unheard-of in NBA history. That's exactly what Zaire and Zion helped me see the very next morning after the loss, by barging into my room and not letting me slink under the covers but instead waking me with the messages of "We love you!" and "Time to get up!" and "Let's get ready for summer!" They even encouraged me to indulge in watching my favorite movie, *Coming to America*. Don't know why but I laugh nonstop watching it, no matter how many times I've seen it.

By the time Father's Day arrived, I was back to feeling overjoyed at being able to do my most important job in life. We had summer fun planned. My sons were excited to get to see their mom and we were also going to plan visits with Dada.

Ever since I'd gotten custody of Zaire and Zion we had really missed having Dada as part of the family, as he had become early on in the visitation process, and he had missed us, too. For a while, I had thought about the possibility of having Dada come live with us. In fact, even before the custody ruling, I had been thinking about a way to do more to help my nephew since he was really a part of the family. Since I'd gotten into the NBA, I had tried to do more for the younger members of our extended family who were living with some of the challenges that I'd experienced when growing up. Dada was the youngest of my nephews and didn't have cousins his age close by. In remembering how important it was for me to have brothers when Tragil took me to live with my father, I thought maybe this was my way to "pay it forward" and step up on his behalf, as others had for me.

When summertime came, I decided to bring up the possibility and see how everyone felt. Zaire and Zion were immediately in favor of having their cousin join our household. Then I ran everything by Tragil to see if she would take the lead in having our nephew come out and she was happy to do so. Finally, I went to my sister Deanna, Dada's mom, to ask if she would agree to him moving in, letting her know that he would be raised with the same love, parenting values, and expectations that were important in raising my sons. Academically, Dada had some catching up to do and I would be working on that with him. She agreed willingly. The deciding factor came down to Dada's desire to live with us and to have me as his father figure.

By the end of the summer, after I returned from trips to meet fans in Australia and China, and was ready to gear up for the 2011–2012 season, my nephew Dahveon had joined our happy home. What could ever cloud this picture?

Well, under the heading of advanced lessons in ebb and flow, the NBA lockout had happened and didn't look like it could end anytime soon. And on the day in October when I'm off work and have time to go pick Zion up, the season is very much in doubt.

Ever since late in the summer, when it became clear that cooler heads were not going to prevail so we could allow the season to start on time, the situation has gone from one of "concern" to "scary." Although the financial uncertainty might not be as tough on me yet as it is for those fellow players who are already on their way to play in Europe, I'm starting to have to think about other options as well. The reality is what it is.

After eight seasons in the NBA, I know this is not a job that can last for that many more years. What, four or five? Maybe six. For me, that is. I mean, as much as none of us want to believe the league could lose an entire season, the real possibility now exists. So finding a way to support my family is obviously a necessity. Another immediate concern is staying in game shape.

For those reasons, my old mantra of "hope for the best but plan for the worst" has become my thought for the day. Yes, I'm an optimist. But life has taught me to be a realist. Life and sports have also taught me that most true of sayings: It ain't over till it's over.

And so, before taking the drastic step of seriously looking to play in Europe or elsewhere, I've tried to maximize Daddy time by doing things like getting to attend more of Zaire's basketball games or surprising Zion as I am by picking him up from school and letting him call the shots for where we should go to have some fun.

We stop by a gift shop not far from the ice cream store and Zion starts picking things out—some cool shades, a microphone, a chain, and then a money clip. He is getting ready to be a performer, I can tell.

"Can I get all these?" he asks.

"Yeah, but you know Zaire and Dada gonna be mad."

"Yeah!"

He puts on his chain and we stroll to get ice cream. In no hurry to get home, we take our ice cream cones and sit outside underneath the Florida sunshine. Wow, it's ninety degrees in October, with a bright blue, cloudless sky, palm trees dancing to a Caribbean rhythm pumping out of a nearby Cuban restaurant. No matter what all else is going on, these are the moments to soak in and let the blessing speak for itself.

"Daddy, can we put the roof down on the way home?"

"I think that can be arranged."

Zion has only one speed he likes to move at: fast. That's something that I got to know during our limited contact early on. The faster the better. Something else I learned is that when the wind is blowing with the roof down, even when we're not going too fast, he thinks we are.

So I put the roof down, get him all strapped into his car seat in the back, and get behind the wheel, first putting on a new pair of sunglasses.

Zion follows suit, putting on his, too. He asks, "How do you like my shades?"

"Cool! Now we ready."

Oh, except for the music. I am stuck on the Jay-Z and Kanye West album *Watch the Throne,* which came out in the summer. It's probably stunted my musical growth. But ready for something different, I start going through the radio dial until Zion hears something he likes.

Roof down? Check. Music turned up loud on the car sound system? Check. Zion and me in our father-son shades? Check. And we are off, driving down the highway toward Miami Beach, laughing and singing along loud and free, waving our hands to feel the rush of the balmy afternoon breeze.

Does it get any better than this? I can't imagine that it does. Until what happens next, when we get back to the condo where we're living while renovations are being done at the house. We ride up in the elevator together and start walking down the hall to the door of the condo to join up with the rest of our crew. That's when little Zion reaches up his hand to give me a pat on my arm—he can't quite reach my shoulder yet—and he says very seriously, "You know, Daddy, I really like you. And I really enjoyed the time we spent together today."

That moment touched my heart so much. Zion and I never had as much of the early bonding that Zaire and I were able to have. But the last seven months have brought us both a long way. And I am amazed how Zion had grabbed the opportunity—just the right moment of timing—to express his approval of me. Parents need that, too!

Timing. A huge concept, so necessary as a secret of success, and Zion was already hip to it. Timing, as I had to learn, is not just about what opportunities to seize but when, not just about knowing that it's possible to turn negatives into positives but how long to wait for that turn and, again, when to change course.

Timing in terms of big decisions has a lot to do with listening to your instincts and listening to input from others worthy of your trust. No period in my life did more to teach me the importance of how to pick up on cues from without and within than back in 2003—not so very long ago.

EVERY BASKETBALL SEASON TELLS A STORY. SCRATCH THAT. Every season tells many stories. Every game is like a season unto itself, complete with a recent backstory, a much longer history, a cast of characters with their own various stories of what brought each to this specific game, this contest, which is about to play out and have its own unique beginning, middle, and end.

Every basketball season has all of those stories, on top of the preseason expectations and buildup, all setting the stage for the most dramatic tale, which comes after the end of the regular season. In college, the NCAA basketball postseason playoff tournament, otherwise known as March Madness, is one of the greatest competitions in all of sports.

At the end of my sophomore year, the 2001–2002 season, Marquette made it to "the dance," but the thrill was short-lived, since we were knocked out in the first round. Going into the next season as team captain, and an all-American with a certain amount of expectations put on me, I was determined to make sure that didn't happen again.

If that wasn't fuel enough, there were other sources, not the least of which came from only thinking of my mom—her courage, her fight, making her decision as she had and not even telling us about the solitary confinement. The only way that we found out was that Mom had written to Pastor Darryl to see about speaking to authorities to provide her with more pencils and paper. By chance Tragil was in the office at the church one day and recognized Mom's elegant handwriting on an opened letter on the pastor's desk.

When my sister learned that Mom was being kept in solitary for twenty-three hours a day, with her food brought in through only a slot in the door, we were all upset and bewildered. Tragil immediately got on the phone to Springfield and was able to grab enough attention to the case that Mom was eventually moved into the prison population. We had to continue to have faith that she could handle whatever was in her path. At the same time, whenever I thought of her spending endless hours alone, the weight was hard to bear.

All I could do was to keep praying, to keep writing her, and to keep pushing.

Once basketball season was over that March, a wave of other pressures took hold: bringing in enough money to feed Zaire (at the top of the list), keeping up my grades, and then also looking for summer work to help keep us going until the fall. Into this mix came the decision by Siohvaughn and me to get married. I wanted to do the right thing and in explaining my reasoning to Tragil—who said she'd support whatever I wanted to do and help with the planning for the wedding—that was my main point.

But Tragil did ask, "Why the rush?" We were struggling to put food on the table so she didn't see why we would put the expense of a wedding on our shoulders, too. We had also talked before about waiting until Mom's release, set for March 2003. Tragil's main concern—

which she never failed to raise—was that I finish college. As far as going to the NBA after that, of course that was never on the agenda. Not in our discussion. T.J. was still teasing me about tripping over my own feet as a kid! All she cared about was my getting the education and the degree—the only way out, as she saw it. Aside from that, there was also almost a taboo for me against saying out loud that if I did well in the next two years of college, well, going pro could be a reality.

Both the drive to do that and the need not to get too far ahead of myself came from being me, Dwyane Wade Jr.—the son of the man who had to convince my high school coach that maybe I'd be as good or better than my brother Demetrius. What did Dad really think of my chances of going further than college? When I asked him in later years how he felt at the time, he confessed, "I was too stubborn to think you could or that you would have the opportunity to make it at the next level. Not that you couldn't or wouldn't find your way. But that was me and my thinking. My focus was never about getting to the next level, you know? It was just about teaching you guys the game of basketball."

Tragil was there on that same page, no doubt, thankful for the educational opportunities and for doors in business and even public service that could open after a successful college showing. The marriage complicated everything, in any case, so she asked me again, "Why the rush?"

Well, I reminded her, I had a son and Von and I were starting a family and committed to the right things. If a wedding was what the Funches women cared about, and they were in a hurry, there was no reason to postpone making the marriage official. Deep down I had misgivings; I'd been hearing a lot of worry and pressure about all of the added responsibilities and I kept up with "I'ma find a way."

What that could mean in reality was far beyond me. The concept of getting a prenup would have made me laugh. Siohvaughn and I were two kids from Robbins, Illinois, unsophisticated, clueless, unprepared for the complications of wealth and fame. Especially at a time when we had nothing. Other than that, if you asked me whether I was in love, enough for a lasting marriage, I wouldn't have known how to answer. I knew that Siohvaughn and I, ages twenty-one and twenty, were head over heels in love with our baby boy. That said, the tension between her and me, on top of the pressures of this period, was a nagging concern.

But being stubborn, once I'd made a decision that was it. So I put a positive spin on my choice, and told Tragil that getting started young was a good thing—that I wanted to have my kids young, while I still had lots of energy to be engaged with them on their level. That meant the kids and I could play together, grow together, and wasn't this how to keep the promise that I had made to be different?

Tragil understood that I'd made up my mind and went forward to help us plan the day. There wasn't enough room for our various relatives at our little half-storefront church but we were able to hold the ceremony at the church right across the street. The first date they had available for us was May 18, 2002.

If memory serves, Dad was the first one to realize the significance of that date. Dad had a thing about reoccurring numbers and dates. His birthday, March 17, St. Patrick's Day, was always a source of pride for Dwyane Tyrone Wade Sr. He would boast that the city of Chicago turned the river green just for him. Of course, my being born on January 17 had made the birth of his only biological son that much more special. So what was it about May 18? By coincidence, that happened to be my parents' wedding anniversary.

We were all mystified but felt honored to be sharing the date with my parents. The thought that their marriage hadn't lasted more than five years wouldn't have occurred to me if Dad hadn't later mentioned his own skepticism about our marriage. I know he wanted the best for us and he thought highly of Siohvaughn and her mom. He also didn't want to tell me what to do. Looking back, he said, "You were growing into a man and I wanted to see what kind of decisions you were going to make." He also remembered telling me some months after the wedding that so much of life was in front of me that he doubted the marriage would last more than five years. Well, if he did say that, I blocked the comment out. Maybe because it touched a nerve.

I also blocked out the fight that happened on the eve of the wedding when Von went off because I'd decided to go spend the night hanging out with the fellas. This wasn't one of those bachelor parties with strippers or crazy drunken wildness. We were just going to hang out at Marcus's and then I'd come to the church in the morning. What was the big deal?

This was an early indication of Von possibly feeling threatened by my closeness to the guys or just her needing to be in charge. It was also an early indication of me pushing back against that control. In the end, I went to Marcus's anyway. He, Vinny, Wug, Donny, and I sat around telling stories about how fast the years had gone by.

Vinny was good at putting everything into context, just saying how it was hard to believe, "You getting married, being a dad, growing up so fast. Seems like yesterday was the fourth grade."

Nobody would have tried to talk me out of getting married. They knew me. Once I'd made up my mind, even with misgivings, I believed my will would be strong enough to make our marriage work.

The wedding day showed Siohvaughn and me how many people cared for us and wanted to celebrate the important step we had taken. The choice before me was either to linger on potential problems or focus on the good and on everything that was wonderful about my wife, and the ways in which we were blessed. True, we were struggling—so much so that we definitely couldn't afford a catered event for the wedding. But we did serve Popeye's fried chicken, my favorite! And we had a support system. My mother-in-law was a devoted and involved grandmother to Zaire, helping out, babysitting, whatever she could do, especially when Siohvaughn and I were studying for finals. We could also look forward to Mom's release once she returned to us and to her becoming Grand-mama, too. We had loving friends and relatives on both sides of our family who were cheering us on. The last thing I wanted to do was let any of them down. Scratch that. The last thing I wanted to do was let Zaire down.

After the celebration was over, however, other realities set in once again. One of the issues is faced by many college athletes or students on scholarship who have to make do on the financial aid supplied by the institution. Room and board is great during the school year. But on holidays and off-seasons, you're left to your own devices. That's hard enough when you're single but for married students with children, the struggle can be very rough. Whether it was a cause or an effect, by summer, Siohvaughn and I were arguing more than ever, and once again the pettiest stuff became heated debates. If not for the joy of playing with Zaire, my best friend in the world, and seeing his rapid development, I would have probably started to question more seriously the decision to get married.

Maybe I was old school about how life was supposed to work. In the story about how boy meets girl and boy gets girl pregnant, wasn't the traditional ending that boy does the right thing, marries girl, and eventually they learn to care for each other and get past the rough patches?

More than that, in my mind the real problem was money. Once we didn't have to worry so much, I was sure, we'd all be happy together. And so I pinned my hope and belief on that motivation, soon transforming that need for better days and the hunger (literal and otherwise) into the pressure cooker at the core of my being.

This was the recipe that stoked the fire to win big that 2002–2003 season. That fire, combined with Coach C's guidance and strategic brilliance, not only roused us to want to go all the way but, more important, it made us believe we could. The belief that you can win is everything.

From the moment we walked onto the floor of the first preseason game, our Marquette colors of gold and blue draping Bradley Arena and making everyone in the stands look like royalty, you could feel that the season ahead was going to be a story to tell.

The word most often used to describe it by others was *magical*. On November 15 in New York City, we put up a W against Villanova and never looked back, cruising to victory through the next three games. Our fifth game was at Notre Dame, and though we played like winners, it was our first loss of the season. Looking to erase that memory, we played our next four games, all of them at home, at a playoff level of passion, handily beating Appalachian State, Wisconsin, Elon, and Grambling State. By early 2003, we had fallen twice, first to East Carolina and then to Dayton, but then roared back in a hard-fought win against St. Louis and a smackdown against South Florida on our home court. The rest of January was glory time, giving us four wins: Tulane, Charlotte, DePaul (always a pleasure to compete against the school that didn't recruit me hard enough!), and East Carolina (returning the favor from our previous loss).

There is a saying that the better it gets, the better it gets.

Such was the case for most of the rest of the season. We went from a win at Cincinnati to a nail-biter of a victory at home against St. Louis on February 5 (the same week that Zaire had his first birthday), and then to earning a win against Wake Forest on the ninth. The icing on that cake was another victory on the twelfth, against DePaul.

Our next game, at home against Louisville, was nonstop ballin' all the way to the end, when the basketball gods smiled down on our opponents, giving them a 73–70 victory over us. But we shook that off and won the remaining five games, which included a rematch on Louisville's home court that gave us a 78–73 win.

The last game of the season, slotted to be against Cincinnati on our home court, held special significance. This was beyond the fact that it would pave the way for our record for the year, to soon stand at 27–6, the second best winning record in school history, and Marquette's first ever Conference USA Regular Season Championship—with the 2003 Conference USA Player of the Year award given to me.

As fate would have it, the date of the last regular season game,

March 8, fell three days after Mom's scheduled release from prison. We were ecstatic about the timing that would let her attend her first and only college game of mine. But after everything we had been through that day when she went to court for sentencing fourteen months earlier, we knew that getting her to the game would be iffy. What was the problem? As we learned, the provisions of Mom's probation stipulated that under no circumstances could she be allowed to leave the state—especially with her history as a fugitive.

My sister and I, along with members of our extended family, enlisted everyone we knew to plead her case and make an exception, with our guarantee, special escorts, extra security. We were desperate. Finally, we made contact with her probation officer. In another surprising coincidence, his last name so happened to be Wade. No relation. After much deliberation, Mr. Wade granted Jolinda Morris Wade special permission to attend that last game.

Excited and still somewhat in a state of disbelief, I was almost nervous. This was at a much different level from high school, for one thing. Not to mention that Mom was no longer in her madness and could savor the seeds she had planted, the result of her belief in me and her having once told me, "Go get you a game."

Mom was even more excited and nervous. When she departed the penitentiary early on March 5, they gave her money and she took the train into Chicago by herself. Tragil went to pick her up and was shocked by what she saw. Mom had hips! Being clean and having three square meals had made her thicker and rounder, more womanly and motherly—and had given her face back the beauty that drugs had stolen from her. But because of the solitary confinement and lack of sunlight, Mom had come out with dark circles under her eyes. And her hair, which had grown thick and bushy, had not been given the benefits of salon styling.

The first thing my sister did was to set up appointments to get Mom's hair and makeup done. During our brief reunion held privately before the game that night, when Siohvaughn, Zaire, and I were able to see Mom, I had to say that the woman I saw before me was more beautiful and put-together than in all my memories of her.

We cried. We hugged. Siohvaughn and Mom hugged. And thirteen-month-old Zaire, already talking and trying to get in on adult conversations even then, added humor to our brief though emotional reunion.

My mother thanked me again for the letters. She reminded me that I had called her my hero. "Do you know how that made me feel? The woman who dropped the ball, me?" she asked. "Me your hero? I was not only able to do my time but I was ready for anything—like, how much time y'all got?"

Words will never do justice to the experience of coming out onto the floor later that night and looking up to see my mother's face. She was in awe. Tragil warned her, just so she would know, "We're not his only crazy fans."

Mom kept looking at Tragil in amazement. Around her were the banners painted for me, the people chanting my name. Let me rephrase that. It wasn't my name. It was the name of her son. Even if no one knew that she was my mother, Mom later said that she felt like a celebrity—and was extra happy that she'd had her hair fixed so pretty.

The win against Cincinnati at home was the fairy-tale ending for the season.

Whatever my stats were for the night, I haven't gone back to check. But I know that I played well. That was out-of-body surrender, me suspending the laws of gravity and taking flight. In that game, I felt that Dad's nickname for me had proven true. After everything, after where I came from, I had to be Lucky.

More than lucky, I was blessed—the most blessed and the happiest son alive.

As the final buzzer sounded and the crowds rushed the floor to surround the team, I looked up in the stands and Mom was on her feet, like Rocky, tears running down her face, nodding her head in triumph.

I catapulted over whoever was standing between me and her, ran up, and hugged her so tightly and so long, time stood still. Fans and team-mates were gathered nearby and pressed in, surrounding me, Mom, and Tragil. I had to yell above their voices and the lingering cheers from the game, telling her, "I love you!" And then I hugged her again.

In remembering that triumphant moment, Mom would remind me, "After I had my hair fixed so pretty, when you grabbed me and swept me up like that, my hair went all crazy and then the photographers starting snapping away!"

I forgot that part. We both would be able to laugh, reliving a high-light together that would shine forever in our lives. As Mom puts it, "We were just so into the moment. And it was the most exciting moment of my life."

Mom would say again and again, in later years, that she found her strength behind the walls. Because through the solitary confinement she was able to commune intimately with God and come to her under-standing of "binding and loosing," as it is explained in the New Testa-ment, she sought the path of self healing before ministering to others. She began by writing down what are known as warfare prayers. Mom put it this way: "I lived a life of fasting behind the walls. I learned to be a warrior. I built up a bulldog mentality. I hate the Devil and I found out he don't like me."

After Mom moved into the prison's general population, her minis-try evolved naturally just by her sharing her story. That was the jour-ney she continued in studying to become an ordained pastor after her release. Her message to all was simple, whether they were struggling with addiction or hopelessness, whether it was a family member or loved one. "To anyone caught in a bad place, I'm here to tell people not to give up. My kids never gave up on me. They prayed for me. Believe in the power of prayer. I'm living proof."

Jolinda Wade would say that on March 8, 2003, when her hair got messed up in front of the cameras, the road to her redemption was not at its end, but it was also not just starting. She'd come through this last regular season, at long last, as the MVP of her life. Now she was gearing up for a championship run. One of many to come.

THE CURTAIN ROSE ON MARQUETTE'S DRAMATIC 2003 quest for the NCAA basketball championship in Indianapolis, Indiana, on March 20. Before tip-off, more than a few backstories were getting ready to collide on the court in a first round that would determine our fate as well as that of our opponent, the College of the Holy Cross. At a conference record of 24–5 we were third-seeded; Holy Cross was seeded fourteenth. Marquette hadn't gotten past the opening round since 1996; the Holy Cross Crusaders hadn't gotten past that hump in decades. Though the expectation was that we were in a stronger position to win, part of the madness of this March tournament is that many a favored team has been known to fall to a lower-ranked team. In fact, in the two previous years Holy Cross had come close to knocking out Kansas (in 2002) and Kentucky (in 2001), both powerhouses. The Crusaders might have been on an even more potent recent winning spree than us, having lost only one of the last twenty-one games. In other words, the end of this story couldn't be predicted or written until the game was under way.

An interesting twist to the tale was that the head coach for the Holy Cross Crusaders was Ralph Willard. Coach Crean had been his assistant coach when the two were at Western Kentucky and Pittsburgh. How was this all going to play out? Anybody's guess, anybody's game.

What I did know, within minutes after finding our rhythm, while I found myself getting into early foul trouble, was that my teammate and road roommate, Travis Diener, had the hot hand. Like we'd never seen from him. The third-highest scorer for us during the regular season, Travis went on in this game to have a career high of 29 points—which included six three-pointers. Often underrated, he raised his game and lifted the Golden Eagles with an intensity and gutsiness that had to be intimidating to the Crusaders. We led most of the game until just before the end. With only twelve seconds left, we had started to pull away when Holy Cross cut our lead to three points. But then we scored in response and went on to win the game, 72–68.

We had done it! We had made it out of the first round!

Two days later, still in Indianapolis, we faced Missouri, who had won a squeaker against Southern Illinois in their first round. Steve Novak, then a freshman on our team, six foot nine and formidable, came off the bench and rose to the neck-and-neck challenge, as did I, going on to contribute 24 points, 8 rebounds, and 7 assists for the game. With the clock ticking down to the final buzzer, the score was tied at 80–80 when Missouri managed to get off a shot. Everything suddenly switched into slow-mo as we watched the ball rise from the key, arching toward the basket and . . . a miss! With new life, we charged into overtime and literally were perfect. Firing on all pistons, we won with a golden score of 101–92. Missouri's coach was quoted as saying, "I've never seen a team shoot perfectly in overtime."

Cue the music. We were on our way to the Sweet Sixteen, last reached by Marquette in the 1994 run, which Duke stopped. No stopping us this time. Not after coming this far. The pressure ratcheted up considerably as we traveled to Minneapolis for the semifinals of the Midwest Region, where we would face the second-seeded Pittsburgh Panthers, known for being a very physical team.

Normally I would welcome that kind of combat. But whatever was happening, and sometimes it just happens, I had a terrible first half, scoring all of two points. We were losing badly enough at halftime that when we went into the locker room, the game wasn't looking good. Coach C went off on everyone, especially me.

And then he gave me a look I'd never seen in his eyes before, one of those eye-of-the-tiger looks, with a do-or-die expression on his face as he said something I never saw coming: "Dwyane, listen, if this is going to be your last game, just go put it on the line."

For a moment I almost didn't understand. Coach had never talked to me about the possibility of my playing on the next level. It had been an unspoken subject, raised only recently by the ESPN guys, who had been showing some of my highlights from March Madness and comparing me to some of the other elite college athletes gaining NBA attention so far. A few of the analysts called me the best college basketball player in the nation but others were still like, *Dwyane who?* The buzz so far was mostly for Carmelo Anthony and the unlikely wins he was giving his team, Syracuse.

So this was the first time Coach C had raised the question, something that I wouldn't have brought up out of respect, and without saying it in so many words, he gave me his vote of confidence. The message was that I had fulfilled his hopes and had a shot of going further, and could do so even at a time when another season for Marquette was on the table. It was between the lines that I heard him tell me—*Son, you're going to the NBA, so leave your mark now. Leave it out there on what could be your last college game.*

Tom Crean knew me and knew how to flip the switch that sent my engine into overdrive. I went out in the second half and scored 22 points and the team rallied, putting away the Panthers easily. The headlines in some of the syndicated sports outlets read, "Dwyane Wade probably ended any debate over whether he is ready for the NBA." One article said that I had turned the game into a personal highlight film.

Besides the thrill of winning the Sweet Sixteen and now advancing with my team to the Elite Eight, I was on top of the world because of what Coach Crean had said to me. I'd revisit that moment often over the years to come, reminding myself to treat every game as if it could be the last one and to always put it all on the line. I also took away the lesson that I would have to relearn at different stages in my career, that just because you're having a bad first half, it doesn't mean you'll necessarily have a bad second half. A metaphor for life as well!

Two days later, March 29, again in Minneapolis, we advanced to the Elite Eight for the Midwest Region Finals, which put us in the role of David versus the Goliath of Kentucky. The Wildcats had swashbuckled their way into March Madness on a twenty-six-game winning streak. Kentucky was a huge, storied basketball program and, in everyone's mind, we had no shot. I went out, playing with a little piece of everyone who had ever believed in me in my heart, and just did what Coach Crean had said to do in the last game. This was when it hit me that I really might be leaving—that this could be my last college game. All the NBA talk from outsiders hadn't gotten to me, but I believed the reality coming from my coach and played like it.

Kentucky didn't see us coming. We had nothing to lose and elevated our game to become the proverbial little team that could. One of Kentucky's main weapons, another future NBA player, Keith Bogans (now with the Chicago Bulls), was playing with a sprained ankle. Kentucky would later say he wasn't at his best. Mainly they were overconfident. When we came out to the court to warm up, I could see they weren't taking us seriously. I nodded in their direction as I talked to my teammates, saying, "Look at them down there. They think this is going to be an easy game. Let's go show them what Marquette can do."

And we put it on 'em, because we believed that we could win, and then we won one for the history books—by fourteen points!

Unbeknownst to me that night, this was the game that really put me on the personal radar screen of Pat Riley. Since Riley went to Kentucky, he would have had special interest in the game anyway, and while watching the game to see how his school did in the tournament, he apparently happened to see me dismantle them. Little did I know how my journey ahead had been shaped by that game.

Though I knew as the minutes flew by that I was playing well, I didn't know how well. Finally, after the game was over and we started running around the court in celebration, enjoying the tradition of getting to cut down the nets and being awarded shirts and hats for the Final Four—our next stop—an awestruck reporter asked, "You know that you had a triple double?"

Wait. Did he just say a triple double? I actually said something like "Huh?"

He repeated his statement that in the game we had just played, I had a triple double: 29 points, 11 rebounds, and 11 assists. In a daze, I learned that a triple double had only been recorded three times before in the history of the tournament. One of the previous records belonged to none other than Magic Johnson, for Michigan State. Still in disbelief, I turned to one of my teammates and blurted out, "I got a triple double!"

He was as flabbergasted as me. Triple doubles were that rare. Our interview wound up being a comedy routine. But our convincing win over Kentucky was anything but funny to Kansas, the powerhouse basketball team we met in the Final Four in New Orleans on April 5.

Not only was Kansas a better team than us, but they did their legwork and prepared for us. We had never played against a team with their style or their speed. They used that disadvantage to their extreme advantage. Whenever we scored they'd get the ball out right away and hustle down and score. We hadn't seen anything like that. Most of our opponents we could outhustle with enough time to go set up our defense. Not Kansas. They didn't let us set up at all. And we got clobbered. Smashed. Killed. We lost to the Jayhawks by thirty-three points.

So many mixed emotions accompanied our trip home from the Final Four. We had to feel triumphant. For Marquette, a small school, to have come that far—a feat only surpassed by the Golden Eagles in 1976–77, when we'd won the championship—was to scale a mountaintop, an opportunity for us to play on the biggest stage of college basketball. But the loss was also a heartbreaker. You get that far, you have a singular focus: you want to win. You want to bring back the trophy for your team and your school. You want to climb Mount Everest and feel what only a select few others have experienced. Yet we had put Tom Crean's Golden Eagles in the minds of the basketball world from that tournament forward. The AP poll ranked us at number six in the nation after our showing.

The AP also named me a First Team All-American, the first for Marquette to have a player so named since 1978. The United States

Basketball Writers First Team All-American was another accolade I received, along with being named a National Association of Basketball Coaches Second Team All-American, as well as being nominated by ESPN as 2002 Shooting Guard of the Year, among other amazing distinctions.

We all took home the sweet with the bitter.

Coach Crean did turn out to be right. The game against Kansas (who went on to the tournament finals and lost to Syracuse) would be my last college game. But I didn't know that on the trip home by any means. Getting to that decision would require some intense deliberation. And nothing Coach said or indicated in the near aftermath even hinted at what I should be thinking about my decision.

Before I could begin to process where this could be headed, I needed to go home and see my family and then lay my head on a pillow to sleep on it. My best decisions have always been made that way. When the moment came, I would listen to guidance that I trusted, go to bed, pray about it, sleep, and then wake up in the morning and know what to do.

"SO HAVE YOU THOUGHT ABOUT NEXT YEAR?"

Coach Crean brought up the question during a flight to Los Angeles, where he was accompanying me for a week of events before the April 12 presentation of the 2002–2003 John Wooden Award, given to the most outstanding collegiate basketball player of the year.

More to the point, he added, "Have you decided what you want to do?"

I knew this conversation needed to happen since nothing had been said yet. As one of the finalists being flown out, I felt fortunate to have Coach C with me. But I was also nervous. Too many unknowns remained. Did the chance of being able to support my family make up for not finishing my degree? If I threw my hat in the ring and found no serious suitors, would I blow later opportunities after another year of college basketball? Answering as unsurely as I felt, I said, "Yeah, I mean, I'm kinda in between."

Coach Crean nodded and took a deep breath. "Fine," he began. "This is what we should do over this trip. You're going to make a list of the pros and cons of coming to school next year or leaving. And I'll do my job to get people's consensus about you as a draft pick."

I smiled, thankful yet overwhelmed.

Coach continued, "If you're seen as a lottery pick, then we know what to do. If not, we'll have a decision to make."

With that in my mind, I spent the week savoring the possibilities, hanging out with fellow finalists who were already projected to go to the NBA, and starting to get a feel for how I would maybe thrive in that atmosphere. By the end of my stay I had stars in my eyes and was thinking, *Man, I do want to go to the NBA!*

At the main event, I didn't get the John Wooden Award. In fact, I finished fifth in the voting. I thought that my stock should have been higher, but going under the radar was nothing new. And it was still an honor being in contention.

On the way home, Coach Crean didn't bring up the NBA move at all. We barely talked the whole flight back. He was tired, he said, and since we had taken a red-eye, we both just went to sleep. After arriving early the next morning, I had to get to class in a few hours so he drove me back to my apartment with enough time left for me to clean up and be on my way.

After pulling up to the curb, Coach, wearing a serious expression, leaned over to me and stuck out his hand.

I looked back in confusion—what was he trying to do?

Without an explanation, he grabbed my hand, shook it, and then finally said, "I just want to thank you for everything you've done for Marquette University." He elaborated on what the past three seasons had meant to him. Eventually he came back to the fact that what he had heard from the scouts was that I was a projected lottery pick. "So you remember that I told you: that if that was the case, I was going to have you pack your bags?" He paused. "And I'd be the first one to help you pack them. I just want to say congratulations."

My heart was pounding. Words wouldn't come close to describing my excitement, because in my heart I wanted to go, but I also didn't want to disappoint him, and had anticipated a more gut-wrenching conversation. Instead, he let me off easy.

"The one promise you have to make is that you cannot announce it. I want you to finish the school year. Keep going to class and focus on your education. You leave here the same way you came in—as a good student."

Smiling, I remembered that redshirt year and how my academic eligibility had improved so consistently that I soon had the highest GPA of the starting line of our team. Coach Crean had made that possible.

I promised him to do as he asked. He didn't want me to go the way some other guys have done who enter the draft and stop their schoolwork, or don't even go to class, and basically drop out. Keeping the promise, I didn't announce for quite a while. Eventually it got to be too much to have to lie. Everybody around the school was bothering me and asking if I was coming back. Teachers would interrupt their own lectures to ask me for an update in the middle of class. The drumbeat for an answer was terrible! So after a month of this, I conferred with Coach C and arranged to hold a press conference so I could announce my decision.

By this point in time we were already late in May and I was setting up meetings with different sports agents. For a kid from Robbins, just twenty-one years old, this was all foreign to me and I only knew to go by my instincts.

Just as I had never forgotten how Coach Crean was the first recruiting phone call from a college, I was impressed by Henry Thomas, who originally called during the regular season, even before March Madness. Hank, as he was known, had followed my high school stats and had heard from my AAU coach that I had potential and that he should "keep an eye on Wade." He did just that and eventually reached out to both Coach Crean and my mother-in-law, introducing himself with a packet of materials: articles, a brochure, and an impressive résumé.

Hank showed genuine interest, first by calling to speak to Darlene, who, once I'd made my decision to leave after junior year, helped him arrange a meeting with me at Marquette. Actually, this was on the same day as my press conference to publicly announce leaving for the NBA. Besides Tom Crean and my mother-in-law, Siohvaughn attended, as did Tragil. We all loved Hank's enthusiasm and conviction that I was going to be a first-round draft pick. While others at the meeting asked more questions than me, I listened intently to Hank as he talked about himself, his background, and how he liked to work.

Hank Thomas was nothing like the stereotypical sports agent that I had been expecting to meet. Some of the other agents whom I later met could have been modeled right after Jerry McGuire. Tom Cruise look-alikes and everything. Not Hank. He did appear to be much younger than his age (somewhere around fifty) at the time. He was cool, down-to-earth, perceptive, energetic, yet protective and fatherly. From Chicago, too. Hank had played basketball in high school. As captain he had led his team to the city championship before being given a scholarship to play for Bradley University. After taking a course in business law, taught by a professor who was also a sports agent, Hank found his calling—a way to combine his love for basketball with a business career.

"Everything I did from that point on was to be an agent," he told us. That included not only getting his law degree but also coaching during summer leagues. His first job after law school was as a tax accountant. Four years later, after taking a teaching fellowship at DePaul's law school, while pursuing a master's in law and taxation, he created a sports law course. Hank explained that by teaching sports law, he would have to learn everything he needed to know once he was fortunate enough to get a client. That day arrived in 1989 after he joined a law firm as a practicing lawyer and was approached by Tim Hardaway for representation. Before long, Hank's success on behalf of Tim led to opportunities for him to become a full-time agent. He went on to have his own company, which he ran for ten years before selling it to CSMG—whom he had just joined before meeting me.

What impressed me most about Hank in that first meeting was the time he had taken to get to know my track record. He pointed to my skill level, and compared the work ethic I had, and the ability to work harder than anyone if need be, to Hardaway's—a great compliment. But more than anything, I appreciated his approach to developing opportunities beyond only negotiating contracts. A career in the NBA wasn't an end unto itself, he observed, but a means to achieve a great running start in life—a first really great job after college. He explained: "The opportunity is more than to be an NBA player, but to use that as the leverage point that will allow you to take care of yourself and your family for the rest of your life."

Tragil, still not fully in favor of me leaving without a degree, asked how Hank had helped clients establish foundations. She also asked him about his own practice of tithing or giving back. This was the main question she had for all the agents I was considering. Hank spoke about his faith in a quiet, personal way that connected for us, how he tithed with money and with his time, and he shared with us his values of giving back to the community. As a father himself, he talked about me having a positive influence in promoting fatherhood. Tragil and I could see that he knew where we came from, without knowing the full story at the time, and that he understood the desire I had to be able to make a difference for kids and families in struggle.

Without giving Hank Thomas my official decision to sign with him or not, we invited him to attend the press conference that day. I appreciated him giving me encouraging feedback afterward and letting me know I could call on him with any questions.

The other sports agents I met were all excellent. But the one thing that Hank Thomas conveyed that the others hadn't touched on was the sense that he looked to help cultivate the whole person. When I told Tragil that Hank was my guy and she asked me what clinched it, I told her, "I went to bed, slept on it, and woke up knowing."

Call it a vibe, a gut instinct. I just knew. That became one of the most important and best decisions of my career.

Surprised but clearly delighted, Hank sprang into action on my behalf.

The first order of business was to line up tryouts. This involved reaching out to certain teams while fielding offers from certain teams reaching out to me. Hank's confidence in me was contagious. These individual workouts, he believed, could be treated like a job interview. That meant not only getting ready for drills on the court and being thrown into actual practice with members of the team but also preparing for sit-downs with coaches, general managers, and other key personnel. Hank made sure that I knew their rosters and any history that might be relevant for an interview.

We knew going into the process that as teams were starting to take a closer look at me, my draft status was somewhat questionable because I was a 'tweener—still between a point guard and shooting guard in height. The question to Hank was "So what's his real position?"

This was a real hurdle to overcome, even though I've always been a shooting guard. Hank believed that teams did themselves a disservice trying to fit players into strict categories. But that did happen to me to an extent. From the initial hoopla after the Final Four I dropped a bit and was not in as certain a position as that of, say, Chris Bosh, the other player Hank was representing in the same draft. The input from the number crunchers was that I could go as high as fourth and as low as twentieth.

My job was obviously to shoot high. I went on to work out for a crazy number of teams in a two-week span—something like thirteen teams in fifteen days. Most of the workouts went well in my estimation. On some I did really well; others were just okay. The Memphis workout wasn't great for me. Hank heard that I didn't play particularly well and that wasn't a surprise. But the rest of the feedback was good. I felt strongly about the possibility that I could go to my hometown Bulls, who had the seventh pick that year. As for the Miami Heat, when I called Hank my feeling was "I didn't awe nobody."

With the fifth pick, Miami would have a jump on Chicago. But unlike other franchises that might telegraph their interest ahead of time, the Heat were known for playing their cards close to the vest. One thing I did know was that the little I saw of Miami was something out of a dream. Year-round summer? That was, after all, my favorite season. My thought was, I could get used to that! Then again, no invitations appeared to be in the offing.

From Miami, I went directly to Orlando, where my workout was very good. The coach, Doc Rivers, had gone to Marquette, so there was a connection that appealed to me. But Orlando had a fifteenth pick and I hoped to go higher than that.

Still, I had to work out with everybody that was in the lottery or close to it. With three days left until the actual draft and more workouts to go, I called Hank and said, "I wanna take these last days to just chill." I was confident that whatever I'd done so far should have been enough. What I'd done over the past two seasons at Marquette and in March Madness, plus how I had showed up at the workouts, ought to have shown the serious buyers what kind of player I was and how I'd fit with their teams. There are times when you have to keep grinding and other times, like this one, when you have to know your worth, knowing that others will, too.

Hank was in agreement. His next assignment, as I went back to Chicago to get my head together and prepare for huge changes, was to obtain permission for sixteen-month-old Zaire to attend the June 26 ceremonies in New York City. Apparently, players as young as me didn't typically have children.

There were many family members and friends whom I would have loved to have had there with me. The same group of fellas from home—Marcus, Vinny, my cousin Antoine (Wug), and great friends from college—had been part of the home team all this time. Then, of course, there was Dad, my first coach, and Mom, my first and most devoted cheerleader, and Grandma, my first mentor. The problem for my mom was that per the conditions of her parole she couldn't leave the state. Though I could have argued that Dad and my brothers should have been there, there were only so many spots and I'd pushed the envelope already to bring Zaire. It didn't occur to me that Siohvaughn was making the decision about who to have there and that my family, other than Tragil, weren't priorities. That wasn't her fault; it was mine. The whole crew really should have been with me.

But the logistics were beyond my pay grade at the time. The only extra tickets I could get were in general seating and those went to a few of the fellas. With a limited amount of places at the table, I decided that along with my wife and mother-in-law, Tragil should attend, as should my coaches, Jack Fitzgerald and Tom Crean. And Hank would be going back and forth between my table and Chris Bosh's.

During the workout period, I had gotten the chance to meet some of the other players who were in the draft. Chris—or CB as I would later call him—was entering the draft after a year at Georgia Tech. Since Hank represented the both of us in the draft, CB and I had become friendly at the start, grabbing dinner together and exchanging contact info to stay in touch no matter where we ended up. One of the things I would come to admire so much about CB is how different he can be from everyone else on and off the court. He doesn't care that he's different. If everyone else is listening to music to get ready for a game, he'll be reading. I love his game of skill and finesse, but I also know he has a place where he gets fired up, and plays with a passion that teams feed off of, and I love that even more.

Before heading to different cities for tryouts, I had met LeBron James and Carmelo Anthony at the weekend of medical and physical evaluations in Chicago that were required before our workouts took place.

As I was preparing to have my knee examined, the first player I met was this young man who walked into a waiting area and introduced himself. That was LeBron. For an eighteen-year-old high school phenom whom everyone was talking about, he was surprisingly down-to-earth and approachable. As time went on, I was always impressed by LeBron's gracious personality. When you go to his hotel room or house, he's the guy who offers you cookies or pretzels or whatever you want and then gets it for you! L.B., a.k.a. Bron, as I would also call him, is a great host. Most of us guys are lazy—like, "Want something to drink? Go get it in the fridge!" Not LeBron. He was that way from the start and never changed.

Carmelo Anthony was also someone I'd gotten to know early on in the draft process. During March Madness, I had watched him and Syracuse win the championship and had been out on Bourbon Street during the celebration to congratulate him. Once you've met Melo in person, you can't *not* like him. In fact, as I would later say, Carmelo Anthony is so cool and so, well, Melo, that if you could choose to have a personality—like in a video game when you can create your own character—you'd want to be him. He is just who he is, bringing that Puerto Rican charm even into the game.

While I was happy to be going to the draft with players I hoped to know in the future, I sort of kept to myself in the time leading up to the actual event.

The wild range of emotions I was having caught me by surprise. Maybe because I am a different person, the way I'm assembled and the way I chose to be, I opted out of the typical partying that always takes place on the eve of the draft. The party makes sense when you think about it because it's really like you're about to get married to someone you barely know and they get to do all the choosing. So that night before is almost like a bachelor party; and so, like at a wedding, players notoriously show up hungover or wiped out for the big moment. But since I'm not a drinker or an excessive partier, that wasn't for me.

Instead, Jack Fitzgerald, my high school coach, and I decided to go do something. Was I hungry? Well, yeah, we all know the answer to that. But what did I want to eat? I didn't know. So Jack said, "C'mon, let's just go out," and we headed out into the cool summer night air and walked the streets of New York together. We just walked and talked and walked some more until we passed by a piano bar, windows open to let us hear the sound of someone performing jazz inside. Wow, when we went in, I stepped through the doors into another world. On a budget and spending most of my time in gyms, I couldn't recall ever having been in a piano bar. We ordered something to drink, no alcohol for me, but beverages for both of us with lots of ice that we could clink as we toasted the future.

Being the tough Irish guy that Coach Fitzgerald is, he held it together well, but I can report that watching him sitting there that night was the closest I'd ever come to seeing someone almost literally bust with pride.

With everybody else out partying, we headed back to the hotel early because I knew the next day was going to be a long one. Besides the anticipation, I had agreed to have *USA Today* follow me around the whole day. Finally, the hour for the draft arrived and my group and I made our way into the Theater at Madison Square Garden, everybody decked out for the occasion and the room pulsing with excitement.

Strangely, any nerves that I might have had were gone. Other than that, the suspense was killing me!

Because the Cleveland Cavaliers had won the top pick in the May lottery, I knew as well as everyone else that LeBron James would be the first pick. The Detroit Pistons had the second pick and the Denver Nuggets had third. There had been talk that Darko Miličić could go to the Pistons but no one knew that for a fact. I knew that Carmelo Anthony would be the third pick. Other twists could happen but for me the draft most likely was going to start with the Toronto Raptors, who had fourth pick. The tea leaves said that Chris Bosh was going to go fourth. And if that happened, my gut told me that I'd go seventh to the Chicago Bulls. I'd worked out twice with the Bulls and all the talk kept circling back to that scenario—which I was happy about. Once that order of the top four was in my head, I realized that the draft really started for me at position five.

Like clockwork, meaning just how I'd called it, LeBron was 1, Darko 2, Melo 3, and Chris Bosh 4. As the handshaking and ceremony continued for Bosh, my agent Hank left his side and came over to my table, pulling up a chair to sit by me. Still relaxed, holding Zaire, who was taking all this pomp and circumstance in, I was thinking that my number was at least a couple of picks away if Chicago was going to take me. In mid-thought, I heard Hank's voice as he leaned over and said, "Don't change your facial expression, act calm, I just got a call from Randy Pfund at the Miami Heat. They are gonna pick you at five."

Cameras were all around us and though I was trying not to tell anyone, I didn't expect to be drafted so fast and something came over me—I had to tell somebody—so I turned first to Siohvaughn, and said under my breath without looking suspicious, "The Heat are about to pick me at five. Don't change your facial expression."

Then I turned to my other side to tell my sister. The point was to prepare us. Instead, not only did Siohvaughn and Tragil change their facial expressions but the two of them started crying with hysterical happiness. Just to make sure everyone was in the loop, I looked back into the crowd and nodded at the fellas, letting them know that I was about to get picked.

Just then, NBA commissioner David Stern appeared at the podium and announced, "With the fifth pick in the 2003 NBA draft, the Miami Heat select Dwyane Wade from Marquette University!"

Well, that was what he might have said, but the excitement was already such that I couldn't hear at all. Hank nudged me and smiled. This was happening.

My wife and I hugged, Zaire started cheering with everybody else, and I made my way around the table, embracing everyone. Hank had said before that with a young team in the process of rebuilding, I was going to have a better chance of getting to start. The full impact of how perfect my selection was hadn't even hit me as I ran to the podium—euphoric!

All of what followed was an out-of-body experience to the umpteenth degree. So many dreams had led to this moment to get up there, finally, to take the hat welcoming me to the NBA and Miami, shake hands with my future employers and go in front of the microphones. All the struggle, all the years, now felt like they'd flown by and at long last I had found a way out, could prove myself and quiet the doubters.

Everything felt new. An amazing story, without hardship and obstacle, could now be written.

At home in the Southside of Chicago, Jolinda Wade, Willie Mae Morris, my older sisters, and nephews, nieces, aunts, uncles, cousins, and longtime friends from our church were somewhere gathered together singing praises about one of their own having got himself a game. And not too far from there, in downtown Chicago, Dwyane Wade Sr. used an accident settlement he had won to throw a draft-watching party at the ESPN Zone for everyone in his family and Bessie's family. His prediction that I would go fifth actually made the local papers. At the time, Dad wasn't able to put into words how he felt, but later he would say that he couldn't have asked for a better scenario as far as Miami being a place for me to grow and mature.

Tragil was the one person without whom none of this would have been possible. I knew that her hope was that I would have had that diploma—and it's something she's still hoping that I can complete one of these days. She is the first to say that at the time, her knowledge of basketball wasn't deep enough to evaluate my abilities. But there was no way she ever would have thought that I was going to go in the first round, forget whatever was to come next. Still, when I asked her how she felt after the end of draft night, she looked at me and just shook her head, asking, "What more could a sister want?"

• • •

of the major lesson that I had learned during halftime in the locker room after my miserable first half against Pittsburgh in March Madness.

Oh, but I didn't know that until the middle of the Heat's season.

The NBA team that I had joined in preseason that summer of 2003 had fallen the year before to subbasement levels. The record for 2002–2003 was something awful like 25 wins and 57 losses. The Miami Heat, founded in 1988, had risen to heyday levels by the late 1990s with Pat Riley as coach and legendary players like Alonzo Mourning drawing in the crowds. But those days seemed long gone.

Now in this rebuilding, reinvention period, Pat Riley was looking for a way to retrieve the winning DNA that was lying dormant in the Heat all along. As a new kid trying to find my place in this new world of the NBA, I can now report that being coached by the iconic Pat Riley was scary. The respect I held for him was immeasurable—both as a basketball genius and as a person. All I knew was I didn't want to screw up! And he was very hard. His game was *game*.

Coach Riley did something that put me right at ease. He wanted to just let me play and didn't mind the usual mistakes that happen in the early going. I found that very refreshing.

But then, just as I was settling in on the eve of the season, Pat stepped down to focus on general management duties and Stan Van Gundy became our coach. To have two coaches right before a first season was challenging. And these were two very different guys with two very different approaches.

Coach Van Gundy has a voice that rings in your ears and gets underneath your skin. Always on edge, he coached from a state of high alert. From practice to games and in-between. Also always in tune to the momentum of a game, he let me go on the court similar to the way Pat did. That was going to be good for me in the long run since I was given the opportunity to be a contributor and to find my stride.

Because of Stan, my toughness and drive showed up early on, thankfully. In what could have been a great omen, I was actually the scoring leader for our first game of the season. Even though we lost, I wasn't worried. Then we lost the next game and the one after that. We went 0–7 for the start of the season. Time to worry? I felt sick. After that we continued to struggle, winning here and there but mostly losing for a solid couple of months. Some of those games I had to miss on account of a broken wrist.

But lo and behold, as the holidays approached it was like we had all gone in the locker room and realized that for the second half of the season we needed to put it out there on the line. And we started to win. By March 2004, we were on a tear, winning seventeen of our last twenty-one games for the season. Being able to help make the difference in going from the subbasement to a winning record of 42–40 for the season was incredible.

The learning curve for me over the course of the season had been steep. Everything that had powered me in the past became intensified. The stakes were much higher—especially with the pressure I put on myself—as were the risks, rewards, and opportunities. All of that crystallized for me when we went into the first round of playoffs against New Orleans.

By now I knew that once the story of the postseason begins, all that has come before is backstory and playoffs are really where the world pays attention. The chance to prove myself on that mega-stage was energizing. In the past, I'd done well in crunch time. But I'd never had the pressure of an NBA playoff moment with a game on the line. That moment was given to me at the end of the first game of the series. Final possession was ours and we went into the huddle. The play was called and Stan Van Gundy surprised us all by going to me to make the basket. The rookie in me was nervous and scared but the competitor in me was up to the challenge.

On the playback, I can hear the shock of the announcer's voice as he describes the play, the inbounding of the ball to me and "Wade puts it up, it's good! Stan Van Gundy went to the rookie and he did it!"

In that moment, I arrived. From then on, I was seen as a player to watch and, eventually, a force to be reckoned with. We went on to win the dramatic series against New Orleans, four games to three. That was the first time that the Miami Heat had won a playoff series in four years. In the second round, we battled the dominant Indiana Pacers in a six-game series, including two phenomenal Miami wins, but in the end we couldn't overcome all that they had in their arsenal.

Disappointed not to have gone even further, I had also gotten a taste of rarefied air and hungered for more. A year earlier anyone who had suggested that the Heat had any chance of winning a championship in the near future would have been thought crazy.

But you have to be a little crazy sometimes to believe.

Hank Thomas came to me about planning for the future, on the court and for opportunities starting to come with that. After the playoffs, he felt that I was finally starting to get the recognition I should have had from the start. The fact that I still wasn't being given headlines that LeBron and Carmelo were getting annoyed him as much as it did my teammates and me. After all, Hank noted, most of the teams with picks that had gone ahead of the Heat hadn't made the playoffs. Cleveland, Denver, and Toronto had all failed to make the playoffs. But Miami had gone to the second round.

He was right. By any standard, I had enjoyed a monster rookie season. And if the lack of attention to me could lend some motivation to my game, so be it. Not like I hadn't used naysaying as fuel in the past.

At one point I had complained to Lamar Odom, a.k.a. L.O., one of my best friends in the sport and a mentor on and off the court as well, about how the team as a whole and myself in the process weren't getting our due. We were on an airplane together as this conversation came up and we had a long ride ahead of us to talk about my complaints.

Lamar predicted that the tables would turn eventually and then the expectations would be so stratospheric that not living up to them would seem catastrophic.

"Highs and lows," L.O. explained. "The NBA is all about highs and lows." He charted his own ups and downs with a lengthy story that went along with his point. The idea was simple though: One minute you can be on top of the world and the next minute on the bottom. Or vice versa. Part of what he was saying was not to become thrown by the adoration or the hating. The other part of his point was that whatever it is that you think you've attained as a high could be taken away at any minute. The solution he had found was to try to stay on the middle ground, between the highs and the lows.

L.O.'s talk with me on that flight was like handing me the keys to the kingdom in terms of physical and emotional endurance over the long haul. I don't know how much he remembers of that talk or if he realizes how much he influenced me—even to this day.

In fact, I credit much of my development as a player to L.O. and teammate Caron Butler, who were true mentors to me my first year. I would stay in touch with both of them but I don't think either are aware of the extent to which they empowered me and gave me so much confidence and knowledge. Caron Butler was the big brother I needed and, as I had learned, had paved the way for me to go to Miami. Both saw the big picture—that you have to love the game but also know that one day you won't be the gold and shining star you might have been, and to make plans for what's to come after basketball.

Well, since I was just making a name for myself after the rookie year I had turned in, my focus was not to be changed by whatever people were or were not saying about me. My approach was to close the lane on the doubt and the doubters. I was just going to keep playing my game and, being my father's son in the end, just keep working at getting better.

None of this is to say that I didn't make rookie year mistakes or that all of life was ready to be lived happily ever after. One of the worst mistakes would come back to haunt me: when I had come into the NBA, wrongheaded thinking of my own convinced me not to allow anybody to handle my money.

There were a few reasons for this. First, I had some trust issues after growing up without any money or examples of how to handle money. So when Hank brought up the names of top financial planners, I didn't even consider the possibility that they could have shown me how to save or to invest wisely. Second, as for a financial adviser who would handle banking and bills, well, Siohvaughn kind of had that department covered.

As time went on, Hank would bring this up with increasing concern, asking whether I had access to those accounts. Usually I'd laugh and say, "She handles the money, I shoot baskets."

That was naïve. In hindsight, I know that. In theory, I believed that we were partners and that we both worked to contribute to our family's well-being. Why take a job away from her, especially one of control that she cared about? At the same time, why would she discourage me from getting financial advice?

The reality was that the marriage wasn't on solid ground. Obviously, during our struggles in college, we'd been through changes, and those were multiplied when I got drafted and we entered a whole different stage of newfound everything—not just the money but the fame, the status, the attention that goes along with that, and options for riches and rewards that grew over time.

Everything was different. We might as well have gone from Robbins to Milwaukee to the moon. On one level, this was amazing and we could enjoy pinching ourselves that all the work had paid off. But on another level, because our relationship wasn't tight from the get-go, other, bigger compatibility issues set in—such that we became even less close the more success there was.

Starting in 2003 with getting into the draft, we'd spend the summers apart with different schedules, basically going our separate ways. We never discussed breaking up. Summertime just came and we had other plans and chose not to be around each other, besides the shared time we had as parents.

That said, I saw these issues as things that I could fix. Just like me saying I could find a way to take care of the family. So the idea that we weren't going to make it work as a team, well, I couldn't think about that.

Besides, money was supposed to make things better, right? All those years of not having any and now we had the freedom and peace of mind to let go of the worry. As a father, I could finally feed my son—who was growing like a weed and continuing to amaze me as the little person that he was becoming. As a couple, we could soon afford a nice home and do things for friends and family that we never could before.

Did it bother me that Siohvaughn didn't seem to always think to involve my family and friends in some of those fringe benefits? Yes and no. Yes, it bothered me; and no, I chose not to look at the negatives.

Being stubborn, I was going to make it work. That's all I knew. There was trouble brewing, unfortunately. But I kept trying to get to that middle ground.

OCTOBER 27, 2011
THURSDAY EVENING
AT HOME IN MIAMI

ZION AND I ARE BARELY THROUGH THE DOOR AFTER OUR afternoon's adventures when Zaire and Dada appear as if out of nowhere with greetings and salutations.

There's so much to do and discuss. Both have excellent schoolwork to show off.

Dada has made progress and we all congratulate him. What's the secret? Just working hard and not giving up, he tells the other two.

The key to Zaire's recent good grades seems to be his ability to focus better at test time and, when he isn't sure what the teacher has explained, his willingness to ask questions.

Underneath my serious expression, I'm trying to keep my face from showing a big happy grin. So many of the conversations that we've had at length are now coming back from out of the boys' mouths—like they've discovered them on their own. And that, as a father, is as good as winning a jackpot.

Because, in the end, the old saying that you can lead a horse to water but you can't make him drink is true. Nor should you want to make him drink.

That leads me to one of the biggest fatherhood or parenthood discoveries that I've made—you don't empower your children by taking credit for their successes. Even when you deserve some credit. Let them own their victories.

How do you do that? Praise helps. Always. Although, it's not always so simple when you're also trying to set boundaries and offer guidance and motivate kids to reach high. But in the end I think the best way to help your children seek out opportunities and make the best of them is by modeling the behavior.

If you as a parent live your life and pursue your goals, always remembering to put it on the line, even if you haven't had the greatest first half, that rubs off. If you put your heart into whatever you do, playing with the will to win of a rookie who wants to do well, kids will cut you some slack for caring.

These are fatherhood lessons I'm still learning. In those weeks, when from all appearances we were in real danger of not having an NBA season, I had to think about the example I was setting and come up with some Plan Bs and Cs.

For parents and kids, families and individuals, the importance of planning, whether short or long range, can't be overemphasized. Should there be any doubt, this is where Daddy gets to have a say—in the next chapter.

CHAPTER NINE

MOUNT EVEREST

MID-NOVEMBER 2011
IN THE BLEACHERS
MIAMI

WALKING INTO THE COMMUNITY GYM WHERE THE LOCAL BOYS basketball league holds their games, I have to stop and inhale the memories: the smell of sweaty jerseys, the echoing rat-a-tat-tat of who knows how many basketballs being dribbled out of unison, the sounds of coaches blowing whistles and calling drills, and the squeak of sneakers on the old wood floor.

I'm thinking of all those games played as a nine-year-old myself when Dad used to pile as many of us as he could into the car and take our Robbins team to compete against the Southside kids much older than some of us. Thinking back, I guess there was a method to the madness.

"How's my son?" Dad's unmistakable voice surprises me as I turn and spot my father, looking very GQ in his shades and Jordan brand warm-up suit. For a guy in his early to mid-fifties, Pop's not doing too bad keeping in step with trends. I have to give him credit for that—as well as for some other tough accomplishments. Ever since he moved to Miami, six or so years earlier, after his divorce, he's mellowed out considerably. Dad's sober these days and I'm proud of him.

Of course, it's weird to have a kinder, gentler Dwyane Wade Sr. sitting up in the stands with me at Zaire's games. The boys actually have a lot of respect for his basketball knowledge. Even if, whenever Zaire asks Pop to show him stuff, he ends up fuming to me afterward, "Grandpa's mean!" But then my son will do something impressive on the court and I'll ask, "Where'd you learn that?" and he'll admit, "Grandpa."

With the NBA lockout dragging on, I'm still making the most of the extra time and maxing out my hours as Daddy. With options running out, some fellow players (L.B., Melo, and Chris Paul, a.k.a. C.P.) and I are planning a series of exhibition games as charity benefits for our foundations in our hometowns. So travel is on the horizon. Before leaving for the first of these, however, I'm getting a chance to go watch almost all of Zaire's games.

Zaire loves having me there. He genuinely wants to please me and see me proud. The fact is, he is good. It's not for me to say that he's the best kid on the floor, but let's put it this way: even though he is one of the youngest players, when he's playing well, his team wins. I mean, Zaire's really talented and tenacious. And he likes when I praise those traits.

At first, I started with the mentality that I wasn't going to say anything or be demonstrative in any way. I was going to sit there with my hat on, with the brim low, and just watch the game from up in the back. It didn't turn out that way. For one thing, when he plays, he looks for me and then he looks at me. It got to the point that I said, "Zaire, stop looking at me, look at the game."

He'd be dribbling and glancing over to see if I approved. And I'd have to mouth the words, "Look at the game."

That said, I couldn't help but be entertained whenever he did something, something good or unexpected, or pull one of his antics. He is so animated. A showman who has all the antics in the world, and funny visual takes to the crowd, he'll turn around after making a basket and do his special cool move and everyone will cheer and then he'll look at me.

Pretty soon, I realized there was no way I could be that polite version of a dad sitting with the brim low and up in the back. I mean, if I could sometimes be the player to kick up the excitement on the court, why wouldn't I share in Zaire's excitement? What I would not do was be like those other overly involved parents who stand up and try to coach their kids from the bleachers. Instead, I go for positive reinforcement—a thumbs-up for a great play, a nod and a smile for any kind of effort, and big applause before a break, when he can see me on his way to have a seat. The bottom line is that I'm a huge Zaire Wade fan. Of course, I'm going to be engaged as a spectator. I'm *that* dad.

We had made a plan at the start of his fall season that as long as his grades were in good shape, he could play basketball on a real team. We were also clear on other considerations for the plan. We had already discussed the fact that the pressure of being my son was going to make it hard for him no matter what. So the deal was, "Listen, if you gonna play basketball, the only way I can say yes is if you play and have fun. Don't worry about what anyone says. Don't worry about being better than this person or that person. Right now, you're in the fourth grade, and the terms are that you're only playing to have fun, to enjoy yourself and the game. You play hard, you be respectful to the coaches, to your teammates and the refs. But that's it. Don't worry about nuthin' else."

Before my dad and I take our seats in the bleachers before the game, just to make sure, I go check with Zaire to see if he's in pain from his groin. The day before, Zion had kicked him accidentally, or so I was told, and so I have to remind Zaire, "Listen, if you're hurt, I don't want you to play."

"No, Dad, I'm fine."

"Cool. But if I see you run up and down funny I'm gonna stop you."

As soon as the game gets under way, Dad and I both notice that Zaire appears to be having an emotional game. Not sure what's going on, I'm concerned that he is hurting from the injury. Oh, and then I remember there's a girl his age he really likes who is one of the cheerleaders at this game.

Whatever it is, I'm watching a nine-year-old playing under a lot of pressure, very emotional, and evidently not enjoying himself. Worse, every time the ref makes a call, Zaire goes running to him, asking, "What'd I do? What'd I do?" and even arguing with a call, saying, "No!"

After the coach says something and Zaire reacts by becoming sensitive, I can see that he's getting ready to cry. Pretty soon, even though he's on the court, he's not playing. Rather, he's just out there, barely into the game.

I keep seeing this behavior that we'd planned to avoid, but I hold back from saying or doing anything. Finally, during a timeout I turn to my dad and say, "Go talk to him." Then I suggest maybe he can stretch him out, too—in case his groin is bothering him after all.

Dad heads over to the floor, where Zaire appears almost to be sulking, and pats him on the back before having him tuck one leg in and stretch out the other. Then Dad leans down and says something that seems to get my son's attention. I have no idea what my father has just said, but I do know that he doesn't talk to Zaire the way he used to talk to me. Not even close.

Zaire looks at Grandpa after the talk and nods solemnly.

I later had to ask my father what he had said to his grandson. He said, "I told Zaire that the way he was acting, with that attitude, no one was gonna want to see him play basketball like that. And I asked him to think about how his mother would want him to play." Dad was aware, as everyone who knows Zaire is, how much he loves his mother and wants her to be proud of him. Dad felt that was the one way to get him to understand. Looking back, I seem to remember similar lectures about making my mother proud but delivered in much stronger fashion and colorful language when I was having emotional games at age nine.

Dad's talk seems to help initially, but as the game goes on, Zaire reverts to being upset by calls and playing without any enjoyment. With no improvement, I get up and start to walk over. Again, I never thought I'd be like this as a dad.

"Zaire," I say quietly, in my normal, soft-spoken, no-drama voice, and gesture over to a spot on the floor, "come here and let me talk to you."

Then I get into him with a stern tone that's important to me to right our ship together. "Listen, son, I know this attitude is out of character. If it doesn't change, we're going to get into the car and go home." I continue and remind him that how he is acting on the court is a reflection of us as a family, first of all, but more than that, "That's not what we do. That's not what we promised each other we'd do if you played basketball. You were only going to play to have fun and all this emotion and all this stress you got right now is defeating the purpose. Zaire, this is your outlet, this is your enjoyment, but not right now."

Reacting the same way as he did to my father's serious comments, my son nods in understanding and sets his jaw with a resolve to do better.

So then I change my tone a bit and add, "Good. Now—go out there. Let me see some of that swagger. That Zaire swagger. Let me see you enjoy yourself. Let me see you smile. When your teammates do something well, you make sure you let them know they did something well. Don't mope around. And when your coach says something to you and when the ref makes a call, you respect them and you listen."

That's the dad-sideline-private-chat-with-son I wasn't going to resort to. How'd that approach work? Well, Zaire comes out and has a fantastic second half. I'm talking about scoring, stealing, rebounding, all of that, passing the ball to his teammates and high-fiving them when they do well. And then maybe because he has found the inner joy again, he reclaims his ability to delight onlookers—shooting the ball, having it go in, and then celebrating with a little move and a signature look to the crowd.

Of course, now I'm fired up. Forget the nod and the light applause. I'm all up on my feet, letting him hear me: "Yeah, that's what I'm talking about!" My dad's next to me doing the same thing, too, cheering loudly for his grandson.

For the baller in training, there will come a time when, if he's open, I can offer more instruction. But the priority of enjoying himself is tops for now. Besides the fact that this was his first year to play and I don't want him to lose this as an outlet, I do want to prevent him from getting into the pressure of being my son, or having to think he has to score twenty points for me to be proud of him.

My plan to be the dad who would just show up to watch didn't play out, on the other hand. Apparently I can't do that.

Still, on the theme of being a father first and understanding that life is bigger than basketball, I have found that the most important feats start with a visionary planning approach—whether we're talking about being a parent or pursuing a dream.

I'm hard-core on having a plan. At the same time, as I learned after my rookie year in Miami, the ability to adapt a plan in the face of changing circumstances—off or on the court—is ultimately what wins.

WHEN I'D FIRST ARRIVED AT THE HEAT, I WALKED INTO THE gym and saw this fierce warrior on the court. His hair in braids and with a powerful build, all cut, he looked like somebody you would not want as an opponent.

"Who's that?" I asked someone standing next to me.

"That's Udonis Haslem."

Wait. Udonis Haslem? I'd known him from when he played as a Florida Gator. Udonis Haslem was not cut like that. "You mean Udonis, fat Udonis?"

"He ain't fat no more."

So Udonis had come into the league at the same time as me (in tiptop shape) and would journey with me through all the highs and lows on and off the court together as a tremendous basketball player and friend. U.D. or Udon often comes across as this big tough, gruff guy, but take off that mask and he is all caring, all heart.

In those early days, U.D. also liked to point out the surprising side of me as one of the quieter, more soft-spoken guys who at the same time could come out and make some pretty strong statements about how I felt, whatever it was.

True. With me, what you see is what you get. I have been known to wear my heart on my sleeve and, even with my teammates and coaches, not to hold back from telling them how much I care about them. You know the "I love you, man" guy? Sometimes I can be that guy. Other times I can be the best at compartmentalizing and setting aside whatever is hurting me—whether from the past or elsewhere—and not let it jeopardize my playing time.

That's where I was after finishing up a promising rookie year—trying to forget any negativity at home and putting my focus on the fastest way to get to the mountaintop—yep, the Big One. Being realistic, I knew it could take many seasons. When you think about Michael Jordan, who had come into the league in 1984 and didn't win a championship for seven years, that gives you an idea of what it can take—and that was with the best player in the world.

Of course, I had high hopes for us. Considering how far we came in one season from the year before I arrived, we were moving fast. Yet no sooner had we started to really mesh than all the dynamics shifted when a decision was made to trade Lamar Odom to the Lakers. When I talk about the highs and lows of the NBA, that was a low for me. However, it also turned into a high because as a result of the trade the Heat brought in Shaquille O'Neal, one of the greatest centers in the game.

It was Shaq who decided that I needed a new nickname besides "D-Wade" and would eventually coin one while watching a block-defying dunk over defenders much taller than me. How'd it come about? Just from him saying, "Wow! When you go, you go like 'Flash.'" And from then on I'd also be known as Flash.

When Shaq first came to the Heat he brought with him a history of sometimes clashing with the other lead teammates—with Penny Hardaway at Orlando and with Kobe in Los Angeles. So he wanted to make it clear that he and I would share in making things happen for our season ahead. At the same time, he took me under his wing. On and off the court, he was totally generous and gracious.

Almost immediately after Shaq's arrival, the Heat went from being a team that no one really took seriously to being on TV almost every night. When we traveled, no matter what city we were coming into, throngs of fans and reporters would be on hand, taking pictures, asking for autographs from Shaq and the rest of us. Shaq-Diesel gave us license to think, act, and play big.

The way that Shaq felt free to use his humor and his big-man swagger was invigorating. I'll never forget the Miami masses who turned out to welcome him to our city and how he stood on a stage promising to bring a championship to the Heat, and after not getting enough of a roar, repeating, "Do you hear me, Miami?"

Wow! That promise worked for me.

Shaq also helped open up my eyes to another side of the NBA— to the obvious and more hidden opportunities in endorsements, of course, as well as to the concept of being not just an athlete but also a brand, an entertainer, and a public figure with the privilege of using those fifteen minutes of fame to do some good. In the process, he encouraged me to allow my authentic personality to get out there more. Yeah, I was the real quiet, shy guy. But Shaq kept pointing out that I had style and charisma and a creative side with pretty good instincts.

Hank Thomas—who would remain based in Chicago but eventually move to the sports division of Creative Artists Agency with his stable of NBA and European players—started hearing a certain buzz about me early in the season after Shaq's arrival. Endorsement deals were floated, the talk-show circuit beckoned. A whirlwind awaited. Hank had a plan. He said, "Let's be strategic and not accept everything."

I embraced that approach completely. It's easy to become overexposed as the new kid on the block or be aligned with products that don't really make sense. Hank wasn't in a rush and neither was I. The approach was golden, as only time would tell. In terms of publicity, my story as a young father drew a lot of interest from the media, as did some of the elements of my journey in overcoming the odds.

However, during these years, I rarely talked about childhood or the more traumatic aspects of my story. Those, too, became compartmentalized. Maybe the reasoning was, you know, hey, if I'm only at base camp preparing to scale Mount Everest, no way do I want to think about being back in the valley, no way do I want to carry that with me.

At twenty-two years old, going on twenty-three, I wasn't ready to bare my chest and show the scars. Instead, I wanted to savor the blessing that my mother was rebuilding a life, a purposeful life; that my sister could finish her degree in education; and that my dad was beginning to look at making a new plan for himself. The pleasure of being able to share my adventures with the fellas, or I should say the "Flash Crew"—my brothers Demetrius and Donny, my cousin Wug, and my two best friends, Vinny and Marcus—was another blessing we could celebrate, even if we didn't see each other as often as I'd like. Marcus actually moved to Miami shortly after I did. None of my close family and friends ever needed to remind me where I came from. We all came from the same place, after all, and now they could be part of the trek up, too.

I started to have a sense of momentum but still had no concept of how much was going to change over the course of this second season. Hank did, however. That fall of 2004, he decided to add someone to his team who was based in Miami and who could coordinate the various off-the-court activities that were being added to my plate.

In all honesty, I didn't think that having a "go-to" was really needed at the time. Since I wasn't that big of a player yet, I wondered if we weren't getting ahead of ourselves. Obviously, I didn't know the big picture or how radically the tempo of life and work can change.

As we put the word out, the first name that came up as a possibility was Carmen Green-Wilson. A veteran in the industry, she had gone from the Heat organization to work for Nike and manage their athletes. Carmen was also married to Ric Wilson, who was at Converse and was instrumental in bringing me on board with them. But since she wasn't available, Carmen recommended Lisa Joseph, a young woman who had been working with Alonzo Mourning. (As fate would have it, Zo would end up returning to the Heat at the end of our 2004–2005 regular season.)

Here's the "what a small world" piece of this story. Hank Thomas remembered Lisa Joseph from some years earlier. With a background in PR and communications, she had graduated from the University of Miami and had earned an internship at the Heat back in 1997–98, when the team was on fire. Pat Riley had come to South Florida to build a championship team and guys like Zo and Tim Hardaway were making Heat basketball must-see TV—with an epic rivalry against the Knicks that was burning up the airwaves, too. As Hardaway's agent, Hank was in Miami frequently and crossed paths with Lisa at the time.

When her name came up now as a candidate, Hank remembered liking her cool-under-pressure attitude and arranged to interview her. On paper, she sounded impressive. About twenty-eight years old, Lisa had been overseeing the day-to-day of activities of Alonzo Mourning Charities, Zo's foundation, which included a youth center in Overtown, one of the poorest neighborhoods in Miami. Her main focus had been running the development and fund-raising programs for the youth center, raising millions while serving the greater community with vital services, and also doing publicity for Zo.

Alonzo had actually left Miami to go play for the New Jersey Nets the same year that I arrived, so Lisa wasn't very familiar with me. "Well," she would recall later, "I knew you wore number three." Other than that, before she went to meet Hank, Lisa had to Google me and print out my bio. Hank discussed the responsibilities entailed in the job and felt she could easily handle them.

That was more or less the rundown he gave me before I interviewed her. If Hank approved, I was ready to say, "Let's go with her." But I went ahead with the interview, as I often joke, just to make sure she wasn't crazy!

When we met at Perricone's in Miami, I could tell Lisa was not just cool and someone who could clearly keep things on an even keel; she was also extremely smart, a strong woman like the kind I was raised by, tough, no-nonsense, and with a great heart. And important to me, she had an awesome sense of humor.

However, Lisa wasn't sure that she wanted the position. Mulling it over with her friends and family, she famously insisted, "I'm not going to quit my day job over a rookie after nearly seven years with Alonzo's foundation!"

Meanwhile, I went with my gut and told Hank to cancel the other appointments he had lined up. I knew she and I would click.

So Hank proposed to Lisa that she work for me part-time and continue her work for Alonzo. Lisa agreed and came aboard just in time to be part of an explosive season for me and the Heat. As my right-hand person, she helped coordinate my activities in the areas of business and philanthropy. Soon enough, her part-time job was more than full time, but because of her loyalty to Alonzo and her commitment to the important work of his youth center, she just kept juggling these different responsibilities—for another six years.

Lisa helped in ways that I couldn't have imagined at the start. As my mouthpiece when dealing with everyone from the press to brand partners, she could be assertive when I needed to be relaxed. We had a kind of brother-sister relationship from the start, though in terms of handling logistics, you might call it good cop–bad cop. I could trust her to level with me, even when it meant taking me to task on something I could have handled better. That became a key to my staying grounded as the heady days approached.

Early on, Lisa took over my calendar and became the point of contact for anyone trying to get in touch with me. Siohvaughn saw many of the areas of responsibility she used to handle now go to someone else.

At first, a problem arose, as my wife tried to persuade Hank that Lisa wasn't needed.

In her professional way, Lisa was able to handle the fact that she was seen as a threat. At times, Von did value Lisa's ability to get things done and would lean on her for advice on navigating all things Miami—what was then still a new world to us. But that was as close as they got.

The question of a financial adviser came up again and this time I insisted we bring someone in to review our accounts. Siohvaughn finally agreed but then when that particular adviser expressed concern about some numbers not being right, she insisted we fire him. Fine, I thought, we'd get someone new. But somehow nobody was good enough. I tended to see Von's points when she brought them up. She could be very convincing.

Meanwhile, thanks to the vision and planning of Hank Thomas and the day-to-day handling of the details by Lisa Joseph, I could focus on the demands of the season in front of us. From the beginning, the chemistry of the team was unbelievable, not just between Shaq and myself, but with everyone playing well and with a confidence that energized me even more. After winning several games early in the season, we fell into the normal rhythm with highs and lows. Then something different began to happen right about December. It was like there was something in the water—or in our bottled sports beverages, to be more precise. During that month we scored fourteen consecutive victories, a Miami Heat record. That month I was named NBA Player of the Month and Stan Van Gundy was named Coach of the Month.

And from there we kept on soaring higher on into the new year. Everyone on the team, from players, coaching staff, to front office, to our fans, started to feel the ascent. Suddenly, the idea that we could win a championship sooner rather than later was looking doable. Why not? As in—when you're hot you're hot!

Besides the good news that after being traded to Toronto from the Nets, Alonzo Mourning was coming back to the Heat, I had also enjoyed the honor of being elected as an all-star, for the first time, and went to Denver for the All-Star Game, coming off the bench to help contribute to the East's decisive 125–115 win over the West. Slowly the league was beginning to pay attention.

By April 2005, at the end of the regular season, the Miami Heat was not the same team we had been six months earlier. With 59 wins and 23 losses for the season, surpassed only once before by our franchise, we had the best record in the Eastern Conference. As the first seed, we could sense the basketball gods smiling down on us with a first-round matchup against the New Jersey Nets, which we felt played to our strengths.

But in taking a page out of lessons from the past, I remembered how Kentucky made their mistake in not taking Marquette seriously. That memory helped in game one of this first round when we allowed New Jersey to get ahead of us early in the game. We responded, went hard, took the lead, and never lost it. Before long, the shooting contest on the floor was taking place between me and my teammate, Damon Jones, who scored 30 to my 32, as both of us wound up with 67 percent shooting from the field.

In the second game of the series, the Nets' plan to contain Shaq worked and he scored only 14 points. They didn't plan for Zo, however, whose gifts, including nine rebounds, kept on giving—right along with his 21 points. We were now winning the first round of the series 2–0 but there was no doubt that New Jersey was poised to adapt with new firepower in the next game. Sure enough, Jason Kidd was in warrior mode and went on to record a triple double for the Nets. After not one but two overtimes, and final-stretch prowess from the Heat, including clutch plays from Udonis and Alonzo, we went home with the win.

The next game, obviously, had to be New Jersey's fight for its life but ours to shut the series down and move up the mountain. Between my 34 points and 9 assists, Eddie Jones's 21 points, and Shaq's second-half dominance, along with every Heat baller, we got out the broom—

winning the game by 13 points and sweeping the series four games to nuthin.'

We were hoopin' now, on our way.

The next round of the playoffs pitted us against the Washington Wizards and threatened to be much tougher. Then again, the first game of the series gave us hope that the well-oiled machine that we had become could keep on chugging. After being knocked out in the second round the previous year by the Pacers, however, I refused to take anything for granted. Even when we won the first game by a lop-sided 105–86 margin, I knew that, just like when scaling the heights in any treacherous climb, the weather can change drastically and quickly.

The fact is that when you're playing at playoff ferocity, there's an even greater potential for injuries that can stop even the best team. True to my fears, though we pulled off a win in the next game—which included great performances from Eddie Jones and Damon Jones, plus 31 points from me, as well as a postseason record of 15 assists—Shaq was injured with a deep thigh bruise that would prevent him from playing in game three. Worried as I was, we adapted successfully, with large credit going to Zo, who stepped in for Shaq, and to Udonis, who gave us 12 points and 12 rebounds.

So we were up 3–0 in the series and in game four, the Wizards were in do-or-die mode; we had the chance for a sweep again. At halftime, we were down by four points and had to make a familiar mental adjustment in the locker room about leaving everything we had on the line for the second half. With that thinking, I just went Flash, living up to my nickname and spurring the Heat to score 40 points in the third quarter alone, a record high for our franchise; 22 of those points were mine, also a Heat record. For the game, I delivered a postseason career high of 42 points. But if not for a three-pointer from Eddie Jones in the final seconds of the game and Zo's block of what might have been a game-winning shot from the Wizards, we might have not left there as we did—victors and moving on to the Eastern Conference playoffs!

As I learned so well at this next stage of NBA championship play-offs, each of the four rounds that must be played to get to the top is a season unto itself. Until you've been there, there's not much else that can really prepare you for the sheer physical and mental demands that invariably begin to weigh you down and wear you down. You live almost nonstop in the zone, from game to game, practice to practice, city to city. You sleep, you eat, you guard against any distractions, good or bad. It's a crazy marathon made up of forty-eight-plus-minute out-of-body sprints along the way that can make or break you and your team. At every pinnacle, you literally can't rest on any laurels or you will fall.

Everything that's come before, once again, is only backstory.

Such was definitely the case for the opening of the 2005 Eastern Conference title series—the Miami Heat versus the Detroit Pistons, defending NBA champions. All bets were off. As a new team built to win, we had astonished everyone by coming this far in one season. Shaq never promised he'd bring home a championship as quickly as we were moving. But now we were here at this third round, coming into the playoffs as first seed and then sweeping not one but two earlier rounds, and we were feeling the mojo, amping up to go for it all. The major question for the skeptics was whether we really had what it would take to overcome that which we lacked: experience.

The veteran Detroit Pistons had proven to be a nemesis for many a franchise. They had been to the top before, including just the year before, with more or less the same lineup. How important was that experience? Well, judging by the first game, it was critical. In spite of the fact that Shaq was back and had a great game, I had one of my poorest showings to that time in the NBA, and as a team we fell badly behind in the last five minutes of the game.

Down 0–1 in the series, the wake-up call provided plenty of incentive to adjust in the next game. Earlier in the season, after a game against Seattle in which I clashed with Ray Allen and didn't deliver for the team, Coach Van Gundy had some choice words for me the next day at practice. He began by drawing a star on the board and then pointed at me, saying, "So that's our problem, you think you're a fucking star now."

He didn't have to say anything else. I brought that memory into our second game against the Pistons and redeemed myself from the previous game's performance with forty points. The Heat won the game, tying up the series 1–1. Buoyed by that success, we returned for the next game and hooped our way to victory with everyone contributing, as if we'd erased all memory of the first-game loss.

Up 2–1 for the series, we had to feel better than ever about the wave we were riding, although the game reflected the combined efforts of a Detroit team that was firing on all—well, you know the rest. And yep, the Pistons ruled, whuppin' us by ten points.

On June 2, we played game five as the champions we believed we were—with everyone on the Heat cranking up the energy and delivering. The great news was that we won by a dozen points to lead the series 3–2. The terrible news for me was that with a little less than five minutes to go in the third quarter, I'd gone up for a jump shot and let go of the ball, nothing out of the ordinary, but to my horror suddenly felt a red-hot flame of pain sear across my rib area.

For a minute or so, I ignored the abdominal strain and soldiered on. Mind over muscle? Oh, yeah. That's what you do up here in rarefied air. You keep going. That's what I'd been doing so far, in fact, playing with sinusitis, flulike symptoms, and a knee strain. But as the pain began to intensify, radiating across my core and whole torso, I couldn't just push on, because any effort at shooting the ball was going nowhere. With the crucial fourth quarter still to play, I was taken out of the game. The Heat forged on, led by Shaq, and we won.

Injuries, unfortunately, weren't new for me. But this was the first time I'd ever faced the possibility of not playing in a playoff game—when we were so close to going to the fourth and final round—and I was sick over it. The team doctors and coaches went back and forth over my eligibility to play on June 4 in game six. Finally, the decision was made to sit me out and I watched from the bench feeling helpless as the Pistons defeated us 91–66.

So on June 6, with the series tied 3–3, and though I wasn't back 100 percent, the doctors cleared me to play in game seven. During the first two quarters, we played come-from-behind basketball, closing the gap to within five points by the half. For the third quarter, I put on blinders, seeing the basket and the remaining minutes as the only obstacles standing between us and moving on to our final push for the championship. Even though I had helped us capture the lead going into the fourth quarter, much of my stock-in-trade—the ability to take over a game at crunch time—had been shut down, not by the Pistons, but by the injury. With three minutes to go in the game, our slight lead eroded and the clock, showing no mercy, ran out.

In the locker room after the game, Shaquille O'Neal spoke to reporters about the loss of the game and the series, mourning them like you would a death and talking about how the postseason had been allowed to slip through our fingers.

Of course, in the wake of a heartbreaker like that, you second-guess everything that happened, developing all kinds of questions about what you could have or should have done differently, revisiting decisions and asking how they might have played out if you did x or had tried y. For me there were echoes in this experience of getting stopped at the Final Four by Kansas. I tried to take away that same feeling of thinking that now that we knew the rigor of the heights, that knowledge could be power. In terms of conditioning and training, there was more work to be done.

The lesson was not easy to swallow. Nor was the other eye-opener from this season: that even when it seems that all the planets have aligned in your favor, and you are well on your way up the mountain, you are not assured of anything.

Hard as these truths were to accept, they were my answer to everyone who had predicted the outcome of this first attempt to go all the way. How so? Because I knew without question that we'd be coming back and going further. Soon.

AFTER SUCH AN EXPEDITION, YOU TEND TO RETURN TO CIVILian life, as you come to think of it, craving comfort and calm and no more pressure for a little while. All of that was there for me in the company of three-and-a-half-year-old Zaire Wade. The sun rose and set on that child for me. Everyone knew it. But because of the summer schedule, shortly after the season was over, Siohvaughn took him with her to Chicago to spend time with her family and friends.

Part of the reasoning for that was because summers were busy for me with photo shoots, commercials, charity work, and various exhibition games, all part of what I did for a living. Since she didn't want to hang around Miami during the hottest time of the year, either, I understood her position.

That is, until I was doing a photo shoot in Los Angeles and an incident occurred, which involved Siohvaughn getting jealous, as I understood it, and sending a message to Lisa Joseph that she was on her way back to Miami to slash my tires and bash in my car windows. Feeling like this was not an idle threat, I flew back home to try to stop her—too late. When I arrived in Miami, Udonis Haslem picked me up at the airport and we raced over to the house to find that the damage had been done.

At first, I didn't think we could get past this. I'd seen instances before of what I perceived to be anger issues and a volatile personality. But more and more I seemed to be the target of her resentment, which resulted in things in the house getting broken, my trophies and shoes and things being given away, and my clothes having holes cut in them or being ruined by bleach. She would deny doing these things or even being mad at me. But she also couldn't say who or what was causing all of this.

Other reports weren't as alarming as upsetting. When I wanted to fly some of the fellas in for a visit, I got the impression that she wanted to make sure that Lisa would book their tickets with connections, almost as if she wanted them preferably in cargo. Instead of sending a Town Car to pick them up, the implication was that she wanted them to have a van without windows pick them up. Later on, she would go on sprees, flying her girlfriends into town, booking them into fancy hotel suites and then paying for spa services at ridiculous expense.

The tire-slashing incident was a symbol for her being mad and wanting, as the expression goes, to hurt me where it hurt: in my pocket. As in financially.

Every time I'd get to the place of thinking *This is it, I'm going to have to file for divorce,* I'd lose it and end up crying because of the thought of being separated from Zaire. I didn't want him to have to grow up being shuttled between homes. That was the life I was trying to protect him from. Just like I was going to find a way to support us, I believed I was going to find a way to fix us.

The money thing I was sure we could handle. We were married, two halves of one whole, and I couldn't distrust her as my wife. But for my peace of mind, I insisted we bring in a financial adviser who could help us get control of our spending. Soon afterward the guy came to both of us and said, "There is a lot of money that is being moved around that I don't understand." When he mentioned the amounts, I was in shock. Could we be spending that much?

She denied that could even be possible and as soon as the adviser left she got into my head and once again convinced me that this was how people lost money: by having outsiders come in and make such accusations. At the time, her ability to turn my thinking around, what I now know was a kind of brainwashing, convinced me to fire him the next day.

But as the marriage deteriorated, with the summer of 2005 coming to an end, I asked Hank Thomas and Lisa Joseph to bring in a financial adviser who could get to the bottom of what had been happening and make sure that I had better access to my money.

Lisa and I met at a Chili's restaurant not far from the arena. With paperwork from the bank in her hand, she sat down with a sigh, saying, "We need to talk."

She, Hank, and the new adviser had confirmed that a large sum of money had been moved out of our accounts. The numbers in black and white on the page couldn't be contradicted. After all that time I'd been saying, "My wife handles the money, I shoot baskets," I finally realized that in a way she had put that attitude in my head so I wouldn't question her.

I was sick. Where was the trust? Our money was for us and Zaire. Fighting back tears, I was angry at myself more than anything. What could I do? By this point, Siohvaughn and Zaire were back in Miami. But she and I were already bringing up the possibility of splitting up. I didn't want that. Except—how could I get past this? I was beside myself.

Just then a young man came over to our table and in the most polite, excited voice asked for an autograph. As I wrote my name on the piece of paper he gave me, the young man was so thankful and happy. I realized he couldn't have imagined that someone in my position could be sitting there having a really rough day. A lot of folks think that every day must be an amazing one if you've reached a certain level of stardom and success—as if you're not even human.

"He has no idea," I remember saying to Lisa, thinking back to a time when I might have thought the same thing. This wasn't how things were supposed to be.

Then I told Lisa, "I'm calling my mom. We need to fly her down here. Have her bring her Bible."

If talk wasn't getting us closer, maybe the spiritual path, the place where we began in making our commitment to get married, would steer us back to where we needed to be.

When Mom arrived, I went over to the house and she had me get Von on the phone, trying to help us establish some calm. Before long, Von and I were yelling and unloading resentment that had been stored up a long time. In the middle of my loud phone call, the doorbell rang. It was Lisa Joseph, whom my mother ushered upstairs, asking her, "Do you pray?"

Lisa is very spiritual but also private. She said, "Yes, but usually by myself."

Mom could be heard to say, "Well we gonna pray today!"

So they were upstairs praying loudly and downstairs I was on the telephone fighting even more loudly.

Drama-trauma. That's a phrase I didn't know at the time but would later.

Eventually we did calm down. And prayer did help. Mom agreed to work with us and see where that went. Suddenly, Siohvaughn, who had not been that connected to my family, did look to my mother to help us salvage our marriage.

Around this time we happened to have a long-scheduled meeting with Hank and Lisa to discuss setting up a will. We didn't have one and needed to talk first before sitting down with an attorney to draw it up. Since we weren't really speaking at the time, Hank just finally said, "We need to talk about what's happening with you two."

Going beyond the call of duty, Hank and Lisa all of a sudden found themselves trying to give us marriage counseling. One of Siohvaughn's complaints was that I wasn't home enough. She admitted that she wasn't feeling great about herself and her self-image. Those kinds of insecurities are easy to have in the splashy world of South Beach and I tried to be reassuring, telling her that she was beautiful, a wonderful mother to our son, and a really good cook. Without a doubt, I thought we could both work on our communication. And the bottom line for me was that I wanted to keep our family together. Zaire meant more to me than anything in the world. Whatever I had to do, I was willing to make the sacrifice.

The stubborn side of me believed, for better and worse, that you're not supposed to run at the first or second or third sign of trouble. You fight until you believe in your heart that you can't anymore. I was willing to give it more chances than I probably should have, and even logic couldn't change me.

Siohvaughn made it seem that she wanted that, too. The one idea that came up that appealed to both of us was to find that dream home we'd always talked about. That actually gave her an area to oversee and control and she threw herself into the task of finding and remodeling a home we purchased in a new, more exclusive neighborhood.

Were we happy? That was a question that wasn't in my capacity to answer. My duty was to keep proving that I could make a way in this world. Somehow I convinced myself that happiness should take a backseat to that.

The love that I hadn't forgotten we had shared was when we came together to welcome Zaire into the world. As time went on, I started to wonder if perhaps another child might bring back that sense of joint purpose. In a way that's what had happened with my parents, even though that hadn't in fact kept them together. I thought they had other issues, including a lack of financial security, that kept them from building a lasting marriage. But that was, again, naïve.

In the fall of 2005, the thought of divorce after three years still went against the plan I made long ago not to follow the negative examples that had been set for me. So I kept on those blinders and got ready for another climb up the mountain.

SO MUCH FOR BEST-LAID PLANS.

Once again when we returned after the off-season, Heat management had done a remix to achieve what they saw as the new edition of a team built to win. In what was the biggest trade in NBA history, given how many teams were involved, Miami brought in veteran superstars Gary Payton, Antoine Walker, James Posey, and Jason Williams.

Jokingly (but not completely), I initially commented to Hank and Lisa, "Are you kidding me? They've blown up the team that was one game away from the finals and brought in some old guys."

The season lacked the magic and flow of the previous year. It was just tough all around, let alone in contrast to that euphoric feeling we'd enjoyed in the wake of Shaq's arrival. We were up and down. Trying to get it together. With a record of eleven wins and ten losses, injuries (Shaq's) already incurred, I felt that we weren't much better than the average team.

Then, to throw in another wrench, or shake up the lackluster energy, the news hit that Coach Van Gundy was leaving to deal with personal concerns and Pat Riley was going to return to coaching duties. Say what? No one explained exactly the strategy or the thinking. But the major theme that Coach Riley wanted to emphasize with us at this point in the Heat's journey was the power of team. He introduced a phrase that he called "15 Strong," and then brought in this little bowl and gave each of us a card with names of our loved ones on it and philosophical statements that meant something to us as a team and individually. He wanted us to remember that this season was going to be about all fifteen of us on the team. "You are only as strong as your weakest link" was one of the statements he used. We weren't stars and bench. We were 15 Strong. Then Coach Riley covered up the little bowl with some kind of cloth and swore us to secrecy about its contents. Immediately, the press caught wind of this strange bowl in the Heat locker room but we said nothing.

We improved overall in the next weeks, although we'd lost that sense of mission that had reverberated across Miami when Shaq promised to bring the championship home. We were no longer believers in ourselves—especially in our contests against the kinds of teams we might be facing if we did make it past the conference title and into the national playoffs. Teams like the Spurs and the Suns rolled over us and Dallas beat us by a humiliating thirty-six points.

For the rest of my life, I will never forget Coach Riley standing in front of the team after the bloodbath by the Mavericks and how he seemed to be speaking to each one of us individually and all of us together. He pointed out all the talent within our ranks. But the one thing he was beginning to question was whether we had heart. For the answer, he asked us to look deep within ourselves.

I couldn't answer for anyone but myself. There was never a question for me about my heart or lack thereof. And to prove it, come the next game, which so happened to be against the Detroit Pistons—our very nemesis that had stolen our championship dreams in the game seven loss of the Eastern Conference Finals—I found my answer in the last quarter and took it out on them. Whether Pat Riley had decided the time had come to test my leadership, he would never say. But watching the Pistons increase their lead over us, the switch flipped and I went Super Flash, pulling my teammates with me until we had scored seventeen unanswered points to win the game. That was my answer as far as the heart that we all had in us. We were 15 Strong.

That game proved to be a rite of passage for me. Kind of like being handed a new sword to wield, I had found something that was more powerful than I maybe knew how to handle yet. But I was ready to learn.

From that game on, the made-to-order team found its heart and began to click. Pat brought in a bigger bowl with a bigger tablecloth to cover it. He filled it with more cards that mattered to us, reminding us who and what we were playing for. As if overnight, we began to play like a team and then began benefiting from the leadership of the new "old guys"—whose veteran expertise was the factor needed to balance those of us "young" guys who'd been on the journey as a team the year before. Surprise, surprise, we finished the regular season as the second seed in our conference, with a 52–30 record.

At that point, going into the postseason, in addition to our heart we found something else to connect us: each of us *wanted* to win a championship. None of our veteran superstars had been to the top before. And so, behind that unifying desire, we were transformed. Clearly we knew we had talent, but it didn't gel during the regular season. We had hoped we would get it together and had struggled to get there. But when it came together and was about to unfold, wow, it was a beautiful thing!

Pretty soon the big bowl became a huge vat with a blanket wrapped over it to keep anyone from snooping. Fifteen Strong was only for us.

One of the changes in planning for our win this time by Pat Riley was to limit Shaq's time on the court to keep him healthy—since injuries had cursed us before. Critics wondered why Shaquille would agree to do that when it could hurt his stats.

Famously, Shaq responded, "Stats don't matter. I care about winning, not stats. If I score zero points and we win, I'm happy."

His vision on that subject would stay with me and impact future decisions for myself.

In the meantime, the first round of the wild ride had begun. We were pitted against the Chicago Bulls—which we took in six games, winning 4–2. With greatness from the veterans who upped their game and showed why they'd been brought in, those of us who'd been to the playoffs the year before could elevate from where we'd been the last time around. There was plenty of drama in the Chicago series—including one miserable loss caused when we got into foul trouble and a hip contusion that threatened to keep me on the bench before I rallied enough to return to the game. Yet in that crazy mix, playing against the hometown team, I was having so much fun!

Our team's talent continued to mesh in the second round, when we met up with the New Jersey Nets, who hadn't forgotten the previous year's sweep. In game one they said as much by beating us badly. In our house, no less. But from then on, we were unstoppable, ballin' all the way through the next four games, cruising to a 4–1 victory for the series. Besides the leadership from Shaq and memorable contributions from Alonzo and Udonis, along with tremendous scoring from our newer additions, a highlight for me came in game five at home when I sealed the one-point game win and the series by stealing an inbound pass that could have otherwise let the Nets score and win—with nine-tenths of a second on the clock.

Back again at the Eastern Conference Finals, one year later, we faced a familiar foe. Guess who? Yep, the Pistons—who after beating us had gone on to lose the 2005 championship to the Spurs—and might have hoped that they'd be able to put us away quickly so they could go back and reclaim the throne they'd won in 2004. Well, obviously, we had different ideas that were spelled out in game one in Detroit—a Miami win! In a rousing game that had contributions from everyone (compensating for the limited time that both Shaq and I had due to foul trouble), we won, 91–86. Sticking with what had worked, we played game two in Detroit, with heavy lifting from Shaq and Antoine Walker, and a good game for me, but we lost, 92–88. In game three, we returned home to Miami, where the fans gave us extra octane for sure. I had 35 points for the game and a crucial block in the fourth quarter that added to the combined effort from the rest of the team—which delivered an eyebrow-raising 98–83 score. Leading the series 2–1, we rode a wave of enthusiasm into game four, again on home court, and with big plays from Shaq and Udonis, we went up one more game.

In the Eastern Conference Finals you always want to be in the position of leading 3–1 in the series going into game five. But this is, as they say, a slippery slope. As dangerous as it is for the team that faces elimination with every game and must win all three remaining games to survive, the threat of complacency or overconfidence is just as great. Not only that: since we didn't have home court advantage, we had to return to Detroit for that fifth game. And sure enough, we had ourselves handed a thirteen-point loss in front of a sellout crowd of blood-thirsty fans in Michigan.

The stage was thus set for game six, on June 2, 2006. Ghosts of the Eastern Conference battle of the past came back to haunt me when I went to bed the night before the game feeling sick as a dog. For the last year I had wondered what would have happened if I hadn't missed game six and returned less than 100 percent in game seven. The night before the game was brutal and in the morning when I awoke there was no improvement. In fact, I felt so lousy, I had to be rushed to the hospital. What made me feel worse was the prospect of not playing. The only way I could convince the doctors and the coaching staff to let me play was by agreeing to have my time in the game limited.

All I could hear was Shaq's voice echoing in my ears that we had let a championship slip through our fingers. At the game, however, my eyes and head still blurry from the flu symptoms, I watched Shaq and Jason Williams take over, along with Antoine Walker, who scored in the double digits, James Posey with game-changing rebounds, and Udonis Haslem with a key jumper. For my time on the floor, I was able to add 14 points and 10 assists, a double double—not too sorry for a man who had to talk his way out of the hospital earlier in the day. In the fourth quarter, we took a small lead and stretched it out mercilessly until, by the power invested in the clock, yes, yes, yes, we won the game by seventeen points.

We had done it! We had won the Eastern Conference title! We were on our way to the NBA Finals—to Mount Everest! For the first time in Miami Heat history, we were advancing to the fourth and final round of the playoffs, to battle for the championship.

And the strangest thing was that whatever had threatened to knock me on my ass and keep me out of that last game was instantly cured.

I HAVE A CONFESSION TO MAKE. IN MY LIFETIME, EVEN though I believe that life is bigger than basketball, I probably won't attempt to climb the real Everest. Nothing against heights. They don't scare me. But I don't love high-flying birds and I have a fear they'll swoop down and knock me over or remind me that their wings are real and mine aren't. Yeah, I know, it's weird. Blame it on scary stories and Hitchcock's *The Birds*, which I have been much too freaked out to watch.

That said, what I know of getting up into the rarefied air of the NBA Finals is that you win as a team—just like mountain climbers who are connected by that rope. If one falls, the others may go down, too. You hold each other up. You depend on each other and you know the others are depending on you.

There is less oxygen up in the heights of whatever you are climbing toward, or at least on that last ascent, because you have already crawled and scratched your way up to get to where you are and you are running off the air and fuel that you've been storing in your being since you ever dreamt this incredible dream. You're not always thinking when you need to be hyperfocused and every move matters.

Now, if that's true for you and the other members of your team, imagine that it's also true for your opponent, who is climbing with the same fury to get to the top. And only one team gets to reach it.

In the case of the Heat and the Dallas Mavericks, neither team had ever won the NBA championship before. So the thing that unified us as players earlier in the season in our desire to win was no longer the antigravity force that was working for us. We needed something more powerful, the proverbial fire in the belly, to take everything we had been doing and turn up the dial—several notches.

We were not the same team that the Mavs had embarrassed early in the regular season. They knew that. They weren't the same team, either, of course. They brimmed with game- and series-winning confidence, big, lean athletic ballers who looked like they felt damn fine to be opening the series with home court advantage as they stampeded onto their floor on June 8 for game one of the series in Dallas. Between Jason Terry, Dirk Nowitzki, Josh Howard, and Jerry Stackhouse and the rest of the Mavericks, they appeared to be ready to rumble.

So were we, obviously. But by the second half, the momentum swung in their favor, helped along by their bunch that killed ours. The 90–80 win for Dallas in game one wasn't disastrous. We left their arena resolved to adjust, shake off the loss, and come back to turn the tables on them in game two.

Instead, on June 11, still in Dallas, we got slammed even worse! Crushed by nightmarish proportions. Oh, yeah, the fourteen-point loss could have been worse. At one point we'd been losing by twenty-seven! No matter what we did, we couldn't catch up to bring us any closer than twelve points behind.

So we traveled back to Miami like we were the payload in a hearse. Knowing the importance of home court advantage, we had assumed we weren't going to win both games in Dallas. But we had planned on winning one of them. We were good enough to do that and we had allowed the Mavs to control both games.

We didn't want to think about how sharp the incline just got and how the oxygen was running low. We could only hope that being back in front of our fans on home court would level the playing field. Not that we needed to be reading statistics at this stage, but the track record for reviving and winning a series after losing the first two games of a playoff series wasn't at all heartening. Only two other teams had ever done that before. Uncharted territory? Almost.

Before tip-off of game three, on June 13 in Miami, I'm taking my moment to do my pregame ritual—three pull-ups heavenward through the basket, letting myself come up through the rim and see above it, marking this zone as my turf. I've got my three pieces of chewing gum ready and my three bottles of Gatorade. (Endorsement alert!) The patterns of the number three make me joyful, reminding me that this is, after all, game three, and this battle is far from over.

That's what I'm thinking. We're all alive and playing but the Dallas Mavericks have apparently decided they can sweep the series and will have all but the last few nails in the coffin after this game, with a 3–0 series advantage. Well, the first half is a struggle but we hang in. By the second half, that awful piercing pain in the gut starts to suggest that we aren't going to pull this out. Coach Riley wears a look of bewilderment, as if he doesn't know how to get us back to the moment of truth we had earlier in the season. Then I realize that we're allowing ourselves to be defined by a team that doesn't think we can beat them. In my brain a big red warning light turns on that makes me angry. Down by 13 points with only 6:15 to go, at the end of a timeout I say to no one and everyone, "I'm not going out like this."

Now, add to that anger a whole bunch of unspent currency of pent-up rage—the fear and loneliness of childhood, the hunger that lived with me daily, mixed with the pride that kept me from asking for food when it was there, the poverty and absent fathers and mothers, not passing my ACT, struggling to feed my son, I mean, all of it—and I went and took all of it out on the Dallas Mavericks.

The rest of my team felt that moment and brought their own fury into the game and with 9.3 seconds to go, when we were locked into a 95–95 tie, Gary Payton sank a basket to let us take a two-point lead. With 3.4 seconds left, Dallas had the ball and we fouled Nowitzki, giving him the chance to tie us up again. Dirk missed the second of his two free throws, putting the score at 97–96, with our razor-thin one-point lead. Then I went to the line to shoot two free throws and missed the second as well. Dallas had the last possession. With three-tenths of a second remaining, the Mavs took the ball down the court to in-bound it, hoping to get it in and tie the game, sending it into overtime, or win with a three-pointer. As soon as the inbound happened, I stole the ball right before the buzzer. We won game three, 98–96. Like Shaq said, stats don't matter if you don't win. For this game he had five critical assists and I had 42 points—15 of them in the fourth quarter—and 13 rebounds.

Game three turned out to be just as fortuitous and pivotal as I had imagined it might be. In game four, on June 15 in Miami, three of us—Shaq, James Posey, and I—each recorded a double double and everyone in our ranks soared as we fed off the love of the fans. We did unto the Mavs exactly as they had done unto us in game two, and won, 98–74.

But wait. Maybe you think that you know how this ends. Well, remember, we did not. The series now was tied up, 2–2. Once again all bets were off. Game five, played in Miami on June 18, left so many milestones for both of our teams and had so many twists and turns that everybody came out of the arena with whiplash.

We had been down by as much as 8 points at halftime and found ourselves trailing by that amount as we were finishing up the third quarter. A burst of effort gave us 23 points in the fourth quarter, 17 of which came from me, including a long bank shot that helped tie the game at 93 all and send the game into overtime. We went neck and neck until Gary Payton helped push the score up by one. Nowitzki answered with his own basket, giving Dallas the edge, 100–99—with 1.9 seconds left in overtime. Then I was fouled and made both free throws. We won, 101–100!

We traveled back to Dallas for game six, which took place on June 20. Now that we were up 3–2 in the series, the momentum had shifted to give us the edge. Theoretically, Dallas could use the same advantages that had given them wins for games one and two. But now that we had been in the trenches over the last five games, the odds were slightly better that we could win at least one of the two games and take the series.

We had a better plan than just going with slightly better odds. We went to win, to take the series in six games. Pat Riley announced he was only bringing one tie for the trip. I did the same and said so to reporters when I arrived in a cream-colored suit and walked to the locker room, telling them, "This is all I've got. I'm not packing anything else. This is our game seven." After that, I went to change, saying to some of the press standing by, "Hope to see you at the party later on."

That's what I mean about oxygen deprivation from playing in higher altitudes. Traveling with one suit was very risky. But in hindsight I think that the fearlessness of being willing to risk all to win all was where I'd been coming from. That thinking gave me the confidence to try to put my team on my shoulders—to get us back into the series when we had been counting ourselves out.

I did do that. But game six, however it played out, was going to be won by the best team—by whoever showed up to play. For most of the first half, the Mavericks held the lead. Then we went up with less than a minute before halftime when Posey made two free throws. In the second half, we never fell behind, even though we found ourselves tied more than once. But I knew the outcome would be in our favor. I've never played with a greater feeling of relaxation, or at least not in a playoff game. Yes, I found my shots and made them, 36 points' worth, yet there was no anxiety or fury. The expectation that we would be champions when the game was over made everything feel effortless. All fifteen players on the Heat contributed in some way. Udonis had 17 points and 10 rebounds and Antoine Walker scored 14 points and grabbed 11 rebounds. James Posey scored 6 points, including a three-pointer at a critical moment in the game, and made 5 rebounds. Alonzo Mourning will always be remembered for 5 blocks that were considered game-altering, as well as for 8 points and 6 rebounds. Shaq had 9 points and 12 rebounds, a team high, and Jason Williams had 7 assists, also a team high.

In the last seconds of the game, we were up 95–92, and when the Mavs missed their possible tying shot, and I realized that we had won the game, I grabbed the ball, heard the final buzzer, and threw the ball high in the air—something that I'd only ever fantasized doing.

The power of 15 Strong added to the most unforgettable celebrations for us as a team, at home and everywhere else. There is no way that I could have imagined any better party than the parades and fanfare and jubilation that lasted until the next season. That's a high you just don't want to come down from. Oh, and when the press finally gathered in the locker room to see what was in the bowl turned vat, they couldn't believe that no one had come close to guessing. Everyone was shocked. How could cards in a bowl with sayings and pictures on them fire up a team of guys so much? However it happened, they did. Pat Riley had orchestrated this, using his powers of unpredictability, which are part of his secret for success.

Certainly, for me, being awarded Finals MVP, after averaging

34.7 points per game and being given the trust of my coach, my team, and my fans, was humbling and more rewarding than even words can say, and definitely career altering, too—if not life altering. Winning MVP, after only three years in the NBA (the magic of number 3 again), shot me into the stratosphere like a rocket. I was suddenly on all kinds of magazine covers, on talk shows day and night, and had millions of dollars of new offers flooding in.

There's nothing like the view and the exhilaration of being at the top. Nothing. Even if eventually you have to come down to the ground and start planning the next expedition.

The 2006 NBA championship finally seemed to put to rest the question "Dwyane who?" But just to be sure, I made up some wristbands to remind everyone. Some said, "I ain't going out like that." The others read, "Any more doubters?" For a while, at least, there weren't many.

As rough as some of the patches had been on the way to the top, the lasting lesson was one that I would hold close. I knew now, as an adult, that even in the darkest hour there is still a reason to believe anything is possible.

Little did I know in those happy days after winning the championship how much I would need that lesson again—as much off the court as on it.

MID-NOVEMBER 2011
AT THE CONDO
MIAMI BEACH

THE LESSONS OF TEAM AND 15 STRONG HAVE BEEN WITH ME throughout my life, not just during the year of the 2006 championship. So it's no surprise that as the boys and I get ready for Thanksgiving and

Christmas, I'm thinking of creative ways—like Pat Riley—to motivate each of them individually and together.

Zaire, Zion, and Dada have been troopers from the start, willing to adjust, as long as they're given a heads-up. Children really are much more adaptive than we give them credit for.

The idea of having a family plan, much like a team, has been a helpful concept in our household. When one of us has an accomplishment we consider it a family win. When one of us is going through a tough time, we can all be there to boost each other's spirits.

And we all have our challenging days. The fact is that for children like mine who have had to deal with their parents' divorce and/or with parents who live in different places, there are going to be tough times and difficult conversations.

How to talk to kids about divorce? Honestly, of course, and also by being careful not to alienate them from the parent they will continue to love and need—no matter how mad or resentful you might feel toward that spouse.

I say this with all sincerity, for reasons I'm about to reveal.

CHAPTER TEN

OLYMPICS

EARLY MORNING
NOVEMBER 19, 2011
PORTLAND, OREGON

THE SOUND OF A POUNDING THUNDERSTORM WAKES ME UP IN my hotel in Portland.

My first thought is—where am I? The next is—can I please stay in bed and sleep a little longer?

Not a chance.

I'm expected early at Nike headquarters along with a handful of the other players who, like me, are represented by CAA. With the lockout dragging on, our agents decided to sponsor a training camp to make up for the inactivity that could lead to injuries down the road while getting us in shape for our December tour of charity exhibition games. CAA approached the Nike and Jordan brand executives who agreed for us to have our training there at the grown-up wonderland that Phil Knight and his team have created in nearby Beaverton—a world unto itself.

Ever since Michael Jordan honored me with an invitation to be the public face of his line at Nike, the Jordan brand, I've appreciated the opportunities to provide input about products and promotion. So while we're here, we're also going to be talking to designers, testing new products, and jumping back into some training that we're sorely missing as a result of the lockout. *Sore* being the operative word.

Yeah, the NBA lockout. As one of the lows that Lamar Odom had warned me about, this was one of those times for continuing to find the middle ground and not letting fears of missing an entire season overwhelm any of us. But, since that's now looking like a reality, my frustration is that, in my opinion, the players have been the only ones who have come to the table with real concessions. In these rainy early-morning hours, I'm not optimistic that the owners will come back with anything that would allow us to salvage the season.

Checking texts, e-mail, and twitter, I see that Associated Press writer Tim Reynolds, a sports journalist I greatly admire, has a piece about the tour and the lockout that quotes me.

"I'm sore," Wade said. "But that's why we set it up this way. We want to get into work mode. When we get into the tour, we want to play. We want to be equipped to do that. We don't want to just run up and down the court and jack up shots. We want to get into the things we need to do when it comes to strength, defense, all those things you usually do in training camp. So we're getting into that mindset."

There's been no shortage of exhibitions featuring NBA players during the lockout, which is now in its 21st week and has already led to the cancellation of more than 300 games roughly one-quarter of a full season. Talks broke off last week after players declined an offer that the NBA said would have raised salaries considerably, which apparently wasn't enough to convince player reps that it was the right deal.

Other media are running stories on the number of players actually leaving to go play overseas. The word on me is that I'm thinking about it seriously. Why? Because as I was quoted in a few sources: "I've missed a year of basketball in my life before. I'm not trying to miss another."

That's pretty much what's on the schedule after this training effort and our tour. Wow, I didn't think we would get down the road so far. But then again I should know better.

On the other hand, in the midst of this thunder right now in the early morning as I rouse myself from bed, I have to remember that there is always hope that what's right and just will eventually come to pass.

Beyond basketball, I know that's a big statement and I say it as a proud African American, who has grown up seeing so much injustice and senseless violence. The fight for justice and equality continues. But I have to believe in justice, as a faithful servant of God. That's what I've tried to be and will continue to be. That's a belief to fight for as a father and as a citizen.

Hope for justice? On a personal level, have I always felt that? Honestly, my preparation in life, feeling the unfairness, being scared all the time, worrying about people I loved, gotta say—the world I saw wasn't always just. And on another personal level as a veteran of a protracted divorce that continues as of this writing, at times I may have come close to giving up on what was just.

As my story has shown, over the years I've had to keep my faith in a positive outcome when there was little evidence to support my belief in such a possibility. After so many tests, I never expected that a divorce/custody battle could bring into question my convictions that justice for my kids would eventually prevail. But there was a time when I came close to giving up.

That was in the darkest days of the custody case, when new tests of faith were in front of me. If the toll had been only on me, I could have dealt with it, but not when people I hold dear were being put through pain. Was it shocking that a mother who loves her children would distance them from the same father she had once praised to the skies? It was. Was it my fault for believing that she would never alienate her children from their father, even if a divorce came to pass? It was.

My error was not understanding that people who feel wronged, justifiably or not, can talk themselves, or be talked, into making choices of retaliation or vengeance, which is not in their or their kids' best interests.

But, and I say this with no lack of forgiveness in my heart, I believe in the cardinal rule of breakups when there are children involved. That rule is simple: you have to make sure, no matter what, that the children know it's not their fault. To use them in any way to get back at the other parent or to make them responsible for fixing the problems of the marriage—well, that's not okay. It's not their job.

Looking back, I take full responsibility for being naïve. And I take responsibility for being, at age twenty-five, at a point in life of deciding once and for all to be selfish and for just wanting to be happy.

BY THE LAWS OF NATURE, WHAT GOES UP MUST COME DOWN.

That was the backstory to the Heat's 2006–2007 season. And there were other problems. We came back as the same team, of course, since we'd just won a championship. We were the same guys, yeah, but after spending the summer partying and riding the wave of accolades and adoration, we were out of shape. Now the guys who were already older were playing that way. Other teams came after us in the regular season and we weren't at all ready.

While that was happening with the Heat, the rest of my life had good news and bad. As for the good, these were heady, heady days.

To have gone from being the NBA draft underdog to being called the greatest player in the game by former skeptics—that was crazy! Awesome and crazy!

Of course, I knew there were going to be highs and lows. So I braced myself. Still, I had every reason to be ecstatic. Coming out of the 2005 playoffs, I had already been fortunate to have the top-selling basketball jersey, and those sales soared even more after I won Finals MVP in 2006; despite the Heat's sluggish next season, my jersey continued to be the top seller long into the following year. Another pinnacle in 2006 was being awarded the *Sports Illustrated* Sportsman of the Year Award; for me to receive that after only three seasons in the NBA was humbling and thrilling at the same time. Then there were developing business relationships with companies like T-Mobile and Pepperidge Farm, in addition to Converse and Gatorade, who made deals with me earlier. And others started swarming.

The endorsement opportunities that we sought were, as Hank had planned it, strategic. To give me room to grow, I didn't have to be on TV selling everything. Only products that I was passionate about and companies that were interested in building long-term relationships with me. This part of my career and the business lessons I was learning were rewarding for many reasons. Mainly I was being given opportunities to appreciate that my life was bigger than basketball. I liked the sense of fun and accessibility that marketers could tap in me. If I could inspire a new generation of D-Wades, using my story as the underdog who made it, that was keeping the promise that I'd made long ago not to forget kids like me.

Because my brand partners were investing so much in me, I believed in making an investment in their goals. In cultivating loyal relationships, I took what I learned from the court about 15 Strong and the importance of team in general and came up with the idea of a team for Brand Wade. Since I was the common link between the different partners, I hosted retreats and strategic planning meetings where they could all get to know each other, have fun, and bring together the best of all of our combined creative thinking for mutual success.

The Heat organization and my brand partners always were such a part of my life, sticking by me and letting me know they had my back. I wanted to honor that and the fact that they cared about my input and collaboration, treating me as far more than just another athlete promoting products. So it came naturally to me to treat them like family and connect them to each other.

When we began, most of the marketing executives said this was unheard-of. For me it made a great deal of sense. I wasn't just taking their check. Besides that, they were counting on me and my name. Over time, the Brand Wade retreats would become a highlight of my off-the-court career; I began to thrive wearing my business/ creative hat.

So all of that, in terms of basketball and career in general, continued to be on the up-and-up in a big way. For a minute, during all the celebrations and the thrilling whirlwind that came after the championship, the good times extended to my home life. Zaire at four and a half had a chance to take in the excitement with me. And Siohvaughn, seemingly in a good space now that we'd moved into our dream home, also joined in to savor the festivities and the fruits of my labors.

But that minute passed. Regaining the trust that had been lost for me the year before hadn't been easy. Then summer came and I was off to Japan for the World Games with Team USA. Whenever I called to check in with Siohvaughn, our conversations went instantly from all business to shouting matches and me being berated for everything and anything. After one too many of these talks, I realized we'd probably come to the point of no return. In my mind, nothing was working and maybe it never would. That left me to feel we could go one of two ways—either call it quits now or try to reclaim what it was we shared when Zaire was born and have another child. He was almost five years old and a brother or sister would make his life more meaningful and joyful. The one thing that Siohvaughn and I seemed to do well together as husband and wife was give love to our child—so maybe investing ourselves in that higher purpose would help us heal.

When Siohvaughn arrived in Japan to join me there, at first, she said, "Well, I don't know if we should do that. I don't want to be a single mom with two kids."

The more we talked about it, however, the more we saw the possibility of working on our marriage as part of the decision to have another child. That was to take the pressure off the idea that having a baby could fix us. We would fix us and be worthy of the son we already had and the child we hoped would be on the way.

Caught up in the romance of trying again, we conceived right away, as we learned back in Miami just as the season was getting under way. But we were already falling back into the same patterns that had been problematic before. Whatever the idea of working on our marriage and our communication had meant in theory, it didn't translate to reality. The thought nagged at me that we were more roommates than anything else. And every night when we went to bed, I became more and more aware of the gulf between us.

Literally.

In those days, I had this massive bed that had been custom made. In a normal-size bedroom it would have taken up the whole space. For me, a little under six and a half feet tall, this was designed as the height of cool and comfort. The bed was so big, though, that when she and I were both in it, the space dramatized how far apart we were. We had reached a time in our relationship that the distance was mutual—and that we wanted Zaire in the bed, in between us, as if to fill that gulf.

At the same time that I saw we weren't getting better, any thought of breaking up was out of the question now that we had committed to having another child. The responsibility was on me, I thought. As in the past, I saw our problems as my failure to make things better—that I wasn't trying hard enough.

By September, we were either arguing or I was being given the silent treatment. When I got a call from a friend who was in town briefly and wanted me to come over, hang out, and have a bite with him, I said yes. A chance to hang out and not be in the house for a few hours getting either ignored or yelled at? I was there!

When I came back later that night, our bedroom door was locked and, oh yeah, I got the message. Rather than have an argument and upset Zaire, I made sure that my bag had what I needed for the trip to Los Angeles the next day for my T-Mobile commercial shoot, and I went to sleep in the guestroom.

The next morning all hell broke loose, with Siohvaughn asking what girl I'd gone to see the night before. No matter how honestly I tried to offer explanations and tell her she could check out my story, the more furious she became, fussing and yelling at me, until I was so freaked out by her level of anger that I couldn't wait to leave. When my cousin Wug came to pick me up to go to the airport, she switched into silent mode, not talking to me or looking at me. Needing to get out of the house without a confrontation, I left Wug in the other room and, walking on eggshells, went to grab my bag to leave. Siohvaughn exploded again, accusing me once more of being out with another woman. All I wanted to do was get out of the house. But before I could leave, she went even more ballistic, as she leapt across the room lunging and swinging her fists at me.

I'm telling her to stop while dodging blows, covering up my face, as she goes for what's some kind of uppercut, misses, and hits her own face.

Next thing I know, she's saying that I hit her when, in fact, I hadn't touched her and never in a million years would I have hit her.

All of sudden, the stuff that I'd been in denial about became very real. How was I going to fix this shit?

Wug and I headed to the airport as I tried to chill for a minute, glad to be out of the tension. My cell rang and I picked up to hear Lisa Joseph with one of her usual "we need to talk" greetings, which signified she had something of concern to discuss.

Lisa dove right in. "I got a call from Siohvaughn and she said that you hit her and she has pictures. I hate to even bring it up, but what's this about?"

"What?" About to laugh, I told her what really happened. The scary part was how convincing the story must have sounded to Lisa. But there was more. Lisa then informed me that Von was threatening to send photos to Pat Riley to show him who I really was.

Again, I could have laughed but this was too painful.

At the airport where Wug and I were met by Lisa and Tragil, the three of them waited until we were on board the charter flight and then they expressed their serious concern. Of course, I was worried but I had seen Siohvaughn through a depression before and this reminded me of that.

After returning to Miami following the commercial shoot, my thinking was more along the lines of just weathering a bad storm, much like a bad season. Certainly as the pregnancy was confirmed and we got through the first trimester, I could see that the hormonal changes were intensifying Siohvaughn's anger issues. My guard was up, however.

What should have been amazing news for us to share, that we were going to have another baby, seemed overshadowed by how distant we were. The good memories we both had of our early days, when we got through arguments by laughing them off, were being wiped away.

Two overriding thoughts kept me from seeking legal advice about steps to officially end the marriage. First, there was my desire to be a family man and I had my sense of duty to set an example. That was big, right there in my hardwiring. Along with that was worrying how the perception would be, what the public and others would think and say—*Oh yeah, he got to the NBA and he decided to leave his high school sweetheart, just the typical pro athlete thing.* The story was more complicated, needless to say. But still.

Second, and more important, was concern for Zaire and the baby we were expecting. Even at five years old, Zaire made comments that showed he was afraid of divorce. However he came to those feelings, I refused to do anything to make him fearful. And I was the one who had pushed for a second child. My old refrain held on: I'ma find a way.

LIKE I SAID, WHAT GOES UP MUST COME DOWN. IF THE DETE-rioration of my marriage wasn't bad enough, just after the all-star break I dislocated my shoulder. Not just any dislocation but one of medical history's worst sports-related shoulder dislocations. With the constant threat of injuries that can be season-ending or even career-ending, I knew the range of choices. The options were (1) contemplate leaving the season for surgery or (2) do the rehab route, with the hope of playing again in time for the postseason while ultimately having surgery in the off-season. Going with the latter option, I missed a lot of games but managed to come back and contribute, helping to improve the Heat's record for the season.

We appeared to be poised for a comeback and, in defiance of predictions, got into the playoffs. But, lacking the chemistry of the previous season, we were swept in the first round by the Chicago Bulls. After an epic vault to the top of the Himalayas, this drop was epic, too. In the history of the Heat, we had never been swept 4–0 in the playoffs. Not since 1957 had a defending champion fallen that low the very next year.

Like L.O. said, highs and lows.

The new lessons from this season were not to be ignored. The biggest lesson was that each year is its own. Just because the right ingredients worked last year, they won't necessarily the next. Now I knew better, with my injuries, that anything can be here today and gone tomorrow—a rite of passage and a leap forward in my thinking, unlike my younger days of feeling immortal. Being only human—and realizing it—is always a lesson worth relearning. In turn, I began to reevaluate everything, with a lot of soul-searching about career and business and what I wanted out of life.

As much as getting swept in the first round is not a feeling I ever wanted to experience again, I never thought my days in the sun on the court were over. No one in my circle would have suggested that the various injuries I'd sustained up until now were going to derail my career forever. On the other hand, none of the surgeons who examined the shoulder (and the knee that had never healed) would come out and say they could make me like new again. The risks were high. I knew the stories of young phenoms having to retire following multiple surgeries after only a few years playing at the top of their game.

That said, after the loss in the playoffs, I went to bed, prayed, slept on it, and woke up in the morning with the decision to have the dual surgeries. Thankfully, I was blessed to have gifted surgeons. Even though Siohvaughn was getting close to her due date, she was very attentive while I was recovering from surgery, cooking for me in the days that followed, and standing by to make sure I was well fed. With faith, I had to believe that if I worked hard, as always, I could be ready for the next season without missing a step.

Once I came through surgery on both the shoulder and the knee, the reality of needing time for extensive rehab hit me. But I knew that for the long term the surgery had been the right thing to do and I wasn't worried. Part of this thinking, in that period, had to do with a new bright light that was shining in my world, too—young Master Zion Malachi Aramis Wade. The one and only. He burst onto the scene at 8:45 P.M. on May 29, 2007, in Chicago, where Siohvaughn and I had decided to be for the delivery so we could be closer to our families in welcoming Zion into the world.

Nobody could take away the joy of now having not one but two sons to call me Daddy. Added to that feeling of fulfillment was how excited Zaire was to have a baby brother. He wanted to know everything—how soon before Zion could talk, walk, and play with him? That lifted my heart so much because all I really wanted was for us all to be happy.

However, wishing and wanting do not always find their match in reality. When Siohvaughn first went to the hospital, accompanied by our friend Andrea, godmother to both our boys, I picked up the phone to hear my wife say not to rush—that she'd call me when the doctor said she was getting close. After I did get there and had a chance to meet our brand-new baby boy and fall in love with him, as the hour was getting late and everyone else was leaving, my wife said, "You don't have to stay the night."

Did she mean that because I shouldn't feel obligated or because I was still on the mend from my surgeries two weeks earlier and might be uncomfortable? Before I could ask or argue, Siohvaughn said, "It's fine. You can leave."

After I did go, in the car ride home I started to remember how different my role had been allowed to be when Zaire was born. With his birth, I'd driven up from Milwaukee after a big game for Marquette and had barely left their side for two days. Why was she pushing me out after Zion's arrival? The more I thought about it, the more I knew that there was no willing ourselves back to a better place.

What marriage was there to save?

That harsh reality wasn't going to keep me from being Daddy to our new son. The next morning, I drove to the hospital to pick up Von, Andrea, and baby Zion. He was as perfect as Zaire, just as alert if not more. I strapped him securely into his infant seat in the back and helped the ladies into their seats. Siohvaughn, understandably, was tired.

On the drive home, just as a car in front of me came to a sudden stop, I had to react quickly and come to a sudden stop, too. For a second my heart started pumping to think of the close call that had just occurred with baby Zion only a day old in the backseat. But fortunately I have good reflexes. Or so I thought. Not Siohvaughn. She went haywire, screaming about the sudden stop.

Just wanting her to be quiet, I didn't yell or say anything other than to please not scream, with our son having to hear that on his first day of life. Calm and cool, I pulled up and parked at our house, went back to pick up Zion, and carefully started inside, where we had done our preparations and had everything ready that a newborn could need. I was no more than ten steps from the car when I turned to see Siohvaughn jump out of the car and then run to the driver's seat and then speed away.

She didn't return for a couple of hours. When she did, she was nice and cheerful. Nothing should have shocked me but I was left with emotional whiplash.

For the next few months, I worked and traveled as needed for my summer commitments but tried to spend as much time with Zaire and baby Zion as possible. Siohvaughn was hot and cold. We had no big blowups but the end was near.

We weren't even good roommates helping to pass the time. There was no question: we were done.

In late July, I happened to be in Hank's office in Chicago when Lisa was in town. In the middle of discussing something else, I finally heard myself say, "Well, I guess I'm going to have to make the move."

My reason was not hard to explain. "I don't feel comfortable in my own home."

Since I was traveling for photo shoots and commercials over the next month or so, I didn't make any attempts to officially separate or move out. But I had a lot of time to think about what really mattered.

From as far back as I could remember, all I wanted to do was to be happy. Willie Mae Morris had told us well enough what was important: not to be no trouble, but to be good to others and find a space of happiness. Whatever wasn't working, I had seen Siohvaughn's problems getting worse but I couldn't figure them out; I knew I couldn't fix them. All I knew was that I wasn't happy.

After the struggles, overcoming so much, was I missing something on the happiness test? The injury and surgery that I'd been through were a reminder that nothing is promised. Nothing, that is, but death and taxes. And if life is so short and it can be taken away in the blink of an eye, I wanted to enjoy the present.

Maybe selfishly, I admit. At the time my feeling was that God gave me opportunities and He didn't give it all for me to be unhappy. If I couldn't be the person He wanted me to become, how was that living up to my promises? Facing hard truths, I didn't like the unhappy person I was turning out to be, a man who wasn't the way I had dreamed of one day becoming.

My decision was a huge relief. In the Olympic trials of life that come to each one of us, in some shape or form, I had to accept that not everyone is great at everything; I had to accept that I had failed at this marriage. Selfish or not, the truth set me free: I didn't want to be unhappy anymore.

There were still some conflicts in my mind that were clogging up how or when I was going to act on my decision. In August, when Siohvaughn and the boys moved back to Miami so that Zaire could get started in kindergarten, I stayed at Marcus's for a while rather than move back into our house. Every time I visited the boys, I avoided interacting with Siohvaughn.

In doing so, nothing changed my mind about us having a chance to stay married, even just for the sake of the kids. The timing was such that it would be better to split now rather than keep trying to hold on for my sons' sakes and become more unhappy and less of the father I was supposed to be. If this tough passage happened while Siohvaughn and I were still young, we could create our own dreams while still being loving parents to our boys. With the kids being young, rather than in adolescence when divorce would take a greater toll, they, too, would be better served.

Those were all my thoughts when I got myself a suite at the Four Seasons, still not ready to move my stuff out of our house. There was no point in making excuses or casting blame. This was a decision that was for me, not something that I expected my kids to ever understand. But at the same time, if I wasn't happy, I felt that the boys would also sense that and feel that something was not right. The clarity came for me from the realization that the unhappiness was going to affect them anyway, even if I was in the house.

Clearly, none of the process was easy. But the hard part, now behind me, was that I could at least be at peace with my decision to go find my happiness.

"I'M READY," I ANNOUNCED TO MY LAWYER, JIM PRITIKIN, IN his Chicago offices in September 2007.

When Hank Thomas met my request to find the best divorce and custody attorney he could for me, he was thoughtful in recommending someone like Jim, who had the sensitivity that he did.

In fact, as we talked about how to proceed, Jim wasn't convinced that I had fully made up my mind. Through the conversation, I admitted that a divorce would mean that I had failed—that I didn't try hard enough. Also, I explained, there were my promises in childhood to be different, to be there for my children at every step of their growth. Even though I knew the statistics, how one in every two marriages ends in divorce, I didn't want to be a statistic. A deep concern was that marriage in the black community had been on the decline for generations while the rates of divorce and out-of-wedlock births and children being raised in homes without two parents, dads in particular, were increasing. As I said to Jim, "I do *not* want to continue this generational curse."

His recommendation was that instead of filing for divorce or raising the issue of separation, I could sign a document called a praecipe and leave it as a legal placeholder, signifying the intention to file for divorce later. That would be important because this legal form would show that I was the first to file and would allow me to lock in a jurisdiction.

Even with that as a viable option, I couldn't bring myself to go forward. For the next two months I wavered. In my mind, I kept running down lists of new action steps I could take to salvage some kind of marriage, but without putting blame on either of us they all seemed too little too late.

With that in my thoughts, I went ahead and signed the praecipe in November. Nothing was announced. No one knew. Not yet. Before I could go forward with the next steps toward filing a petition for divorce or backing away, I did have a season of basketball to play.

"WE NEED TO TALK." LISA JOSEPH STARTED OFF A LUNCH meeting with me and Hank Thomas in the early spring of 2008 at Tempo's in Chicago.

If you didn't really know Lisa, her "We need to talk" would have sounded as the most matter-of-fact, no drama, no worry, everyday takin' care of business, no more chitchat kind of statement. But knowing her as I do—and as I did in that period—I braced myself.

The deal with Lisa is that over the nearly four years since she had come on board, just after my rookie year, she had proved there were few problems she couldn't handle on her own or with Hank. And so on that rare occasion when she couldn't address a thorny issue without my participation, I would hear those four words from her, "We need to talk."

Then again, I had so much trust in her and in Hank that there was no point in building up any more stress than what was already in the mix.

By mix, I should confess that in the grand sweep of highs and lows, the 2007–2008 season that had just ended was the subzero low. Forget what was happening with my marital problems. Basketball-wise, pretty much my take on it all was *Whoa, everything just sucks!*

That's saying a lot for me, because if there's growth to be gained and wisdom to be learned, I'll usually find that silver lining. No, this was just the sludge. One mistake of my own had been to come back to the game without being fully recovered from surgeries. The season hadn't begun well and Shaq wasn't so happy with the newer talent on the team. The veterans were gone and the Heat was in a necessary rebuilding stage. Seeing their struggles, I rushed the healing process to get out there and try to help. But things only went south. After Shaq was injured, he wound up being traded in the middle of the season.

The fans mourned the end-of-the D-Wade/Shaq-Diesel era, as did I, and I attempted to go it alone, playing hard but still impaired from injury and surgery until finally, in March 2008, the decision was made to shut me down so I could get healthy. A month later, Pat Riley, again without much explanation given for his change in thinking, had stepped down from coaching to focus on his role as president of the team. Riley had retired as the third-winningest coach in NBA history. Erik Spoelstra, the thirty-seven-year-old assistant coach for the Heat—who had begun as a video coordinator before rising up through the ranks of the coaching staff (and who worked with me on my shooting when I first arrived)—was catapulted to head coach for the remaining weeks of the season.

The atmosphere was like a morgue. We won fifteen games the entire season. Two years after winning a championship we won fifteen games! A low for the organization, it was pitiful. Worse than pitiful. When the Heat didn't make the playoffs, something I'd never experienced before, the low became all the more pronounced.

Given that fiasco and the new hurdles that were being thrown up to keep me from seeing the boys, I had some real heart-stomping days when I felt that despite everything I had nothing to show for myself. Walking around Miami brought more rude awakenings. There was a time when I had to go places incognito not to get mobbed, but it sure didn't seem like everybody was screaming my name anymore.

Wow, Lamar Odom had been more right than he could have ever guessed.

The stress over deciding whether to fully file for divorce was building. When Lisa began to go over the list of items we had to discuss at our lunch at Tempo's, I was relieved to hear that nothing about logistics with Siohvaughn was on the agenda. Instead, Hank explained that the main focus for our meeting was to discuss the profile that AP writer Tim Reynolds was going to be doing about my participation in the Olympics.

"Great," I said, exhaling, so thankful *that's* what we needed to talk about. "What are my travel dates?"

Hank and Lisa glanced at each other, like something was up. A hesitation followed. Seconds seemed to stretch into minutes.

Was there a problem? No, there couldn't be. I mean, I'd been a shoo-in since being co-captain of Team USA with LeBron James and Carmelo Anthony for the 2006 FIBA World Championships (FIBA essentially means International Basketball Federation). There'd never been a question. In fact, when USA Basketball turned the reins over to Jerry Colangelo for team selection before the Worlds, there had been much to-do about some top NBA players deciding not to play; when those of us like Kobe Bryant and I announced we would compete in 2006, we were asked to make a three-year commitment that would allow us to build back into a powerhouse capable of winning gold in Beijing.

The strategy for asking for our commitment was to prevent another fall from grace that Team USA had experienced in the early 2000s. The story in 2004 in Athens was that nine out of the twelve NBA superstars originally slated to go—who were on the Team USA that had qualified as first-place finishers in the 2003 FIBA Americas Championship—changed their minds about going to the Olympics. That opened the door for some of us younger players like Melo and Bron and me to be brought in at the last minute. Between inexperience and a lack of time to get up to speed, in the early games we had lost to teams like Puerto Rico and Lithuania. We fought back hard enough to win against the solid play of Australia and to give the undefeated Spain its first loss in the quarterfinal game—only to fall to Argentina in the semifinal match. We did revive to win against Lithuania in a game that earned us the bronze. Even so, Greece 2004 would rank from then on as one of the worst showings for Team USA in the Olympics. After the Dream Team of the 1990s, during the 2004 Olympics we'd been humiliated badly enough to be known as the Nightmare Team.

But that was all water under the bridge, and I'd already been getting mentally prepared to be part of what planners hoped would be called the Redeem Team in China.

Of course, in my thinking, there would never be a problem with me being on Team USA.

"Well," Lisa began after that moment of awkwardness passed, "we're not sure about the logistics yet." Her face told all. There was a problem.

She went on to say that a friend of hers who worked for one of the advertising sponsors for the Olympics had called with a heads-up. Apparently, in their marketing meeting while going over plans for Beijing, my name hadn't come up. From the sound of it, other names were being floated to fill my spot. Lisa, not easily rattled, had already been upset in hearing of photo shoots that had included Kobe, Melo, and LeBron but not me. When she followed up to see what the real facts were, she was told that, yeah, I wasn't a shoo-in. Worse, it didn't look good. Being practical, though, the point was that the tone needed to change for the profile with Tim Reynolds. Instead of the piece being about me absolutely going to China, the focus should be about how much I hoped to contribute to Team USA.

As Lisa broke the news, Hank Thomas studied me closely. In his expression was a combination of caring and concern over what Lisa had just conveyed. But as a father figure who knew the competitor in me so well, Hank also had this challenging glint in his eyes. He watched what must have been a reaction of complete shock on my face as it fell, with the wind being knocked out of me at the same time. And then, saying nothing, Hank locked into my eyes, as if to say, *So, Dwyane, what are you going to do about it?*

In that instant, I wasn't sure. Had the doubters really gotten to me?

When we left Tempo's and we started down the short walk to where I was staying, I remember telling Lisa, "You know, right now I wanna disappear and hide under a rock somewhere."

Frowning, she couldn't disguise her surprise at hearing me talk like that. Maybe I even surprised myself.

But in answer to Hank's question, one thing I could do, for starters, was to adapt on the fly and let Tim Reynolds know how excited I was about the possibility of going, rather than acting like a shoo-in.

That being said, I couldn't let the powers that be control my game, my destiny. A younger me might have. Whoever that guy was whose team had only won fifteen games all season, who had come back not fully recovered from surgery, I had to erase those question marks from the minds of the decision makers about whether I was of Olympic caliber. To do so, I had to shut everything down, strip away all distractions, and build my own fortress of solitude so I could focus and get healthy—physically and mentally. If I had to go and try out, I would, however much we all thought I shouldn't have had to do that.

Oh, and if that shock wasn't enough, there was another one that took place in Miami during this period when a call came in from Siohvaughn to inform me that she had just picked up and moved back to Chicago with the boys. Without telling anyone and without warning, she had pulled Zaire out of school before the end of the school year, packed up all their things, and left. She let me know that since it seemed we weren't going to be together anymore, there was no point in staying in Miami.

I knew then exactly what I had to do—to spend time with the boys regularly and to focus on my training. Assuming that I'd see my kids when I wasn't in the gym, I rented a condo in downtown Chicago, close to where I'd be working out. Strangely enough, even with all the changes in my home base over the years, this was my first time living alone. To get me healthy, my trainer, Tim Grover of Attack Athletics, who had worked wonders in training everyone from Michael Jordan to Kobe Bryant, among numerous other elite athletes, had said he would require six to eight weeks. That would be cutting it close for the tryout that would determine whether I would go to China to compete. But if I was going to have faith in anyone, now was the time to have it in myself.

MAY 2008 WAS A RELENTLESS ROLLER COASTER OF HIGHS and lows.

On a high note, one of the silver linings of this period, starting from the time that I was no longer living with Siohvaughn, was being given time to get much closer to my mom, my dad, and other family members who still loved me for the person that I was—in every season. During the last five years, I had been so focused on driving to the basket that I wasn't always aware of what was going on with my family. There was a blessing, without a doubt, in being reminded of how important those meaningful relationships really are—and, yet again, of how life was still bigger than basketball.

Dad, after going through his own contentious divorce, moved to Miami around this time. Before leaving Chicago he had started attending services at Mom's church—which she began in a tiny storefront with forty-seven members, not long after being ordained in January 2007—and he had been moved by her to examine how he had been living. Once Dad got settled into his new life in Florida, he decided to take more active steps toward his sobriety.

The miracle of Jolinda Wade continued to inspire not only our family but also a growing number of people who heard the power of her testimony. Indeed, that growing number could not fit into that small space where she had been preaching. In January 2008, in the middle of trying to fill out paperwork for loans to buy a medium-size space, Mom drove by a larger facility that was for sale. When Tragil paid a visit to practice at the American Airlines Arena in Miami and told me that Mom had found an ideal spot for her dream church that only needed a little TLC (like a lot of us!), I couldn't think of any gift more fitting for her. T.J. confirmed that Mom's testimony had started changing so many people's lives now that she was able to tell her story, offering her powerful message of hope.

In March, when the time came to fill out the paperwork for buying the building, Siohvaughn, then still in touch with Mom and involved with the church, agreed to sign off on the purchase.

My mother wouldn't have asked me for the help. That's not her. Throughout my success she was always so proud and grateful for the smallest things that I'd been able to do for her that I worried she would feel overwhelmed if I bought the church for her. But with the vision that she had for her following to grow and the ways she could serve the Chicago area community, Mom accepted my offer, only on the condition that I stand at her side for the ribbon cutting.

In mid-May, in front of a packed house of hundreds, dressed regally in purple, the same color she had chosen to paint the interior of the sanctuary, Pastor Jolinda Wade and Pastor Ladell Jones held their first service in the new home. Several NBA moms, including Magic Johnson's mother, were there to take part in the celebration. Between the press and the out-of-town guests and the regular congregants, the parking lot overflowed and latecomers had to park blocks away.

I spoke to the press ahead of time and summed up her story by saying, "I respect my mother so much, from the life that she used to live and to see her today in the life that she lives. I'm so proud of her. Everybody thinks I'm the miraculous story in the family. I think she is. I think what I've done means I've been very blessed, but she's been more than blessed. She's been anointed."

Tragil joined me to give praise for our mother and for the new church home. Only six years earlier, the family had gathered in their Sunday best to support our mom when she turned herself into the court. Here we were on a real Sunday to support our mother on what Mom described as "one of the highest of the highest moments in my life."

Tragil and I both shed tears of pure happiness. My sister commented, "All I can say: Hallelujah." The way she described the big move was that Mom and her following were coming from a "space to a place."

Pastor Wade then cut the ribbon. She declared, "Today is the crossover. We're in here today because of God's goodness and God chose to use the heart of my son to do this for us and he trusts the heart of his mama. Ain't that something?"

Everyone shouted, "Amen!" The festivities continued from there. How strange and great. In a life in which the basketball court had always been my sanctuary, now I could sit in a real sanctuary to feel the hand of grace.

In a month that was mostly tough for me, that day was a most loving reprieve. At the time, I especially needed my mother's wisdom and every family member's loving reminder of the power of faith.

When I first confronted the truth that there was no saving my marriage, I never expected my family to be dragged into it. They knew what was going on; they had been through some of the drama before; but I certainly didn't want to disrupt the relationship that Von had with them any more than I wanted to be separated from her mom, who was a grandmother to my children.

But as I saw it, from the moment Siohvaughn picked up and returned to Chicago with my sons, she had done all she could to make me seeing the boys difficult. The custody judgment would cite notes from the court-appointed expert about my ex's efforts to keep me from seeing the children in this separation stage before there had been a court-ordered visitation schedule. The expert expressed concern about Siohvaughn's willingness to foster a relationship between the boys and me, stating: "For a long period of time she made visitations challenging for Mr. Wade and the children beyond what could be explained on the basis of concern for the children's well-being." So the attempt to control my access to the boys ("in a bad way," as the expert put it) had been there even before there had been a filing for divorce.

Before that nightmare had come to pass, I continued to believe that soon enough we'd get past the anger that was coming out during this time. In hearing about divorces that others had been through, I expected that eventually we would find a way to communicate about arrangements that were in the best interest of our sons. But by the end of May, with no hint of cooperation in establishing a schedule, I finally filed a petition for divorce.

I went back and forth so many times. My sense of self, so connected to being a dad and a family man, was in question. That was the most self-conscious I've ever felt in my life. When I was leaving my hotel and going places on my own, it felt like people were glaring at me. In the end, though, that wasn't helping me see my boys.

Asking for joint custody, I looked to a court-ordered schedule to create a fair structure that would let my sons stay part of the time with me in Miami and part of the time with her in Chicago. Siohvaughn was ready and responded by countersuing for divorce and suing for sole custody. She would insist, as I understood it, that joint custody was not in the boys' interest and if I wanted to see them I could do so in Chicago—despite the fact that my work, the source of the income, required me to stay in Miami.

Just as I'd continue to be devoted to making sure my sons never had to want for anything, Siohvaughn knew she would be provided for. That ought to have been clear in the multiple settlement offers that unfortunately were rejected time and again.

None of it made sense. No doubt the psychology of doing anything to hurt someone at any cost was one textbook chapter I'd never studied in school.

Little did we know that this had been only a brief preview of what was waiting in the wings—in which I would be accused of unbelievable outrages. As in: total lies (that would later be discredited) that portrayed me as the most abusive husband and father, doing stuff like throwing her and the kids across the room, and on and on. This tactic was used to bring in allegations that weren't in the least true but were enough to raise questions that would lead to me being investigated by the Department of Children and Family Services. Not once but three times. One comment that came out of those interviews was from an expert who suggested the resources of parenting classes. Based on that recommendation, I did take an informative one-on-one parenting class so that I could learn more about being a better dad in general and a divorced father specifically.

But, in the meantime, even when the accusations of abuse were completely baseless, there on the record were those visits from child services that could raise questions for the custody judge. Later, the allegation would be made that I'd punched my own son in the face fifty-five times. He would be forced to tell that story, too, after being coached to say that it did happen, but only once. Who would punch a six- or seven-year-old—or a child of any age—in the face?

Before that insanity was unleashed, I turned the battle over to my lawyers and went forward with training to prove myself worthy for the Olympics. While I was in Chicago, I trusted that seeing my kids would be overseen by the court. My thought was, how much longer was I supposed to be punished? My heart was heavy for my boys to have to go through this. Surely, though, the worst of the storm would soon pass.

Not a chance. We hadn't seen anything yet.

WITH ONLY ME OUT ON THE FLOOR, I CREATED MY OWN OB-stacle course and became my own unrelenting drill sergeant, with everything reduced to its primal elements—just this ball, this rim, this moment. Revisiting the great coaching lessons that had been given to me by all my mentors, I went back to being the little boy trying to get himself into a game with the big guys. I was my father's son, alone in the backyard willing myself to be the best. I was all my heroes refusing to be undone by challenges that threatened to take them down—Michael Jordan, Magic Johnson, Alonzo Mourning, those just a few of the names that kept me going.

Getting to see Zaire and Zion turned into a major obstacle course, too—even though we were in the same city and even though the court gave us guidelines. There were all kinds of hoops to jump through just in arranging a time to visit; calls weren't returned and changes were made at the last minute. Then, since I could only see them on their mom's turf, I'd drive over to the house only to be made to sit and wait for long periods of time without being told where they were. The experience became so uncomfortable that I decided to pull back, not wanting to make the situation any worse. For the entire summer, I was able to see my sons probably all of two times. But that contact was enough for me to reassure six-year-old Zaire that we would be able to spend much more time with each other soon and to allow one-year-old Zion to be able to know me a little better. Initially I was such a stranger to him that he cried and wouldn't come to me. That killed me.

But these interactions also sharpened my focus on the job training at hand and stoked the furnace inside me. Every day, from the minute I woke up in the morning until I put my head on the pillow at night, my mental regimen was driven by two tasks—getting healthy and becoming the best basketball player in the NBA. Also driving me was some anger. Scratch that. Down in the belly of the beast, I was one pissed-off combatant. So I used that anger, allowing it to just add more fuel to the fire.

The chatter inside my head was mean punching-bag stuff: how *they* (everyone who failed to believe in me and said I'd never be nuthin' from the start) thought I was done, ready to be put out to pasture after an injury, undervalued, a meteoric rise only to crash and burn. I thought of a powerhouse like Penny Hardaway, my former teammate, who had contributed so much to basketball but whose career was slowed by injuries and multiple surgeries, how I was not going to let that happen to me and how I would show *them* because I was going to come back stronger and tougher, an even better, more formidable player than before.

With that blasting on the turntable in my brain, I put myself back on the radar and invited Jerry Colangelo, then the director of USA Basketball, and a few others who along with him would be making the decision for the Olympic roster, to come see me work out. They saw that I was healthy. Reports surfaced later that after the tryout the concern was no longer about whether my body and my heart were back but if I had my head on the way it would need to be.

To answer that question, I had two close friends, Chris Paul and LeBron James, come up to Chicago to put me through the paces. L.B. and I had grown up in the league together since our rookie years. With his infectious spirit and unstoppable positive energy, C.P. had been as close to me as a brother since he had come to the NBA in 2005. Both had played at the level where Olympic-caliber basketball was by now; both knew me before I had become superstar D-Wade. Their assessment mattered to me. After several sessions, they both acknowledged how hard I'd been working. They not only personally gave me a nod of approval that bolstered my confidence even more but also let it be known to others that I was needed in Beijing.

With that I cleared the hurdle to compete in the 2008 Olympics in China. The true tests would come during competition. But in the meantime I couldn't let any negative thinking impair my game. At a less mature point in time, I might have been bothered by not starting; I might have thought too much about not having enough minutes in the game to show that I was on the same level as the best. None of that was in my thinking.

When I arrived in Beijing, I took stock of all the athletes and realized that most everybody had been a star in their field for most of their lives. Everybody had been dreaming gold forever. On the one hand, the reality was daunting to be among so many gifted athletes who had been pushing their training to their upper limits, too. On the other hand, I was inspired and humbled to be there in whatever capacity I could help my team and my country. The first thing I did was to ask our coach, Mike Krzyzewski, to tell me how he saw my role.

"Whatever I need to do," I promised him, "I'm gonna do it."

After that, I had no problem delivering on whatever was asked—

whether it was coming off the bench for Kobe, having to defend like crazy, seizing the right moments to be exciting to the team, dunking, stealing, blocking, and being aggressive and very efficient. Without the ball in my hand a lot of the time, I had to cut and get open so guys could see me. The consensus was that with Chris Paul and myself coming off the bench we were able to be the X factor in giving our team the power it ultimately needed.

As the much-needed Redeem Team we hoped to be, the United States finished first in Group B pool play, winning games against Spain, the reigning world champs, China, and Germany by averages of over 30 points. We went on to the quarterfinals by playing the fourth-place finisher in Group A, Australia, again winning by a sizable margin. In the semifinals we faced Argentina, the team that had won gold and beaten us in 2004. With Argentina's Manu Ginobili kept quiet because of an injury, we won by an emphatic 20 points. A resurgent Spain had fought its way to the finals and appeared ready for us on August 24 when the gold medal game took place. But as battle-tested as they were, we were even more so—and grabbed the gold with a 118–107 victory.

The stats gave me a little something to gloat about when I ended up being the leading scorer of the Olympic team. That was accomplished while coming off the bench and averaging nineteen minutes each game. But beyond the stats was the reclaimed—and in some cases newfound—recognition that in some ways did more to define me than the climb to Mount Everest had. Headlines across the sports world described me as the Comeback Kid of the 2008 Olympics. U.S. men's basketball had reclaimed supremacy and I guess that I had, too. On most lists for the top five All USA, I was named first, followed by LeBron James (Cleveland) and Chris Bosh (Toronto), then Kobe Bryant (Los Angeles) and Jason Kidd (Dallas). While I had been friends with Bron and CB ever since we'd come into the draft together five years earlier, our time in Beijing was the most we'd spent together on a team and the chemistry between the three of us on the court was something we all noticed.

We didn't come up with a plan to play together like that someday on a single team in the NBA. But perhaps the seeds were planted for such a concept to grow later on. And in the meantime, I returned from the Olympics to the Heat's 2008–2009 season with a fury. In spite of the accolades coming my way after Beijing, I couldn't relax or take anything for granted. For the first time, I was really about myself, about proving myself with every possession of the ball.

Because I was dealing with so much bullshit off the court—and it would become only more oppressive—basketball became my only outlet. The shy, quiet guy in me was no more. I was mean. I played angry and I dominated. Stats might not matter if you don't win a championship, but my statistics went nuts as I turned into a scoring machine. After a game early in the season when I scored 40 points, 10 assists, and 5 blocked shots, making me the second player in NBA history to do so, the next record I broke was from scoring 50 points in a game that was lost by the team. (The Heat lost in the end by 20 points.) Then there was the Wilt Chamberlain record of scoring 50 points in a game with 16 assists; I became only the second player after Wilt to attain that. Later, in a double-overtime win against the Chicago Bulls, I scored in the double digits—my seventy-eighth consecutive game of doing so, which meant tying my own franchise record—and again had stats only achieved before by Chamberlain: 48 points (71.4 percent shooting), 12 assists, 6 rebounds, 4 steals, and 3 blocks.

Besides leading the league in scoring for the season I became the first Heat player to score an average of 30.2 points a game and the first NBA player to attain 2,000 points, 500 assists, 100 steals, and 100 blocks in a season. By the end of the season, I had achieved what I and those close to me felt was definitely a MVP kinda year. Still, I came in third in the voting for league MVP, behind LeBron and Kobe.

If that had been the only moment of disappointment in the spring of 2009, I would have been on my knees in gratitude. As usual, this was once again a reason to play with more firepower, as I had all season— explosive, tapping all the anger and nervous energy churning inside of me. I was so grateful for every game minute I had to play, I wanted games to last as long as possible so I didn't have to go back to the vengeance of all vengeance that was being cooked up.

The season was seen widely as a serious success after the Heat came back from winning only fifteen games the previous year and then made it into the first round of the playoffs the very next season—making us the first team to do that in thirty years. In that round, we ran up against the Atlanta Hawks, a really tough team, and we just didn't have enough to go further. Nonetheless, we were also redeemed and ready to continue the rebuilding we had begun.

Without a doubt, I felt energized by these fresh lessons in what can happen when you put your mind to something with focus and clarity about the goals being undertaken. In the middle of the onslaught, I could have sat it out or had my heart taken from me. But I still had too many people who believed in me not to battle back and be the athlete and the man they knew me to be.

STUBBORNLY, AND THAT COULD BE THE CAPRICORN SIDE coming out, up until November 2008 in those early stages of the season, I kept the faith that Siohvaughn would come to her senses and agree to shared time with the boys. Finally, thinking I was asking for a last resort, I sought court intervention because nothing else had worked. The orders were either ignored outright or followed partially but not completely so as to deny me the only thing that mattered—time with Zaire and Zion.

Over the next two and a half years, order after order, motion after motion would be treated as if the law didn't apply to her. Whether or not I was allowed to speak to the boys, mainly Zaire of course, had to do with whether his mom would allow it. My calls were placed every other day or more. We tried e-mail and texting and we set up a prepaid cell phone for Zaire. His mom later told the court that it was my fault for not calling the boys over weeks at a time and that the prepaid phone was not suitable for a child who couldn't manage time or money.

Similarly, when the court asked about the difficulty I was having, Siohvaughn said that visitation happened mostly without incident. One of the judges overseeing that part of the divorce found just the opposite, that the last-minute struggles during pickup and drop-off was causing stress to the kids. The finding, as it was described in the custody judgment, would eventually be that she was engaging in an "escalating effort to alienate" the boys from me and, increasingly, from everyone in my family.

Finally, an order was given that I could see the kids for Christmas 2008 in Miami. Siohvaughn had not wanted them to come to Florida but as she couldn't withhold her consent, she ended up accompanying the boys and staying with them in the house we still owned. I did have a few outings planned with the kids, and we talked about fun things to do for the rest of the holidays, when I scheduled times to pick them up and continue my visitation. On Christmas Eve day, when we were going to go out, she called to inform me that Zaire was very sick and Zion was coming down with something, and they shouldn't leave the house.

Instead, I went to see them there. When I got to the gate and texted her to open up, there was no response. The next thing I knew, local police arrived in force, speeding up as if a crime were about to unfold, approaching the car cautiously, hands on guns, to ask what I was doing there. Apparently she had called to say that a suspicious vehicle was parked outside and that she felt threatened by who might be in it.

When I told them the situation, they escorted me inside and I was, at last, able to see my sons. However, Siohvaughn convinced the officers she didn't feel safe and asked them to stay until I left, just in case. Whatever message was sent to the police officers who had a car outside until the time came to go, I can only imagine. The judge in the custody phase later described this as "drama-trauma," noting, "The presence of the police certainly has a chilling effect on the visitation parent and sends a bad message to minor children."

My original hope had been to take Zaire and Zion with me to see their grandmother Jolinda, who was in Miami, as well as Dada and some of their cousins who wanted to see them. That wasn't permitted; nor were the cousins allowed to come see the boys—who incidentally didn't seem to be under the weather in the least. Since my visitation was supposed to have been for several days, including Christmas Day, I fully expected to be able to pick them up and have them come with me for special activities, including a Wade's World Foundation event dedicating a house to a family that had been burned out of their home and that would have been inspiring, along with adventures planned for my boys who were hurting in this whole process. Nope.

Those kids, as the story went, had been so sick and up all night that she had to take them to the hospital emergency room in the morning. This was more drama-trauma, since the hospital records indicated there was nothing seriously wrong. Aside from the fact that Siohvaughn had been successful in thwarting the court order, as the judge later stated, she reported that I had come alone for a Christmas visit that day. That wasn't true; in fact, I had declined going through another ordeal that felt to me like a setup. The sad truth that nobody could change was that a six-year-old and a toddler were kept from having a loving visit with their dad. And it was Christmas. I hadn't seen them in all this time and couldn't even give them their presents until they returned to Chicago and we shipped them out.

While all this was taking place, I was continuing my intense level of play in our regular season—taking all my fear and frustration out like a battering ram on the basketball court. What was happening with my boys was a constant in my mind. Obviously most fans had no idea of what I was going through, even if the divorce showed up here and there in the news. And there was much more coming.

In hindsight, I should have guessed that my desire to be happy and out there dating, maybe even having a serious romance, would not go unpunished.

BREATHTAKINGLY BEAUTIFUL AS SHE IS, GABRIELLE UNION and I had started our relationship as friends.

Early in my career and hers, our paths had crossed a few times, including in Miami in 2007 at a Superbowl party that we were asked to cohost. During 2008, we started running into each other again, surprised that we had so many friends in common. Eventually, we struck up a friendship on the phone and I reached out to her for encouragement with the challenges that were happening in my life. We probably didn't become involved romantically until early 2009.

Did I sweep Gabrielle off her feet from the start? Not to any degree she'd ever admit. Gorgeous, funny, intelligent, and soulful, she was an actress I'd watched through most of her career. Not to mention a former high school all-star point guard! As we got to know each other, we were mostly cordial in the beginning, but during the time we spent talking on the phone, we really got to know each other. We weren't in a rush to start dating either. I was in Miami; she was in Los Angeles. Over time, we found out how compatible we are and, more than anything, that we genuinely like each other—one of the little-known secrets to lasting relationships.

When Siohvaughn went on a character-assassination rampage against me in this period, Gabby just encouraged me to keep to the high ground, as I had been doing. She was wise to remind me of what I knew—that even if terrible things were being said about me, trying to hit back and disparaging my sons' mother would be hurtful to them.

One of the hardest hits on my character, and one that I couldn't let go unanswered, came on January 17, 2009, my twenty-seventh birthday, when I learned that Siohvaughn and her lawyers had filed a proposed amendment to the divorce petition claiming damages against me because I had been unfaithful during our marriage and had given her an STD. A what? Um, that was news to me. If she had contracted one, it wasn't from me. In fact, I went through a series of tests and submitted medical records to prove it. In early February, the damage some of these accusations caused led me to file a defamation suit against her.

The claims were discredited and her suit was eventually withdrawn. But before that happened, the gossip went global and was relentless. Not being paranoid or anything, I was pretty sure that when I was out and about people were giving me dirty looks.

In the months that followed, once Gab and I were seen as a couple, the media feeding frenzy that had been started by Siohvaughn focused on my girlfriend as the vixen home wrecker responsible for turning me against my high school sweetheart and abandoning my boys.

By that point, with the divorce marathon nearly a year old and getting nowhere, I should have toughened up. But I was shocked, and more than anything, I was hurt for Gabrielle. Her world was different from the fish bowl you live in as an NBA player, where you can expect to get trashed by untruths that come with the territory. When I took a hit on my career and my brand, I could generally hope that after a few news cycles the dust would soon settle. Gabby had to confront the untruths a different way and she did lose some opportunities, it's sad to say.

We grew closer during the deluge. Because we live in a world where people believe what they hear, taking the high road is not always rewarded. Between the rumors and the accusations that were out there, even public statements made to set the record straight weren't always read in full. Even when false claims were soon retracted, it was often too late to unring the bell, as they say.

Any hope of a reasonable compromise with Siohvaughn about anything went out the window. She so angered one judge by failing to appear in court that she was later taken into custody and ordered to pay ten thousand dollars bail for her release. She only became more defiant.

What got me through on a day-to-day basis, besides the support of my girlfriend, my family, and of my close circle, was the same focus that had driven me in preparing for the Olympics.

Every day, I'd focus on the overriding and underlying goal of having contact with Zaire and Zion. Every parent knows the joy of hearing "Daddy!" or "Mommy!" when walking through the door or calling on the phone. When I couldn't talk to them, I would feel numb and empty. When we did talk, and they weren't able to connect or were even negative, I would feel just as lost.

But there was no giving up. Nothing else mattered without them. Nothing.

EARLY MORNING
NOVEMBER 19, 2011
PORTLAND, OREGON

SHOWERED, DRESSED, AND READY TO GO DOWNSTAIRS TO catch a ride over to Nike campus, I look out the window at the rain that continues to fall.

Like always, being separated from the boys even for a couple of days continues to be hard. I thought that by now, eight months after gaining full custody, it might be less of a worry. Of course, as is often the case with single-parent households, I'm fortunate to have great people around like Brenda and Rich, as well as family members who are close by with the kids when I'm gone.

Whenever I do travel, I can talk and Skype and text throughout the day, rarely missing any of the main events. But I do try to make it easy for the boys to talk about any feelings of worry they may have while I'm gone— including any feelings that may come up from the past, given all that they've been through.

That's a question I hear from men and women who've been through a nightmarish divorce process. It's important to say from my point of view that navigating the future, once a judgment has been given, is always a work in progress. Even as estranged parents, the goal is not to give up on the other parent. Although my ex and I aren't in direct contact, whenever I talk about her to the kids I choose to do so always in positive ways—with reminders to the boys to love and respect her.

This brings me to questions about the need to forgive, which I've saved for the last. The answers take me back to Grandma and the stoop, and to the prayers that my sister and I prayed a long, long time ago.

CHAPTER ELEVEN

KEEPING PROMISES, KEEPING FAITH

NOVEMBER 27, 2011
ANYWHERE AND EVERYWHERE

OVER THE WEEKEND AFTER THANKSGIVING DAY 2011, THE basketball world and the public at large celebrated breaking news that ran in media outlets around the globe, like this piece in the *Miami Herald*:

> *Now it looks like it is over, finally. The players and the owners reached a tentative agreement early Saturday that is expected to end one of the longest labor disputes in the history of professional sports. LeBron and Dwyane and the rest should be back on the court by Christmas. It will be a 66-game season,*

*instead of the standard (and seemingly endless) 82 games. The
fans will forgive, eventually, as they always have. And the
money machine that is professional sports will fire back up on
all cylinders.*

The settlement was by no means perfect for players or owners. And in
the coming weeks there would be some unfair decisions, in my view, in last-
minute trades or attempted trades. But the fact was that we had a season.
Everyone contemplating a stint playing overseas or already gone could now
come back and get into shape—and fast—for a season set to begin on Christmas Day.

Not a bad early present to have under the Wade family tree!

In the week following the news, as I cancel all the alternative plans,
the boys and I have some team meetings to discuss schedules and responsibilities now that Daddy's workload just got heavier. Listening to the
three of them express their excitement about having a season after all is
just so touching. They've been praying for this day—for themselves and
for me.

Gratitude overflows my heart. Not that I needed the lockout to be over
to feel grateful. Still, I am thankful for every bit of certainty we can have.
I'm also thankful that Zaire and Zion had a good recent visit with their
mother and that they will have a Christmas visit with her that we're starting
to plan, too.

Zion looks quickly at his brother and cousin and then asks, "Daddy, can
I show you my list?" He's already started the Christmas gift request list, apparently with the help of Zaire and Dada. Not waiting for any answer, Zion
dashes from the room and comes back in seconds. There's a list of several
items. The first is a Christmas tree.

The boys are so excited.

To honor the spirit of the holiday, Siohvaughn has always gone away
from the commercial Christmas celebrations and has tried to emphasize
the season as a time of giving to others. I respect that belief and have told
the boys so. Since they'll have their celebration with her and one with me,

I think a Christmas tree is a great idea and tell Zion he's made another fine choice, too.

Dada's list is much longer, including video games, music, clothes, and a chain like mine. I tell him maybe he'll have to wait until he's older for the chain. But as for the sneakers he wants with his name on them like mine, I give that a thumbs-up. The other two want those as well.

Then there's Zaire, who has some similar requests to Dada. But one of the items is hard to read. I squint.

Am I reading this correctly? "Does this say a 'real live elf'?"

Zion is excited for his brother. I'm suspicious. Is there such a thing? Zaire insists there is. He and Dada suggest that an elf could be helpful with chores and make extra toys they could give to boys and girls who don't have many of their own.

That's a great explanation. I'm so proud of my sons and my nephew. They have been very resilient over the past eight-plus months since the judge's custody ruling.

One of the few times that the older boys ever complained was not too long ago when they both started telling me about how hard their lives were. Seems that too much homework, difficult subject matter, and not getting to play basketball for the next session in the local league was the cause of their distress.

That had been a tough one for me. The deal was that if their grades didn't go down in the fall, they could both play in the winter session. When I saw Zaire's grades slipping, I pulled him out for the winter session, giving him plenty of time to come back and play in the spring. Dada decided he'd wait for Zaire and play when the lockout was over.

In the meantime, both had been going on about how bad they had it, until I finally had to get to the bottom of what was going on.

Neither could really say. "It's just hard," Zaire repeated.

"Really? Because it's important that you guys are happy. That's the most important thing."

Then we decided to take a walk downstairs. In the condo complex where we were living until the remodel was done on my house, there was a back area with a walkway down to the beach that was lit up that night for the coming holidays and looked like something out of a movie.

We strolled down the walkway and out to the sand to look at the yellow moon reflecting on the ocean at night. The stars were out and the early December air was balmy.

"You know what? This is where you guys get to live," I said. "Do you know that I used to just dream of getting to see something like this in my life. For a long time, I didn't even have a backyard and this is your backyard! This is pretty cool."

They both agreed and started to get excited. "Whoa, it is cool!" Zaire said, doing his little dance moves.

With a shrug Dada agreed and quietly added, "It is like our backyard."

After we came back upstairs and said good-bye to Brenda, who had been reading to Zion and then got everyone ready for bed, I started to think about other ways to help the boys deal with the stress of having their moms in a different city and how to deal with whatever unhappiness or anger could be getting stored in them from the past.

That was when I began to ponder this question of forgiveness and how to teach it to my kids—something I've had to learn how to teach to myself, after all.

Actually, my first teacher was Grandma, who taught me to forgive but never to forget. My other teacher was Tragil—who taught me, from her own lessons, that if you seek forgiveness from others or from life, you have to first forgive.

I believe that's true. At the same time, I won't forget what it is that I need to find forgiveness for. This is personal to me not only as a father to my kids but also as a proponent of good parenting. There are too many would-be good parents who may not even know what alienation is, how damaging it is to children, and why the effort to coparent during separation or divorce can and should be successful.

Learning to put the best interests of the kids above all other concerns, like learning to forgive, can be a challenge. But what greater rewards can there be than seeing your children happy and healthy?

In keeping promises made as a child to myself to be a devoted father, and in keeping the faith that was severely tested during the divorce and custody battles, that question ultimately would find an answer.

"WHAT HAPPENS RIGHT BEFORE YOU DO SOMETHING THAT'S like, well, so ridiculous on the court?" Lisa Joseph asked me in the fall of 2009.

We were waiting to meet with Hank before going together to a youth program supported by the work of Wade's World Foundation. Lisa had never asked me that question before so I wasn't sure what she was getting at.

She explained: "I mean, right before you do something that's unbelievable, like when you're going to jump over someone—do you plan it, see it, or how does that work? Do you know that you're about to kill it or does that happen naturally?"

I laughed. At about that point, my laughter was a rare sound to my own ears. "You know," I reminded her, "I'm used to blocking out everything so I don't think, I just *do*."

Lisa then recalled a much earlier conversation, just after she'd started working with Hank for me, when I had first talked about the life that I had lived growing up.

At that time we were meeting at the Four Seasons Hotel with Marcus and Shivani Desai, the rep from Converse, and we had been asked to go around the table to say something significant about our lives. When it was my turn, I began by saying, "Well, I'm a father first and probably everything else after that." At the beginning of my career, that must have caught everyone in the room off guard. Then I went on to describe the nights of waiting up on the stoop for my mom, what it was like to worry for her welfare, how I felt watching her shoot up, the fear that lived in me of having police come in and take her away.

The table became very quiet after that. Most everyone commented that they would have never known that was in my past.

My answer then was "I blanked it out for a long time, like it didn't happen. I tried basketball, did well. I lived." That may have been the first time that I had allowed the past to be part of the conversation about how the basketball court had become a place of escape and refuge, where no one would know what was going on in my life. Tears filled my eyes, Lisa recalled.

The irony that Lisa pointed out five or so years later was that just as basketball had been the one thing that never let me down as a kid, the same could be said now. She wanted to know, "Is it the same process?"

I thought about the heightened awareness of the good and the blanking out of the bad when playing at the upper levels of adrenaline and intention. Kind of the same, I had to admit. Then again, that mental firepower, when you have defenders coming at you from all directions, is hard to explain—you're not just putting a ball into the air to fall through a round metal rim that has a net hanging from it; you are bending time and space to obey your will. The blanking-out process is about surrender, for me. Like the way music can take you away.

More than ever, I had to have that feeling of surrender and sanctuary that only basketball gave me. That had come through loud and clear during the epic home court game in early 2009 against the Chicago Bulls. With three seconds remaining at the end of a second overtime, we were tied and the Bulls had the ball. After dominating throughout the game, I seized the final moment, stole the ball, and flew down the length of the court to shoot a three-pointer off one leg—beating the buzzer, winning the game. Right then, with the roar of the crowd, the blood pounding in my ears, I jumped up onto the scorer's table, all the while pointing down at the floor and hollering, "This is *my* house!"

Yep, I had become that guy.

Nobody was going to take my house, *our* house for all the fans, away. From then on, at the start of every home game, I added a new ritual of running both sides of the court and giving the number-one sign to every single spectator there to be part of the game, to show us the love, and, yeah, to feel the Heat.

Even with the nasty wave of rumors coming at me, I kept on playing like that, powering through the end of the season and into the next. Not thinking, blanking everything out but the finer points of the game.

That's also how the 2009–2010 season was starting, as Lisa and Hank and I discussed briefly that morning. As we toured the youth center where hundreds of participants and fans were on hand, I once again blocked out the worries for the next hour—all amid countless hugs, high-fives, and as many autographs as I could sign for the kids who'd lined up for hours ahead of time in the hopes of getting one.

As we were leaving, a cadre of reporters and photographers followed us in a swarm as we made our way to the waiting SUV. We joked and cut up all the way there and I realized that in the eyes of everyone at the youth center and most of the media, I was living any kid's dream.

Once we were in the car and the e-mails started to come in for all three of us about the legal matters on multiple fronts, I stopped blocking everything out long enough to make a comment to Hank and Lisa that became memorable. With photographers and camera people still shooting away from the sidewalk as the SUV maneuvered through the throngs, I just shook my head and said, "If people only knew what my life is really like right know. They see me and I'm great and everything's cool. But this hell right now, they wouldn't believe it."

Practically in tears, Lisa said, "I can't believe it and I know what's happening." During the Christmas fiasco of the previous year, she had come after I texted her to meet me and had taken pictures of the police cars parked in front of my own house when I was only trying to get to see my kids.

Hank, never one to lose his cool, just gave me that familiar look with the glint in his eyes that asked, *So what are you going to do about it?*

What was I going to do about it? My faith that we would get to a better place was all I had. That's what had kept me going with my mother, and that's what had to happen with my dad. When he was at his lowest, around the time that he came out to Miami, when he battled his adversary—also substance abuse—I kept that same faith. Some days I'd see him and just hug him, rub on his head like he was my own son.

So what I was going to do was to keep fighting, keep pushing, keep praying.

Oh, there was a lot to untangle in my head and block out on the court. To add insult to injury, I had another lawsuit being waged by principals in a restaurant operation that had gone out of business. This was the result of not following lessons I'd learned early on that had come back to haunt me—an investment opportunity that I had recently tried to claim on my own without seeking business advice. I was being sued for $25 million. A couple of smaller lawsuits that came about similarly then were piled on.

Honestly, I had never been one for cussing a whole hell of a lot, maybe because my dad sometimes had the mouth that he did. But I was thinking about picking up the habit.

Somewhere in late 2009, Jim, my divorce attorney, had gently introduced the option of filing for sole custody, since Siohvaughn had gone that route from the start. There were many reasons why I didn't want to do that. Besides the fact that doing so could drag us further away from the goal of coparenting, the high road would be that much harder to stay on, too. In the world where I come from, nuthin' good ever arose from wanting to get back and do to someone else what they were doing to you.

But I slowly began to reconsider the option, holding it out as a last resort. The questions no longer to be ignored were those filled with growing concern and fear for what was happening to the boys. What were they being told about me on top of not being allowed to have me (or anyone connected to me) in their lives? What kinds of influences were dictating how they were being raised without any of my input?

In mid-December, four days after the court issued an updated parenting order, agreed upon by all parties, Tragil—who was legally allowed to transport my sons for pickups and drop-offs for my visitations—went to the house in Chicago to get them. Zion, now two and a half, probably didn't understand what was going on, but Zaire, almost eight, had to watch as a woman spoke in tongues and berated my sister as she broke down sobbing in front of them because, she said, she was a slave to others and following the orders of men.

Shocked, hurt for her, and seriously scared, I told Tragil that she would never have to be subjected to that again, whatever it was going to take. We each talked to Mom, who helped us pray for light to be shone in this darkness. Even my mother, the most faithful of us all in this time period, was bewildered and wanting me to be vigilant in thought and prayer. Mom also knew that I was remembering how she and Dad had maintained a relationship after they split up, in order to give us a sense of family after divorce. But, as she pointed out, "Siohvaughn isn't me."

She wasn't necessarily herself, either, I suspected.

One thing was clear to me, though. In trying to punish everyone around me—and regardless of whether she was being egged on by others who had money to gain or their own axes to grind—Siohvaughn was damaging herself in the process, too. That made me sad. But it was what she was doing to our sons that made me mad.

THE 2009–2010 SEASON FOR ME WAS SIMILAR TO THE ONE before it, giving me opportunities to celebrate milestones on behalf of the Miami Heat—a team that I was prouder than ever to serve as its face. Only my great friend and fellow warrior Udonis Haslem was left from my first year. He and I, along with Dorell Wright, who came in the year after we did, were the only remaining players from our championship season. Also one of my closest friends, Dorell would leave the next year to join the Golden State Warriors. By the summer, I would be a free agent and wasn't sure whether I would stay or go elsewhere. As long as the divorce hung over me and my family, those questions would have to take a backseat.

In the meantime, I continued to play with a crazy intensity and a need to dominate. In the third game of the season, playing against the Bulls, I scored my ten thousandth career point, and then, feeling my wings wanting to soar higher, had a gravity-defying dunk over Anderson Varejao of the Cavaliers. LeBron just shook his head in awe at that one. Varejao and I started to go at it when the whistle blew and we were both given technicals.

The most intense and on fire that I played all season was at my sixth All-Star Game. My excitement was fueled by the fact that the attendance at Cowboys Stadium on February 14, 2010, broke all records when 108,713 spectators showed up to become the largest crowd ever to watch a basketball game in the history of the sport. In planning for this very special weekend—with lots of fun activities lined up for the kids and charitable events that I was going to be hosting or supporting on behalf of my foundation—I wanted more than anything to share the time with Zaire. In January, I had made a motion to have parenting time with him. Grandmama Jolinda would travel there and watch the game with Zaire while I was playing. Siohvaughn objected to this arrangement by saying something along the lines of my mom not being acceptable to care for the boys. Later, when asked about it, Siohvaughn contradicted that assertion. But the bottom line was that Zaire didn't get to come.

Finding my sanctuary on the court and feeding off the energy of the crowd during the All-Star game, I helped lead the East to a 141–139 victory over the West, contributing 28 points, 11 assists, 6 rebounds, and 5 steals. During the presentation of the MVP award, which I was given for the game, I remember smiling and feeling amazing in one minute and then walking away with a broken heart the next. Most of the other players with kids had them at the game. Mine had been prevented from attending. For what?

This weekend had come on the heels of a confusing episode earlier in the week when I went to Chicago for Zaire's birthday. The weekend visitation with both boys had been planned and we were going to celebrate at my mom's house. At the last minute, Siohvaughn texted to say Zion was too sick with a high fever to attend. She e-mailed me a photo of him throwing up. The choice for me at that moment was whether to leave Zion at home with his mother or to have him with me and get him the medical care needed, whatever it was. Trying to be diplomatic, I texted back and let her know that I appreciated being told that he wasn't well, but I would keep the visitation and get him the necessary care because I was his parent. At that time Tragil was on her way to the house accompanied by a representative from the court, an attorney, whose job it was to be neutral and look to the best interests of the children. After the drama with the talking in tongues when Tragil had picked up the boys before, the judge had requested the representative to be there as an observer. Unlike the previous visit, there were signs posted on the blacked-out gates saying things like "We fear no evil." When they buzzed in, the gates didn't open. Eventually, the children's representative called Siohvaughn's lawyer and about fifteen minutes later the gate opened and a friend of Von's drove both boys to the gate and dropped them off. Tragil was confused because earlier I had called her to say Zion was going to stay home sick. But he seemed to feel just fine and was able to enjoy the weekend with Zaire and the rest of us.

The really troubling element that was starting to emerge wasn't so much how Zaire acted around me. Yet. It was the kinds of things he was saying on the phone and, as I learned later, what he said to the court-appointed expert who would eventually testify in trial. Zaire described me negatively in ways that sounded to the expert as if they were embellished or repeated from what he had heard. The expert noted this statement, "Imagine that you're a mother of a five-year-old and you were about to have another child, and imagine your husband walks out on you," as an example of an alienated attitude toward me. Of course that wasn't the story of what had happened but he had heard it as such and repeated it, something the expert said was strange for a child of his age to say anyway.

One judge who was hearing motions and issuing orders at the time described the drama of this period by writing, "Well, the problem is that the same thing keeps happening over and over again. We've got like Groundhog Day where every time there is an order . . . there's drama involved. And I don't know why there has to be drama over putting the child at the gate and saying bye. Maybe the first time you would think, okay, and then it's a second time, and then now the third time, and it's back again. And obviously, every time there is drama, children don't deal well with drama. So we try to keep the drama to a minimum, and obviously that doesn't seem to be happening."

The drama was intensifying. A second judge who had issued an order for me to have visitation after weeks without contact watched every motion I filed—for a phone call—be met with a motion to reconsider. When that was denied and when things didn't go her way, all of a sudden the phone would be off the hook and no one knew where the kids were. This judge's observations at the time: "My concern is that I got two little children and they're in the middle of a battlefield here. And every time it's time to go visit daddy or return to mom, there's tension; there's friction. Why should children have to endure this? What did these two little kids ever do that they have to be in the middle of muddle. . . . I'm very, very troubled by the pattern that is developing in this case."

The breaking point for me had come before the end of the season, on the weekend of March 12–14, when I had two games at home, and Tragil was supposed to pick up Zaire and Zion from school on Friday to bring them to Miami. When she arrived at school, they weren't there. So she went to the house.

"I'm here now," Tragil said on the phone to me. "I'm outside calling the house and there's no one picking up."

"Call Jim and have him get a hold of her lawyers."

A bad feeling spreads through me. Was this more of the same or something worse? Trying to keep calm as I waited to hear for the next couple of hours, I couldn't shake off nervousness I already had about her actions and what she might do to the kids. Tragil checked in constantly and nobody, Von's lawyers included, knew where the boys were.

By late afternoon I'm thinking the worst—that my boys are hurt, that they've been taken somewhere, and no one can tell me where this woman is. So instead of going to practice, I call and admit, "I'm an emotional wreck. I can't make it." When it comes time to decide whether I can make the game or not, I decide to go rather than stay at home and lose my mind. Against the Bulls, of all teams, I get off to a slow start but come on strong in the second half, playing with my angry persona—to the point of being called for a flagrant foul.

After the game, I rush home and sit up until late, worried to death, crying, trying without success to block a terrible feeling that I'll never see my sons again. Finally, I fall asleep for the remaining part of the night.

As soon as I wake up on Saturday, I call Hank. No breath in my voice, I ask, "Anything?"

"We're still trying."

Three hours later the phone rings and we're informed that Zaire is in the hospital.

Thanking Jesus that he's alive and been found, I'm still freaking out. Feverishly, I get the phone number of the hospital and am connected to the doctor assigned to his care. We get to the bottom of the problem that he's having headaches—which the doctor has been informed could be connected to the fall he had when he visited me over Christmas.

I'm thinking—*What the . . . ?* This was a story that began as him horsing around and slipping and falling down, then mutated later on into him banging his head, falling into the pool, almost drowning, and having severe chronic headaches. That was enough to have his safety at my house questioned. The expert in the case called these details "embellishments."

Other facts about how all this had gone down would come out later. Siohvaughn would say that the school had called because Zaire was having headaches and she picked up the boys, went to the hospital with Zaire and one of her friends, possibly after having her mom take Zion—although his whereabouts weren't known by any of us. The reason for not calling anyone? Oh, she had lost her phone but had said she left a message for her lawyer. Then, as we would learn, she borrowed a camera supposedly from the hospital staff and took photos of Zaire on a gurney—which she later sent to me, knowing the horror of my reaction. Apparently she wanted the photos in the hospital records, along with information she supplied that the headaches were caused by the scrape on his head and "almost drowning" back in early December at my house. The eventual diagnosis? Later in the week he was found to have sinusitis. We knew that because six days later she didn't appear in court and her lawyer said the reason was that Zaire was being treated for that.

Not knowing these specifics yet, I listened as the doctor painted a picture of a child brought in on a gurney who could have something wrong with him, based on the description of the symptoms, but couldn't say anything conclusively. He then put me on the phone with Siohvaughn.

Well. Something snapped, big-time. I had been calm and controlled most of the time in our interactions up until this point. But I lost it with her.

The mental anguish came pouring out of me. What I couldn't understand, I said, was why wasn't I contacted? Why didn't she call me? Why didn't she get somebody to reach out to me? She knew it was my visitation. She knew that I would be worried out of my mind. She needed to let me know where my kids were and that everybody was fine. And I went off over the phone like the way that I'd been playing on the court for the last two seasons. Eventually she hung up the phone. I knew that I shouldn't have lost my temper and spoken that way, but I had no more emotional bandwidth for the high road.

And that was my moment of truth.

That night as I sat in bed and asked myself whether I was doing enough and fighting hard enough for my sons, I took a close look at everything else I needed to do to make sure that I could give my kids the life they deserved. With everything that I had worked so hard for them to receive and have, what more would keep them safe and happy and healthy? The answer was that I thought that having them living with me would be better—and I knew that was probably impossible without seeking full custody. Even just the goal of seeing my sons consistently would probably only be possible if I had full custody. We had seen their mom's refusal to follow court orders and what I saw as her gaming the system. There didn't seem to be any other recourse. Above all, I was so scared at that point for what might happen to my kids, I knew I had to fight for full custody. Even if I lost, I'd be in the same situation as we already were.

The decision to fight was ultimately about them doing better in the care of me and my family. Enough was enough. I called my agent Hank, then my lawyer Jim, and they both said, "Yes, it's time." There was no question.

Everyone breathed a sigh of relief, as if they'd all been waiting for me to make the call. We all took a deep breath and started to get ready for the really big battles to come.

JUST LIKE IN ANY OTHER TIME IN MY LIFE, EVEN IN THIS crazy period I never felt rejected or let down by the game I loved. The Heat that season, still in a rebuilding stage, should have gone further in the playoffs but we were stopped by a surging Celtics team. I had some great games in that series, however. The question in the minds of the sports world was whether I had put up my last points for the Heat.

There had long been some thought about me going back to my first hometown and playing for the Bulls. Later that would be an issue in the custody trial when the accusation came up that I didn't make more of an effort to seek employment closer to the boys. The truth is that I would have loved the opportunity to fulfill that dream. But my heart was with the Heat. My career had been built in Miami and everyone in the organization—from Micky Arison, the owner, who once told me he was the Heat's biggest fan and really meant it, to Pat Riley, who had shared his own trials and tribulations with me as a way of stressing that mine wouldn't last forever—had shown me nuthin' but love and support. And then there was the fact that Chris Bosh was coming to the Heat from Toronto. CB's decision helped me solidify mine. Then Bron decided to join us.

As the 2010–2011 season was gearing up, the courtroom was where the real heat seemed to be developing, the worst wars raging. Just when I thought that I had steeled myself and couldn't be shocked anymore, after I filed for sole custody back on March 29, 2010, Siohvaughn fired off multiple lawsuits—starting with a defamation suit against our friend Andrea, godmother to both of our sons. Filed in April, the lawsuit was dismissed in June.

Also at this time, Siohvaughn began filing lawsuits on behalf of Zaire and Zion against the court-appointed children's representative (pretty unheard-of) and, to my horror—against my girlfriend, Gabrielle Union. The lawsuit was for damages in the amount of fifty thousand dollars against Gab, based on God knows what. The motion to dismiss was filed but not granted until August, four months later. During that period, the intended hurt occurred.

In early May, just before Mother's Day, I had finally been given court-ordered makeup visitation time. The order was to allow Tragil to pick up the boys at school on the 5th, and then to allow me to take Zaire to the doctor when I was in Chicago on the 6th and for Siohvaughn to meet me there. Once again, Siohvaughn filed an emergency motion to have the order reconsidered, but it was denied. However, that afternoon when Tragil went to school to pick up the boys, they weren't there. Ignoring the court order, Siohvaughn had picked up Zaire and had someone else pick up Zion. Once again, the opportunity to be with my sons, and in this case to attend Zaire's appointment, had been denied to me. Tragil was frantic about not being able to locate them. Finally, Zaire called me when I was at the airport worried out of my mind.

I was able to see Zaire and Zion for the next few days, and then I returned them to Siohvaughn on Mother's Day and had them bring her flowers. She was still the mother of my children and I knew she loved them, regardless of how she felt about me. Goodwill? Partly, yeah, and I thought it was the right thing to do and the right example to set for my sons.

But as far as I could tell, goodwill wasn't in the cards. This wasn't the same person I knew; it wasn't her anymore. In fact, right after Mother's Day and the flowers, she filed a complaint against me for intentional infliction of mental distress, alleging all kinds of abuse that would be introduced in time for our actual custody trial. In her later filing in the custody case, she went so far as to ask the court to supervise my parenting time with the children. The court would eventually dismiss the complaint of infliction of mental distress even though Siohvaughn would file another motion (ultimately unsuccessful) to reverse the dismissal.

As for the May 5–7 makeup visitation, she told the court it had been without incident, an issue that the judge who later decided custody would raise. That was troubling. But worse to me, it was clear by this point that Zaire's brainwashing by his mom, as I understood it to be, included not only hostility to me but also Tragil. This was TT, the aunt he had adored all his life. By now there were as many as eight signs on the gates outside the house (including one that implied Tragil wasn't allowed to pass through to pick up the children). Although the expert never visited the house or had knowledge of the signs, one of the judges who was deciding motions was stunned that Tragil was barred from entering and that Zaire saw her as a threat because of what he was being told.

This was the shock-and-awe stage of warfare, one that put our sons on the front lines. My hopes rose when we were interviewed by the court's expert, who was present during a question-and-answer session between me and Zaire. It seemed to me that Zaire was asking questions that he had been told to ask. For example, he asked questions about the fall that had happened months earlier, as if he were trying to show that it was connected to his headaches. Then out of left field, he suddenly asked, "What does Zion mean to you?" I wasn't sure why he had been told to ask that but I could hear the anger and accusation in his voice and it didn't sound like the Zaire I knew.

I looked at Zaire and spoke from my heart, saying, "Zion means the same to me that you do: everything. I think of you both every morning when I get up, throughout the day, and every night. I love you. You mean everything to me."

When the initial report was turned in before trial, the expert had said in all her years of evaluating parents and children with respect to alienation, she had never seen a child act as Zaire had. She also noted that I exhibited "patience, empathy, and love" in my responses. They seemed to bode well, as we heard about it, for the trial.

By the end of May, I didn't think any of this could become any worse. The weekend of my visitation in Chicago had been planned by us to celebrate Zion's third birthday and Tragil went to get the boys to bring them to me. In the typical tension that occurred when she arrived, Zaire appeared not to want to go, and as Tragil held on to Zion, the older boy, as though being told what to do, kicked her as hard as he could. Tragil noticed that he was looking back toward someone she couldn't see, as if following directions. In Tragil's effort to calm the situation by telling him to stop and starting to take his hand, she was accused of punching him with a closed fist.

Siohvaughn then filed a restraining order against Tragil and brought a criminal suit against my sister that went to trial the following September. If that had been the only nightmare we had to endure in this period, it would have been unacceptable. Tragil and Siohvaughn had been caring sisters-in-law and close friends.

I could never understand what any of my loved ones had done to deserve any of this—especially Zaire, who was required to testify during the criminal trial and to make the accusations against Tragil that weren't true. At one point, under questioning, he was asked if he loved his aunt and he said yes. When asked if he wanted anything bad to happen to her, he was obviously not prepared for that question, and he replied as a little boy would in a sad voice, saying no. The case was dismissed.

As of June 25 the divorce was finalized in terms of the dissolution of the marriage. There were issues still remaining, including the custody phase and the settlement. Meanwhile, in another courtroom, I went to trial to fight the $25 million lawsuit and was happy to tell my side of the story to the jury. With a settlement hammered out behind the scenes for that suit and the other bad investment cases resolved in the same week, I survived those ordeals. It cost me but I walked out finished with that litigation.

With Siohvaughn, the hits just kept on coming. During my spring vacation time with Zaire and Zion, she would complain that she hadn't been told where we were going and would claim emotional distress from things, like seeing us in Boston at the NBA Finals game that was shown on TV or finding out that I had taken the boys to Disney World at another point. Upon the boys' return to Chicago, she took them for X-rays and CT scans, allegedly because they complained of backaches after going on rides. There was more during a third visit that she claimed involved an injury to Zaire. This time she went after my brother Demetrius as being abusive.

Wedged in between that drama and the actual custody trial that was set to begin in early September, all of the decision making had come to pass for the arrivals of LeBron and Chris in Miami. In such stark contrast to everything else that was happening, I was pumped with anticipation. The younger me wouldn't have been able to share the stage with a LeBron James. The need to prove that I could still be the face and have someone come in and follow me would have been too great. But when you get older, as I was at almost twenty-nine, you understand what it takes to win, what it takes for a team to go the distance. That mattered more.

I was at the place in my career where I could look back and laugh at the need for supremacy. Family and team were now where it was at.

For me to have held on and continued to be the only face of the Heat would have been selfish and not productive for the whole team. Plus it's hard. It's hard on the body—well, my body for sure—and it's hard mentally. Besides, I had proven myself over the last two seasons. What else did I need to put in the history books on my own? If I wanted to keep winning and on a consistent basis, I couldn't do it by myself. Plain and simple. And if I had to give $17 million back on my last contract to get LeBron James and Chris Bosh to come so we could have an opportunity to succeed for everyone, that's what I was going to do. Selfishly, I could have taken all the money but we wouldn't have had the team. And vice versa with the other two.

On all sides there was tremendous good faith shown in the decision to be part of the Heat's next chapter. Maybe I would have been able to savor the experience of the first games more if I hadn't been spreading my time between the two courts: the one where basketball was played and the one where the verdict would come down for custody.

The only address I had in these months was in whatever mode of transportation I had to take to make it to games by tip-off and in my seat in court during trial. There were charter flights, Town Cars, missed practices, crazy sprints out of basketball arenas to make it to airports in time to get to the next stop.

No other term can be better used to describe the trial in which I fought for my boys' lives than *drama-trauma*. The court-appointed expert, on the one hand, testified that Siohvaughn had demonstrated a pattern of alienation of the kids from me. On the other hand, the expert's recommendation was that joint custody be granted. If that was not possible, the next recommendation was to give Siohvaughn sole custody—even though the expert also worried that the alienation was severe and could require intervention.

I was crushed. We all were. After everything that other judges had worried about as to the safety and welfare of the boys, I had never felt so much at the mercy of anyone as I did of the judge who would ultimately make the decision. In hindsight, I knew that because the expert had interviewed my ex before me, she naturally would have been predisposed not to see my side. Besides the general presumption that mothers are better suited to be caregivers to children, Siohvaughn had a very persuasive personality. My status as a well-known NBA player was also not going to help me, especially given the various rumors that she had worked so hard to get out there. Then there was the obvious: Siohvaughn was a full-time stay-at-home mother and I had a jam-packed schedule. Her lawyers had bombarded the court with examples of my limited time. We had countered with a proposed schedule and a support system that was in place to give me more time with my kids than most single working parents have.

The last time I had felt at the mercy of a court of law anywhere close to this was when my mother turned herself in. Those memories resurfaced over the next few months during the slow and painful wait for the final verdict.

In the interim, more drama-trauma followed with more missed visitations. By January 2011, we were back in court, filing a motion for makeup parenting time. That was another torturous story of last-minute illness, this time involving Zion, and my decision not to have him travel if he wasn't well. Siohvaughn contested my motion, claiming I had chosen not to have visitation. The judge would later point out that the arguments against makeup time were not in the best interests of our sons and showed evidence that their mom demonstrated either a lack of concern for their best interests or a failure to understand what their best interests were.

Of course, I didn't know until March 11, 2011, how the judge was reviewing the case and the extent she needed to go for seeking precedent for her decision. In her 102-page judgment, she echoed everything that I believed in my heart, emphasizing that there was no question but that the boys' mom loved them dearly and was a very good mother—but that the evidence showed that "it is her pattern of conduct that is designed to limit, restrict or simply deprive her children of a loving and devoted father that has caused such damage to this family."

If my faith had ever faltered, it was revived, once and for all, on that day when the text came in from Jim and the full judgment was rendered.

And the new chapter could begin.

SO, HERE'S HOW I DREAM: IT'S MONDAY, JUNE 25, 2012, mid-day in downtown Miami, and nearly half a million beautiful fans from South Florida and beyond have flooded the streets surrounding Biscayne Boulevard where a parade is being held in honor of none other than the Heat. In the middle of all this love and joy, along with the blasts of confetti and pulsing music, traveling down the parade route is a long line of big red open-air double-decker tour buses carrying various members of the Miami Heat family. And right up at the front of one of the buses, I'm standing there waving and pointing to the fans with one hand and holding up the NBA championship trophy in the other. Up there standing with me, taking in the incredible sights, are Zaire, Zion, and Dada, along with several members of Team Wade.

Yeah, sounds a little over the top, I admit. But by now you probably know me pretty well and you know that no one has ever accused me of dreaming small! What better ending could I have dreamed up for this story than getting to scale the heights of Mount Everest a second time and getting to share the experience with my boys? The only better ending is to let you in on the secret that this isn't a dream at all. In fact, it's actually unfolding in real time, right in front of millions of people around the world who are a part of this celebration, at the same time that the major events of this past year flash through my mind.

Without question, a few lifetimes have been lived since the end of the

2010/2011 season. In hindsight, I can see that once again the Heat had another updated version of highs and lows that year, with its unpredictable ebb and flow. The high was being a part of one of the most-watched, most-interesting teams to ever play together and to celebrate at the end what we were able to accomplish with LeBron, Chris, and I playing together. Another high was the fun of going through that journey with those guys and our whole roster—from being on a team where nothing mattered, to being on a team where everything mattered, unlike the indifference that preceded it. We were crazy competitive and played with the audacity of fun.

The low was tough to ignore. There had been the scrutiny, the haters, the targets on our backs, unpleasant things said and done, much of it aimed at LeBron that was painful for me to have to watch and not be able to stop. The charge that we had choked avoided the reality that the Mavericks had the edge; it was their time. And again, we went to the championship round, all the way to the finals, and we were two games away from winning in our first year together. But yes, that was another low, when we lost in the end and came away empty-handed. Just another reason to feel hungry and willing to work at the level that we did in the compressed killer of a season that 2011/2012 became—determined to learn from our mistakes and prepare for the postseason, strengthened by the knowledge gained from the pain and struggle of the past.

Off the court, in my fatherhood journey, I've tried especially hard this last year to apply the same principle to the goal of being able to better co-parent my sons with my ex and to improve our lines of communication. Because of my faith, I will never give up on the possibility that we can write a new chapter, even after everything that has happened.

Tragil once told me a story about lessons of forgiveness that helped her. One day in church when she lived in San Diego, the pastor spoke about the weight that unforgiveness puts on your soul. He said that if you carry any unforgiveness in your heart, God won't hear your prayers. Tragil had to clear her slate, she said, by coming to forgive Dad—who hadn't been there for her at a time when she needed a father and who said things that hurt her deeply over the years. They have a much better relationship today, Tragil says, because she decided to forgive him, difficult though it was.

Unburdening her heart of unforgiveness has brought many other rewards, she would say. These days, she is president of Wade's World, my foundation, which serves children, youth, and families mainly in the three states that I've called home—Illinois, Wisconsin, and Florida. My sister is a dynamic and impassioned leader, tackling tough issues that affected our lives when we were growing up. She helps me live up to my promise to come back and try to make a difference for kids and families in underserved communities. Not surprisingly, Tragil is usually a step ahead of me, thinking all the time not of how to meet our goals but rather of how to surpass them.

Unforgiveness is not a known source for bringing blessings, that I know.

Maybe the first step to forgiving is to look in the mirror and take stock of all that you value in yourself and all that you have that leaves room for improvement. That's always been a key for me—looking at ways I've grown and ways I still need to grow. My gift that I do value has been my will—the heart that lets me see good in everyone, the desire to touch and help people, and the patience that I have to do that. My gift that I've tried to develop is my own outlook on life. Somehow I do look at things differently than I feel others might tend to. Because of the tough tests, I've learned to take the hits and the hurt and then get over it fast. A lot of self-talk has been—you know, c'mon Dwyane, pull yourself together, get over it. My patience, however, comes back to bite me as well. Probably I've given more chances to others than I should have; maybe people have taken advantage of that. But I've tried to forgive myself for erring on the side of understanding that we are all imperfect human beings. And I'm on the top of that list. But I will keep on trying to get it better, and get it right.

All of that said, forgiveness requires effort like anything else.

So I sat down about six months after the custody decision came through and wrote an e-mail to Siohvaughn in the hopes of opening up the communication channels. She acknowledged receipt of it but not much else. Still, it's a start that I share in the hopes of inspiring any fathers or mothers who want to take steps toward the goal of coparenting after a breakup:

> The reason I'm writing this e-mail is because of our boys who love the both of us very much. No matter what happens or has happened, they do. So I'm writing this e-mail to ask, or to see, if the time has come when we can move on from the past and move on to the future. I want for our boys to grow up and have an opportunity in life to attack the world with all the tools needed. They will need the both of us as a big part of that. So what I'm saying is that I've forgiven you for anything that has been done or said and I'm asking that you do the same so that we can move forward with both of our lives. But most importantly being parents together. I know it will help a lot to communicate about things that the boys are going through in their lives—school, sports, relationships, etc.
>
> As you know all of our lives are short and our departure time from the world isn't one that we can choose. I say that we move on and try to at least respect who we both are today and become the parents that Zion and Zaire deserve. Even if it's communicating through this e-mail, that's a start. I won't give up on you and I hope you wouldn't give up on me. We both have grown, or are growing into the individuals that we are supposed to be. Good, bad or indifferent.
>
> I hope all is good with you and your family. I'll be looking forward to your response.

FORGIVENESS IS KNOWING THAT WE ARE HUMAN, IMPERFECT, and that we do make mistakes. That's why, as an example to my children, I try to acknowledge my successes as a parent and my shortcomings. I try to know that my gifts from God are being well used. No gift has served me more than my faith—so central to the positive outlook I have on life, my ability to avoid getting into the funk that can last for years, and the belief I have in others to rise about their toughest challenges. Maybe it's because I've seen people I love rise from the ashes that I'm able to hold on to faith in them finding the light in their darkness. In the end, that's where my forgiveness of myself and of others comes from. Staying mad doesn't make me a better father. Encouraging happiness does! Being a blessing to my own children, to my family and loved ones, and to my fellow human beings, as best I can, above all, is a blessing to me.

DURING THE PARADE THAT WILL SOON DELIVER US TO THE American Airlines Arena, I reach over to bring the three boys I'm raising in closer to me. The truth is that I couldn't have done it without them. These kids are so wise and such great human beings that I could not be any prouder.

Zaire, Zion, and Dada are happy and healthy, and see the world as rich with opportunity. Really, that's the ultimate lesson of being a father first and coming to understand that life is bigger than basketball or any other such endeavor. Imagine how great our lives would be as parents if we all sought to raise fine, caring human beings. Love and the belief that they can do whatever is in their hearts is a winning recipe for their success.

Zaire ended his year with an amazing basketball season and his usual very good grades. He is so talented—from the way he watches the game, studying nuances and then incorporating them on his own, to his natural athleticism. He is a much better player than I was at this age. And he is so smart and hip. Here's an exchange I couldn't resist tweeting not long ago:

ths morning convo w/ my son goes alil lk ths Zaire: Dad y u cnt dunk lk blake Griffin Me: why u cnt dunk lk blake griffin Zaire: I cnt jump that high Me: Me either. We both laugh haha kids

That's another reason I say Zaire's one of my best teachers. He keeps me cool.

Dahveon played his first season of basketball with Zaire and did really well. He is one to watch. As the underdog who came in under the radar a lot in my own life, I can relate to Dada's style. On top of that, he's doing well in school, catching up very quickly, and he has such a good heart as he continues to be a steadying force for my sons. Sometimes I joke with him that he must be gaming the system because he does everything right!

Zion just turned five and has the busiest schedule of any of us. He is such a whiz in school that he wants to expand his horizons. The new list of extracurricular activities he gave me to add to his schedule included soccer, hip-hop dance, swimming, basketball, and tennis. Watch out, universe. We're all going to say we knew him when.

Everyone else is doing fine on the homefront.

Pastor Jolinda Wade remains my favorite girl. She is thriving, traveling, and speaking, never ceasing to amaze. Dad is sticking with his program of sobriety and working on self-improvement and growth all the time.

Up here on top of the double-decker bus, I'm thinking about how many of the lessons first given to me by my parents and other family members have continued to serve me all this time, even as recently as the playoffs. The truth is that over the last two months of the postseason, I've needed to draw from guidance given to me by most of my mentors and coaches—in addition to that from Coach Erik Spoelstra, who opened my eyes to new lessons of what being a champion is all about.

Going back to the summer of 2010, when Bron and C.B. first came to the Heat, there had been this assumption that with the two of them playing with me—the Big Three—Coach Spo's job would be easy. Not true. Some people think that having three "superstars" on a roster requires less coaching. The reality is that one of the hardest coaching challenges in basketball is figuring out how to mold and motivate a group of dominant players who are used to playing with the ball in their hands most of the time. Just like when you get a bunch of Alpha type leaders on a mission of any kind, someone has to be in charge to orchestrate the give-and-take.

Knowing how hard that is and remembering how we hadn't figured it out in the previous season, I kept a wait-and-see attitude about whether Coach Spo could meet that challenge. Would he make the necessary adjustments with this particular group of talented players and bring about the needed changes that we weren't able to make last year? Would he get us out of our individual comfort zones to be able to fight for a common goal and do what was needed to win a championship? And could he get us to buy in to his leadership and believe we could go all the way?

From the start of the playoffs in our first round against the New York Knicks, I knew the answer to those questions was *yes*. Spo had found a way to get us to mesh, even with all of the different personalities and egos. He had found the means of molding us to get the job done, to allow the right give-and-take, for each of us to be the Alpha at different points, even when it meant changing or hurting our individual game if that helped another player's game. That's what a coach has to do to lead a team to a championship. And, above all, the team has to trust their coach and believe that the mountaintop can be reached—even when it requires us to change the way we've played during all of our careers.

How did Spo do it? By being willing to get out of his own way and by getting out of his own comfort zone. In setting that example, he made it easier for each of us to do the same, without falling back on playing the way we had in the past.

Of course, there were so many dramatic twists and turns throughout the four rounds that I could probably write a whole chapter on each of the series. But what I can say is that each round brought different opportunities and distinct challenges. I loved getting to play against the Knicks in the first round of the Eastern Conference. Aside from the long-standing Miami Heat/New York Knicks rivalry that intensified in the late 1990s—meeting in the playoffs for four consecutive years, each time in a seven-game series—I love playing at Madison Square Garden. As the first game approached, my excitement grew as our whole city became pumped for the matchup. We also had reason to be nervous. In the past, the Knicks, even with a weaker record, had found ways to beat the Heat—both with their strong three-point shooting and with the firepower of a superstar player like Carmelo Anthony. Though we were confident, we knew there was a possibility of the Knicks turning up the dial on their play and catching us unprepared. In some ways they did, but we made the adjustments and started to find our playoff rhythm, winning the series 4–1. For both teams, the games were fun and social. There was ballin' and playing for the love of the sport. It was pride going against pride from our two teams and our two cities.

Going into the next series against the Indiana Pacers, my main concern was a swollen left knee that had been bothering me. In finishing off the first round in five games, I assumed that a couple days of rest would take care of the problem. And guess what? In game one (which we won decisively at home against the very physical play of the Pacers), I felt much better and even thought the knee issue was resolved. Well, I was wrong, as I found out in game two.

Not only was the knee that I used for elevation more swollen, but the game plan had been seriously complicated by the fact that Chris Bosh had gone down with a series-ending (potentially playoff-ending) abdominal injury in game one. As a team, we now had to figure out how to play and how to win without C.B. My job became harder as well because my minutes went up from thirty-three to thirty-eight a game. Knee swelling and all, I still managed to score 24 points. But then, in a shocker at the buzzer, the Pacers won the game by 3 points on our home court.

So on the morning before game three, on Thursday, May 17, after we had traveled to Indianapolis, I had to decide whether to have my knee drained and get some relief sooner rather than later, or delay having it drained and hope that the swelling would improve. Choosing to have it drained that morning, I expected to get the relief by game time, but instead my knee felt very sore and I was having trouble jumping. In what was one of my worst postseason games ever, after being scoreless in the first half, I scored only five points in the entire game. Worse, we lost by an embarrassing nineteen points, allowing the series to go 2–1 to the Pacers. The overreaction by the sports media, however, was pretty ridiculous. The next thing I knew they were writing my basketball obituary.

What? They were writing about me as if I was over the hill, not a thirty-year-old player in the prime of his career. Ironically, some of the same analysts who had criticized me for being too dominant in the past were now complaining that I wasn't taking over games the way they used to count on me to do.

The challenge, as always, was to tune out the noise and the doubt and clear my head. After all, going back to my rookie year, I knew how to fight for mental toughness and push through injuries. You just do it and deal with the consequences. But in that game three, when Coach Spo and I got into a spat in a third-quarter huddle, I gave in to my own frustration and his. I was playing with everything I had in me, whatever it took to get the ball into someone else's hands if I couldn't score with it, and just having an off night. Some games, hopefully most of them, you overcome the odds. Some games you can't. Our mutual frustration escalated. He might have been trying to see what would happen if he could get me to play mad, which is when I usually play well. But this was me playing frustrated, very different from playing mad. I was bothered by the knee and regretted my decision to have it drained only to feel the opposite of relief.

Coming out of the huddle, the frustration Coach and I were both feeling collided. As unfortunate as it was, sometimes you have to have those lows to reach up for your highs. Afterward, when I heard the press starting to question whether I had the ability to still play the game, I was thrown. I mean, my average of 26 to 27 points a game was down to 23—but on purpose. The objective was to make plays to score as a team and I was delivering. Though the piling on was frustrating and unexpected, it was funny, too.

And I also had to be thankful for everything that went wrong in that game three, even after a public tiff with my coach. It provided the turning point that drove me to look within, dig deep, and find the stuff that I needed to be able to make the greatest contribution I could on the court. As luck would have it, Coach Tom Crean, now head coach of men's basketball at the University of Indiana in Bloomington—where he has been for the last four years—invited me to drive up and visit him on campus. Coach C., recently named National Coach of 2012 by ESPN, was just what the doctor ordered.

One of my first and best teachers, he knew that what I most needed was to step outside of the frustration and get into a different, positive environment. Just like in the past, because he knows me better than any basketball mentor, he was able to work with me to help me feel good about myself so I could flip that mental competitive switch. Coach C. combines the knowledge of being able to show me what I need to do physically with the gift of communication that gets to me to listen.

That visit with my college coach was critical. It recharged me and reset my mental focus about what I needed to do for the rest of the Indiana series and, really, for the rest of the playoffs. I went on to score 30 points in game four, 28 points in game five, and 41 points in game six, which the Heat won, to close out the series and move on to the Eastern Conference finals. Coach Spoelstra was quoted as saying, "The one thing I know about the fabric of Dwyane Wade is that when he doesn't have the game he's capable of, he's very introspective. He owns it. He has shown an ability year after year to bounce back."

After the six games it took to get us out of the Indiana series, we were off to face the Boston Celtics. That series was extremely challenging and we'd had no reason to expect anything different. Yep, we were confident but not so much so that we let ourselves forget just how tough the Celtics had proven to be time and again. Very well coached by Hall of Famer Doc Rivers, the team was made up of Hall of Famers who already had championship DNA in their ranks. But we came in with the belief that we could win, determined to make use of our athleticism. Over seven tough games, we found our edge in being able to wear them down, just by putting enough added pressure on them offensively and defensively. We took advantage of those moments when they were becoming a little tired, especially in the fourth quarters, when we had enough left in the tank to play full-out all the way until the final decisive seconds.

While we were slugging it out against the Celtics, the drama in the Western Conference that pitted the San Antonio Spurs against the Oklahoma City Thunder was taking surprising turns. Of course, we were planning for either team, feeling good to be rejoined by Chris Bosh in time to help us out of the Celtics series and to be able to make a difference in the finals. If not for his return, I might be telling another story today. The Spurs, with home-court advantage won both of the first two games to lead the series 2–0, and many, including me, thought they were going to be unstoppable by the Thunder. The Spurs, by most measures, were the best team in the West and were playing phenomenal basketball. Could the Thunder tie the series at home? Maybe. I was looking at this young, athletic team of unbelievable scorers—Russell Westbrook, Kevin Durant, James Harden—and predicted that they could give the Spurs a run for their money. In my crystal ball, however, I thought it was going to be a seven-game series that would go to the Spurs. The fact that the Thunder won it in six games told us to get ready.

Whether it had been the Thunder or the Spurs in the finals, I believed we would be able to respond and win. Not thinking about my knee (which would require surgery after the finals), I felt that in our arsenal we had the strengths to take on the Thunder and exploit their weaknesses in ways that hadn't been tested before. The schedule for the finals started with two games in Oklahoma City, since they had home-court advantage, continuing to three games in Miami, followed by two games back in Oklahoma. Our thinking at the start was to go to their house and win one of the first two games. In game one, we battled and played well. But we hadn't seen their game yet. Sure, we'd played them in the regular season. But that's different. The game changes and is honed in the playoffs. We hadn't played against *that* Thunder yet. And so in that first game, even though we were ahead in the third quarter, they were able to crank up the energy enough to take us by surprise. They went fast and were very athletic. We hadn't seen that gear from them before. By game two, we were ready to take what they could dish out and kept adjusting with changes they hadn't seen from us. We got the job done in that second game and took the series back home to Miami tied 1–1.

Each game was so tough. Each game meant something different. Game three was huge. We couldn't let them have it because, we believed, it would set the tone for the rest of the series and determine the outcome of the next two games. And we won that game. Game four then became do-or-die, like a game seven in any other series. That's how we played it. And we won.

Game five was all about making a final statement—deciding as a team, hey, let's close this door and not them out. We did that and won the series 4–1. In all, we had won 16 out of 23 games.

And that's how we got to the top of Mount Everest where we planted a second flag for the Miami Heat, and we're all celebrating with this joyful parade down Biscayne Boulevard. We just want this party to last—after all that we've been through as a team and as a city, after all that we've had to overcome since 2010. To me the celebration brings home what being a champion really means this time around: to do something that you've never done before by taking a step back in a sense and giving someone else the opportunity to get there and to succeed. For me that was scoring 23 points a game without getting the ball as much as other times. In 2006 I had done it with the team on my back and that was one kind of triumph. This was different. This was doing it against even greater odds, sticking to the belief that if you stay with your team and your faith in each other, you can get there together. We had stuck to belief, we had trusted each other, and we did it our way.

My heart is full and overflowing with gratitude.

Being able to celebrate with the Heat families, the Arisons, the Rileys, and especially with my victorious teammates, only adds to a sense of fulfillment. The happiness I feel for LeBron is beyond words. First of all, I know how it felt when I got my first ring—what it represents and how blessed you feel when you've been given an opportunity. Second, I know how much he wanted this, how he put everything on the line to get here, and how he took on the responsibility for everything. In the midst of the relentless talk of what the Heat hadn't done, he rose above the fray to do something about it, not doing it with his mouth but with his play.

So this is how I get to wrap up my story, riding down Biscayne Boulevard, feeling the purity of just being happy to be on this journey with one of my best friends, one of the best players to ever play the game.

What's more I get to do it with my boys along for the ride. Since I've had full custody, we've tried to maintain our even keel and a level of normalcy even with challenging drama and excitement like this. I love that they look at everything with an eye to learn from my experiences.

Dahveon sees the possibility for overcoming obstacles and takes risks that he never would have before. Zaire better understands the basketball dream and has the desire to become a champion, while also having seen adversity in his young life and knowing about resilience. Zion pays attention, too, and then keeps everything real, reminding everyone not to take ourselves too seriously. I love holding the trophy, but the best reward for me is having the boys with me, getting their hugs and high fives, sharing the celebration with the ones I love most. They're the ones who give this meaning, and if I didn't have them in my life, I wouldn't be who I am. Our kids and family members are the ones who matter in each of our lives—they're the ones who love us, who help us, and who heal us.

Down the road, there are lessons I hope my boys will remember from this mountaintop: the importance of hard work and of not being selfish. We all want to make our mark on whatever it is that we do. But growing up means learning that it's not just about you, it's about being part of a team. Whatever the quest, it's about everyone involved. It's never just one guy. It's never just two guys or three guys. When this season is remembered, we'll be reminded that history was made as much by Mike Miller's three-point shooting as by the precision of Shane Battier's game and the stepped-up attack of Mario Chalmers.

In addition to striving to be unselfish, I want my sons, my nephew, and all of us to remember that when people say you can't do something, that's when you have to believe in yourself most and prove them wrong. Because, if there is one father-son or parent-child lesson worth sharing, it's that with belief in self, hard work, and unselfishness, you can accomplish anything and everything.

THERE IS ONE OTHER THOUGHT THAT OCCURS TO ME UP on this float as I conclude the journey until now, and that is of another celebration that I was able to share with my boys back in January 2012.

For once in recent years, as my thirtieth birthday approached, Lisa

Joseph didn't keep saying to me, "We need to talk." I knew there was something cooking with a party and was excited. But I had no earthly idea what Lisa was about to mastermind—not one but three separate surprises. With help from Tragil on one of the events and a whole host of other co-conspirators on the others, Lisa shocked me at the second of the three events when I walked in with my lady Gab on my arm to a private dinner attended by close family, friends, and celebrities from around the country who had flown in for the occasion and were being stashed in hotels all over Miami.

All of my teammates were there, as was Hank Thomas, my agent, who has been like a father to me all this time, steering my life and career to this successful stage, and many coaches without whom I wouldn't be the player or the man I am today. Pat Riley honored me with a great toast, as did family members and friends.

After several speeches, Dad announced, "Everyone else says they're my son's number-one fan. But I am truly his number-one fan."

That was shocking, but in the best way possible. Later, I asked Dad to elaborate and he said, "Oh, man, you know as a player, it's been nine years and I still don't know how to feel. You've matured so much from crying in the backyard to being one of the best players in the world. When someone asks me who are the best five players ever, on and off the court, you are exactly what I want to see in a ballplayer."

It's something that my boys have taught me. You are never too young or too old to appreciate praise from your father. Then Dwyane Wade Sr. continued, telling me why he was a fan of me as a father. He said, "I love that you're a leader and that you give your boys a program for leadership. You teach them right from wrong, how to go from struggle to success. And one day, I'm sure you'll tell them everything you went through."

Wow, it was worth turning thirty to hear all that from my father!

The video that was shown had been made with help from much of my Heat family and the basketball who's who of the world also featured special commentary from my sons. Zaire called me "Fantastic!" Zion looked right into the camera and said, "Oh, you know . . ." like there was no point in going into specifics.

My speech was kept short. My heart was full of so much love for everyone who'd been with me all the way. With Gabrielle beaming almost as giddily as me at my side, and Dahveon, Zaire, and Zion close at hand, too, I closed the books on our past struggles and readied for the greatest decade yet.

The after-party that night was an invitation-only extravaganza with hundreds, plus entertainment from surprise artists like Common, Rick Ross, T.I., and Usher and over-the-top gifts that included a rare 1982 vintage bottle of Dom Perignon in honor of the year of my birth, a special edition diamond-encrusted watch from my friends at Hublot, and a custom-made McLaren.

Presented to me by the Collection, a luxury car dealership in Coral Gables, the 2012 McLaren MP12-4C had been assembled in the United Kingdom and designed by—guess who? Me! Oh, yeah, I have to start thinking about my day job in the future. How beautiful and crazy—that I now own a sports car that's better and more outrageous and smarter than KITT from Knight Rider.

I used to say when I first got into the league that I was living my dreams and that maybe I should have dreamed a little bit harder. No longer. My dreams have turned out so much better than I could have ever made up on my own. The best part is that they're alive and well in my children.

For all the amazing surprises that came along with my thirtieth birthday, one that had me breaking down and bawling like a baby took place in the middle of the family brunch on the day before the big bash. Mom, my favorite girl, and I were just settling in for one of my favorite gospel songs, "Never Would Have Made It" by Marvin Sapp, when I felt a hand on my shoulder. I turned around to see Willie Mae Morris, ninety-one years old. Grandma had flown to Miami from Chicago on her first plane ride ever.

We hugged and hugged. We sure had come a long, long way together.

Acknowledgments

In my life and career, I've been truly blessed in being surrounded by people who are not only all-around great human beings but who are also some of the most gifted individuals in their fields. This was definitely true when it came to the team that worked with me on *A Father First*. My lasting gratitude goes to my literary agent, Simon Green, for bringing this book to reality, and to the entire crew at CAA and CAA Sports—for your vision and for believing in mine.

I am also grateful to editor Henry Ferris for your guidance and passion, and to Liate Stehlik, Lynn Grady, Seale Ballenger, Andy Dodds, and the rest of the team at William Morrow. I couldn't have asked for a better publishing home.

Thank you to Mim Eichler Rivas, I am so grateful to you for putting your heart and soul into my story. You deserve most of the credit, if not all, for me being able to shed even more light on this thing called parenthood. I was blessed to have you help me tell my story.

TEAM NO SLEEP! My crew who does double and triple duty working on the business/personal side of my life to make sure I'm good. . . . I could not have accomplished what I have without you. . . . Huge appreciation is due to you who make it possible for me to do what I do as a father, athlete, businessman, philanthropist, and now author.

Henry "Hank" Thomas, aside from all of your wise and valued counsel on every aspect of work, I must thank you for encouraging me early on to tell my fatherhood story. Thank you for believing in me and always having my back.

Lisa Joseph Metelus, thank you for putting up with my nonsense and making sure that everything I should have and dream to have can be possible.

Rubenstein Communications, especially Amy Jacobs and Tisha Kresler, for all that you handle on the public relations/media front and for always going beyond the call of duty.

Sincere gratitude goes to my attorney, Jim Pritikin, and the rest of the firm of Beerman, Pritikin, Mirabelli, Swerdlove in Chicago. Jim, thanks for fighting for me and my family and for making sure that my children remained protected. Ginger Gorden, thank you for keeping my numbers in line and having the hard conversations. . . . It will pay off for me in the future! My stylist Calyann Barnett, thank you for always pushing me to take risks. . . . Your vision has taken us exactly where we wanted to be. Bobby Metelus a.k.a. Bobby Digital, you have captured images on and off the court that will forever tell my story. Thank you for your grind.

And to my home team: Richard Ingraham, master chef who keeps us fed and healthy; Brenda Larson, for your patience and guidance with the boys; and Shellye Martin, for your talents in always making my house a home. Special thanks to Sherif Balogun, my go-to guy I can always count on, and to our housekeeper Elizabeth and her family, for your hard work and loving spirit. You all are the glue that holds my family and home life together.

As for the important coaches, mentors, and fellow players in this game that I love so much, there aren't enough pages for me to name every person who has starred in a meaningful role in my basketball journey. So let me just offer a collective shout-out to the coaches, as well as to the coaching, training, and office staffs, of my teams at Harold L. Richards High School and Marquette University, and of the Olympic teams on which I've had the honor of representing the USA; to the officials of the NBA as a whole; and of course to everyone in the Miami Heat extended family. After nine seasons, the Heat organization has been unstoppable in its support for me in all kinds of weather—good, bad, and indifferent. I am deeply grateful.

Given the added challenges of a compressed 2011/2012 season, I want to specifically acknowledge a handful of individuals at the Heat who've been in the trenches with me during this past year. At the top of that list is Erik Spoelstra, a.k.a. Coach Spo, who has risen to many challenges and who continues to bring out the competitor in me. And to echo Coach Riley's reminder of 15 Strong, I want to acknowledge teammates whom I mention as part of the group but who deserve individual recognition—Joel Anthony, Shane Battier, Mario Chalmers, Norris Cole, Eddy Curry, Terrel Harris, Juwan Howard, James Jones, Mike Miller, Dexter Pittman, and Ronny Turiaf. You are all part of the heart that beats in our team, along with L.B., C.B., and my brother from day one, Udonis Haslem. The fact that I get to come to work every day in the company of your brotherhood goes so far beyond anything I could have dreamt up as a kid. Special thanks to Micky, Madeline and the Arison family, and Cris and Pat Riley—you all are my family.

To my brand partners who have made me proud to represent them over the years, I am so grateful for all that we've already accomplished and what's still to come. Converse, Brand Jordan, T-Mobile, Gatorade, Upper Deck, McDavid, Pepperidge Farm, Hublot, The Collection and Mission Products, thank you for believing and trusting in me to represent you.

These words of acknowledgments wouldn't be complete if I didn't thank the fans. Your spirit fires up mine every time I step onto the floor. Basketball fans, past, present, and future, are the best fans of any sport on the planet. Thank you for keeping me hungry and allowing me to take flight.

Lastly, I gotta give some new and repeated thanks to the family and friends who have always had my back and always will. To the core guys of my Crew, thank you for believing in me and for taking the ride. Marcus Andrews and Vincent Holmes, thank you for the brotherhood that we've all shared since we first met. Marty McGlothan and Rob Jackson, thank you for your lasting friendship and support, and for always showing up for me. For all the struggles of my early life, I was still blessed by the love and caring of aunts, uncles, cousins, nieces, and nephews on both sides of the family. Much love to each of you. And, once again, I have to acknowledge the members of the immediate family I grew up in—Grandma, Mom, Dad, Tragil, Deanna, Keisha, Demetrius, Donny, Kodhamus, Maryya, and Antoine. I'm proud to say that all of my friends and brothers are great dads and take that responsibility very seriously. Though I've said before how much I love you all, it's worth saying it yet again—I love you! Thank you to each of my parents and to Tragil for agreeing to relive some of the more painful chapters of the past in order to help me tell my story. You inspire me.

And to Gabrielle Union—thank you for your love and support when I need it most, for your smile that brightens my world, and for your strength.

My final acknowledgements are to Zaire, Zion, and Dahveon. I love you more than words can ever say and I am so proud of each of you. Thank you for helping me become the man I am today.

FINAL THOUGHTS

NEXT STEPS FOR GETTING INVOLVED

In March 2012, when I had the honor of hosting a Responsible Father-hood Roundtable discussion as part of President Obama's Fatherhood & Mentoring Initiative, our focus was on the fundamental theme of getting involved. In addition to representatives from government agencies and a diverse group of leaders from around the country who were in attendance, we were joined by dads from various walks of life who were recognized for their individual efforts to exemplify and promote responsible fatherhood.

I was inspired after meeting men of all ages who are deeply commit-ted to their roles as fathers and mentors. And I was also very encouraged to hear reports of great strides being made by families and communities that have benefitted from the resources made available by the Initiative's partners, including the National Responsible Fatherhood Clearinghouse (NRFC), the Administration for Children and Families Office of Family Assistance, and the White House Office of Faith-based and Neighborhood

Partnerships. What I learned from our discussion reinforced my own belief that when it comes to parenting, a little goes a long way. The key really seems to be making involvement with the children in your life a priority for your time, energy, caring, and concern. The first step, I believe, is recognizing that priority and the next step is taking action by staying connected to them and their lives.

If you'd like more information on parenting resources and on how you can get more involved as a dad yourself, as a mom looking to promote fatherhood in your family, or as a citizen or organizational leader seeking ways to positively impact your community, I hope your next stop will be the website www.fatherhood.gov. You'll find everything you need, from a DadBlog on a variety of topics of interest to fathers and families, to an interactive map that can connect you to programs on the local level wherever you happen to be. Aside from offering all kinds of suggestions for different activities you can do when looking to spend quality time with your children, the website has a library tab that lets you research books and other reading materials on any parenting or mentoring question you might have. Another section includes information about employment opportunities and community grants, while another provides recent statistics and research about the importance of responsible fatherhood to society at large. As the website states:

> *Fatherlessness is a growing crisis in America, one that undergirds many of the challenges that families are facing. When dads aren't around, young people are more likely to drop out of school, use drugs, be involved in the criminal justice system, and become young parents themselves.*

Of course, when I was first approached by President Obama to become involved with the Initiative, I was humbled. More than that, I was moved by the fact that one of the reasons he was so passionate about this issue is that he grew up without his dad. He, too, has recognized that being a father is his most important role. To acknowledge that, the president is reaching out to dads across the nation to join him in taking a fatherhood pledge. You can make your pledge official by signing up at www.fatherhood.gov/pledge with your name and e-mail address. The pledge is simply a commitment for all of us to do everything we can to be there for our children and for young people whose fathers aren't around. By signing the President's Fatherhood Pledge, your name and e-mail address will be kept strictly confidential and you'll also be sent tips, updates, and information about resources from fatherhood organizations, prominent dads, and experts.

Whether you sign the President's Fatherhood Pledge, write the words to your own pledge, and/or connect with a local parenting program, what matters most is that you've made a serious commitment to *being involved* in the lives of your children and to stepping up as a positive role model and mentor for children in your life and community.

As I have learned from the experience of writing this book, I'm far from having all of the answers. Certainly I've made mistakes as a dad, and hopefully by learning from them I've grown as a parent and a person. And as I grow as a father, I will continue to share more lessons learned.

Until then, I'm sending out my best to everyone who came along on this journey with me, with blessings always from my household to yours.